Studies in Ethnopolitics

General Editors: Timothy D. Sisk, University of Denver, and Stefan Wolff, University of Bath

Focussing on the ethnopolitical dimensions of the security and stability of states and regions, this series addresses theoretical and practical issues relating to the management, settlement and prevention of ethnic conflicts.

Disputed Territories: The Transnational Dynamics of Ethnic Conflict Settlement
Stefan Wolff

Peace at Last? The Impact of the Good Friday Agreement on Northern Ireland
Edited by Jörg Neuheiser and Stefan Wolff

Peace at Last?

The Impact of the Good Friday Agreement on Northern Ireland

Edited by Jörg Neuheiser and Stefan Wolff

Berghahn Books
New York • Oxford

First published in 2003 by

Berghahn Books

www.BerghahnBooks.com

First paperback edition printed in 2004

'2003 J rg Neuheiser and Stefan Wolff

Library of Congress Cataloging-in-Publication Data

Peace at last : the impact of the Good Friday agreement on Northern Ireland / with a fore-
word by Lord Alderdice ; edited by J rg Neuheiser and Stefan Wolff.
    p. cm.
Includes bibliographical references and index.
ISBN 1—57181—518—X (alk. paper) -- ISBN 1-57181-658-5 (pb.: alk. paper)
    1. Northern Ireland--Politics and government--1998- 2. Great Britain. Treaties, etc.
Ireland, 1998 Apr. 10. 3. Great Britain--Relations--Ireland. 4. Ireland--Relations--
Great Britain. 5. Peace movements--Northern Ireland. I. Neuheiser, J rg. II. Wolff,
Stefan, 1969.

DA990.U46 P395 2002
941.50824 dc21   2002025597

British Library Cataloguing in Publication Data

A catalogue record for this book is available from the British Library

Printed in the USA on acid-free paper.

ISBN 1—57181—518—X hardback
ISBN 1-57181-658-5 paperback

TABLE OF CONTENTS

LIST OF TABLES

NOTES ON CONTRIBUTORS

Lord Alderdice was from 1987 to 1998 the Leader of the Alliance Party of Northern Ireland. After the Assembly election of 1998 he stepped down as party leader and was appointed Speaker of the Northern Ireland Assembly.

Alan Bairner is Professor of Sports Studies at the University of Ulster. He has written extensively on sport and politics and is the author of Sport, Nationalism and Globalization (SUNY University Press, 2001), coauthor of Sport, Sectarianism and Society in a Divided Ireland (Leicester University Press, 1993) and joint editor of Sport in Divided Societies (Meyer and Meyer, 1999).

Dominic Bryan is a lecturer at the Institute of Irish Studies at Queens University, Belfast and a research associate with the think-tank Democratic Dialogue in Belfast. He is author of Orange Parades: The Politics of Ritual, Tradition and Control (Pluto Press, 2000). He is presently conducting research into conflict management and the policing of public events and is coauthor (with Neil Jarman) of a series of reports looking at monitoring and stewarding at parades and demonstrations.

Sean Byrne is the Director of both the Distance and Residential Doctoral Programmes in the Department of Dispute Resolution at Nova Southeastern University, Fort Lauderdale, Florida. He is a native of Ireland. He has done intervention work in communities in Bosnia and Northern Ireland, as well as in Fort Lauderdale. He was the 1994–5 Theodore Lentz International Peace and Conflict Resolution research fellow at the University of Missouri-St Louis, and a 1997 recipient of a United States Institute of Peace research grant to explore the role of external economic aid in the peace-building process in Northern Ireland. He has published a number of articles in the areas of ethnic conflict, and children and conflict.

Stephen Farry received his PhD in International Relations from the Queen's University of Belfast. He acted as a negotiator and researcher for the Alliance Party during the multiparty talks. He is currently General Secretary of the Alliance Party and a member of North Down Borough Council.

Cynthia L. Irvin is Assistant Professor of Political Science at the University of Kentucky and Senior Research Associate at the University of Kentucky Appalachian Center. She is the author of Militant Nationalism: Between Movement and Party in Ireland and the Basque Country. A former United States Institute of Peace Scholar, her areas of research include the politics of ethnically divided societies, post-conflict community reconstruction and development, and social movements.

James W. McAuley is Reader in Behavioural Sciences at the University of Huddersfield. His main areas of interest and research are political sociology, political violence and the state. He has written extensively on the conflict and political situation in Northern Ireland and, in particular, on the politics and political identity of Ulster Unionism and Loyalism. He is currently working on an Economic and Social Research Council (ESRC) funded project researching the relationships between 'extra-constitutional' parties and the Northern Ireland Assembly.

Valerie Morgan is Professor of History at the University of Ulster. Her major teaching and research interests are in Irish history and gender history. She has worked extensively on aspects of the Northern Ireland conflict through the Centre for the Study of Conflict at the University of Ulster. She has published widely on issues relating to the effect of ethnic violence on women's lives and the role of education in divided societies.

Gerard Murray is Honorary Fellow at the Unit for the Study of Government in Scotland at Edinburgh University. He is the author of John Hume and the SDLP: Impact and Survival in Northern Ireland (Irish Academic Press, 1998).

Jörg Neuheiser studied History and English at the University of Cologne and at Trinity College Dublin. He is currently working on his PhD in Modern History. His main research interests are British and Irish history in the eighteenth and nineteenth centuries and aspects of collective identity and nationalism.

Camille C. O'Reilly is lecturer in Social Anthropology at Richmond, the American International University in London. She is the author of a number of articles on nationalism and the Irish language revival; gender, nationalism and the Irish language; the Irish language as symbol; the Irish language movement and the peace process in Northern Ireland; the politics of culture in Northern Ireland, and (with Gordon McCoy) the Ulster-Scots language. She is the author of The Irish Language in Northern Ireland: The Politics of Culture and Identity (Macmillan, 1999).

Peter Shirlow is a Senior Lecturer in the School of Environmental Studies, University of Ulster Coleraine. His work has been dedicated to exploring deprivation, social exclusion and political identity within Irish contexts. This work has been published in journals such as Political Geography, Area, Space and Polity, Antipode and Capital and Class.

Thomas Taaffe is pursuing a PhD in anthropology at the University of Massachusetts, Amherst. His dissertation work is on the role of news producers in the political sphere in Northern Ireland in the context of the Good Friday Agreement. He has served as an editor for several small magazines and newspapers in the USA and has previously done research on indigenous/settler relations in colonial America, as well as on the effects of ending Affirmative Action on the enrolment of African Americans in higher education.

Stefan Wolff is a Lecturer in the Department of European Studies at the University of Bath, England. He received his Masters degree from the University of Cambridge and his PhD from the London School of Economics and Political Science. His main research area is ethnonational conflict. He is editor of German Minorities in Europe: Ethnic Identity and Cultural Belonging (Berghahn, 2000), co-editor (with David Rock) of Coming Home to Germany? The Integration of Ethnic Germans from Central and Eastern Europe in the Federal Republic (Berghahn, 2002) and author of Disputed Territories. The Transnational Dynamics of Ethnic Conflict Settlement (Berghahn, 2002). He has also published a number of articles and book chapters on ethnic conflict and forced migration.

Foreword

Even if the Irish problem is not your primary interest, this book is worth your attention. To explain why, as with so many things in Ireland, I need to go back into a little history.

For half a dozen generations my family lived on a small farm outside the border town of Newry. My understanding of the future for Northern Ireland in my early years was much influenced by this background. The province, as it is almost universally known among Protestant Unionists, would survive only for as long as the Protestants could hold out, with little backing from an untrustworthy British government, but in the end the Catholics would win and there would be an independent united Ireland.

In 1968, when I was entering teenage years, the violence of the current 'Troubles' broke out. Like others, I began to appreciate that the bloody violence that had overwhelmed the Civil Rights marches might herald an incredibly costly transition process. This led some Nationalist-minded people to question whether it was worth pressing for unity with the South at all costs, and their demands became rather for equality within the state than for total constitutional upheaval. For some Unionists too, the only realistic future was to be found in a greater accommodation with Nationalists than had previously been contemplated. These views were not shared by more fundamentalist Unionists or by more extremist Republicans, so the aim of the new approach was to build a broad centre including moderate Unionists and Nationalists along with liberals, socialists and other nonaligned groups. This whole approach was based on the premise that if Nationalists could see their civil and political rights fully respected and a good and even close working relationship with the South, they would give allegiance to a new Northern Ireland. For Unionists, it was argued, the prize of peace was worth the price of sharing power with the minority and accepting that Northern Ireland was not just like any other part of the United Kingdom. The only really serious attempt to put this model into practice was during the first six months of 1974 with the brief and turbulent life of the power-sharing Assembly and Executive. It was not acceptable to Republicans but its downfall came because it could not command the support of the majority of Unionists.

The next twenty years saw a series of half-hearted and ultimately futile initiatives but meantime the scene was changing. The United Kingdom and the Republic of Ireland had both joined the Common Market on the same day in 1973, and as it progressed through the European Community to an ever-closer European Union, relations between the two states modified and mellowed. The experience of shared sovereignty and close cooperation affected the political classes greatly, and while it would be easy to overstate the case, a degree of mutual respect did develop both between significant individuals and between the British and Irish governments. At the same time relationships within Northern Ireland slid in the opposite direction. The British government and liberal-minded politicians tried to address Nationalist discontent through strictly implemented antidiscrimination codes and to redress the social and economic disadvantage of Catholics as a group. That this was a serious effort was acknowledged recently by John Hume when he said that the rights that had been fought for by the Civil Rights movement had been achieved. If this model of conflict resolution was working in the way that was intended, the broad centre should have commanded a substantial majority right across the divided community for working a new agreed system, but it was not so simple.

The failure of the 1974 experiment resulted in a descent into increasing polarisation. The Westminster and European elections of 1979 saw old-style Unionism in the ascendant. In 1981 the Hunger Strike and the elections associated with it showed that physical-force Republicanism had now a powerful mandate from within the Nationalist community. The broad centre upon which the model was based was in decline.

The British and Irish governments then proceeded to build upon their own new European relationship and in 1985 signed the Anglo-Irish Agreement. This provided for new intergovernmental institutions that would sustain cooperation at a high level, in the hope that this would create the context for something more constructive on the ground. It was also the beginning of a move away from the 'centreground' model. Nationalists would find influence, not through working with Unionists and others in a power-sharing arrangement within Northern Ireland, but by being represented by the Irish government.

But the arrangement was asymmetrical. The British government would not act in an equivalent way for Unionists. On the contrary, it would be 'even-handed'. All Unionist attempts to bring the Agreement down failed and eventually a talks process was constructed in the early 1990s. On the face of things, it looked like a rerun of 1973, but there were two crucial differences. Even the old-style Unionists realised that they had to be part of the process, and now physical-force Republicanism was part of the process too. Instead of building a broad centre to marginalise and therefore minimise extremism, the new model was 'inclusive'.

One could argue that this new approach was simply making the broad centre even broader – there were after all still some on the extremes of Unionism and Republicanism who would not accept it. In another sense, however, the new initiative was almost the opposite of the previous approach. Now everyone had to be in the process, and the aim was to find a framework which all could accept. The difficulty in fashioning such a framework is reflected in the length of the negotiations. They went on for years. Finally the Good Friday Agreement was signed in April 1998. The differences from the Sunningdale Agreement were small but highly significant. There was North-South cooperation, but this time the very existence of the Assembly was bound to it. There was a power-sharing government, but it had to command not only a majority in the Assembly, but also a majority of both Unionists and Nationalists. The nonaligned were no longer in the centre, but at the margins. The Executive was a power-sharing one, and all the major parties were members of it, this time not through agreement, but through a proportionate mathematical formula.

There was also another difference. Those who had been involved in Loyalist and Republican terrorist campaigns were able to be part of the new institutions to the very highest levels, dependent only on their support at the polls.

There is no doubt that the Good Friday Agreement and the establishment of its new institutions are an extraordinary achievement. Of course, there are problems in its implementation, but, say its supporters, these are understandable teething problems. In one sense they are certainly right. The Assembly has functioned remarkably well, especially when one realises that most of the members and staff have no previous parliamentary experience. The model, if it works, will be a quite remarkable advance in the process of conflict resolution and will eventually have application not just in areas of open violent conflict but also in the more normal processes of parliamentary democracy, which are of course about how to deal with difference without resorting to violence.

If it fails, what then? For Northern Ireland, who knows? There will be a temptation to return to the analysis with which I grew up. More importantly, the message to the international community dealing with other areas of conflict will be a gloomy and unwelcome one, but will also be one that simply cannot be ignored. That is the burden of those involved in the Northern Ireland peace process. The real importance of the Northern Ireland process, and the value of this book which critically surveys it, lies well outside this wonderful, but tragic little offshore island.

Lord Alderdice MLA
Speaker, Northern Ireland Assembly

PREFACE

Four years after the conclusion of the Good Friday Agreement and its subsequent acceptance in referendums, Northern Ireland still figures prominently in news headlines, rarely conveying the impression that a lasting peace has been achieved. This is very much in contrast to the situation in April 1998, when enthusiasm about the Agreement outside Northern Ireland was almost unanimous. Since then, hopes for a permanent end to violence and continuing efforts to address the root causes of conflict in a still deeply divided society have faced unforeseen difficulties both in the implementation of the Agreement and in debates about the interpretation of its clauses. Opposition to the Agreement and to the perceived direction of the peace process from hardliners on both sides of the communal divide has never abated. Even though five years of relative calm and peace after the IRA reinstated its cease-fire in 1997 and the beginning of IRA decommissioning in October 2001 might be seen as evidence for the success of the peace process and the Agreement, sporadic violence – organised and spontaneous – continues to be a feature of Northern Irish politics and society and to threaten Northern Ireland's present and future.

The Good Friday Agreement seemed to offer a way out of the intricate problems within Northern Irish society. However, subsequent events proved the conflict to be more complicated than many had expected. Was the Agreement simply another episode in the long history of confrontation and the numerous attempts to resolve it, or will it still turn out to be the breakthrough to peace for Northern Ireland? In an international context, the uncertain future of the province poses further questions about the nature of its peace process and its significance for other conflicts in the world. Is Northern Ireland a model case for the success or failure of interventions by national and transnational institutions to secure peace in conflict areas?

In the light of these complex questions, the objective of this book is modest. It aims to analyse some aspects of the impact of the Good Friday Agreement on Northern Irish politics and society. How did the Agreement affect the development of parties, the relationship between the two communities, and the life of 'ordinary people' in Northern Ireland? While providing an overview of the history of the conflict, this collection of essays tries to assess the achievements of the peace process after the conclusion of the Agreement and to gain insights into the difficulties Northern Ireland has faced on its uncertain path to peace. In an interdisciplinary effort, it combines studies by historians, sociologists, anthropologists and political scientists from different geographic, cultural and professional backgrounds. All contributors to this volume have been working on questions concerning Northern Ireland for years, and their different approaches combine to provide a deeper understanding of the conflict and the peace process.

The structure of the book is simple. Stefan Wolff's introductory essay follows the history of peace initiatives in Northern Ireland between 1973 and 1998 and gives a detailed analysis of the text and scope of the Good Friday Agreement. The following seven chapters of the volume deal with the 'politics of peace' and the consequences of the negotiations and the Agreement for the political process in Northern Ireland. Gerard Murray and Peter Shirlow examine the position of nationalist parties after the Agreement; the contributions of James W. McAuley and Dominic Bryan follow with studies of the Unionist community. The section is opened by an analysis of the Alliance Party's perspective on the Agreement by Stephen Farry; it is concluded by Thomas Taaffe's study of the politics of media coverage during the negotiations and Cynthia Irvin and Sean Byrne's examination of the role of economic aid in the Northern Ireland peace process over the past several years.

The next three chapters of the book assess the impact of the peace process on society in Northern Ireland and offer perspectives on the often neglected nexus of politics and culture. All follow the question whether Northern Ireland is moving from the culture of conflict to the culture of peace – Valerie Morgan in her study of gender aspects and the role of women in the peace process, Camille O'Reilly in her analysis of the links between collective identities, culture and languages in Northern Ireland, and Alan Bairner in his contribution on conflicts in the world of sport.

Finally, Stefan Wolff's conclusion examines the Good Friday Agreement as an element in the overall peace process. Assessing the current state of post-agreement reconstruction in Northern Ireland, he draws on the wide range of arguments put forward in the book in order to find some answers to our questions concerning the Good Friday Agreement and its significance for the future of Northern Ireland.

The vicissitudes of academic life have placed us in the honourable position of editors. Outlined in 1999, the idea of an international project on the Good Friday Agreement and its impact on Northern Ireland came from Christopher P. Storck, a historian at the University of Cologne. We owe thanks to all contributors for bearing with us on the long, but nevertheless fruitful journey since then. The production of any book like this is not possible without the help and assistance of numerous individuals and it is our pleasure to acknowledge our indebtedness. Jörg Neuheiser thanks Vera Nünning, Christopher P. Storck, W. E. Vaughan and Herman-Josef Verhoeven for their advice and encouragement. Stefan Wolff expresses his particular gratitude to Brendan O'Leary, Antony Alcock, Colin Irwin, Ulrich Schneckener and Mari Fitzduff for productive and stimulating discussions on Northern Ireland, as well as to Lucy Marcus. Special thanks are due to Megan Laura Yoos who read and commented on a first draft of the volume, to Timothy D. Sisk, one of the series editors of Studies in Ethnopolitics, and to Sean Kingston, our editor at Berghahn.

Jörg Neuheiser
Stefan Wolff

LIST OF ABBREVIATIONS

AP	Associated Press
CRC	Community Relations Council
CTG	Cultural Traditions Group
DUP	Democratic Unionist Party
ECHR	European Convention on Human Rights
EU	European Union
GAA	Gaelic Athletic Association
IFI	International Fund for Ireland
IICD	Independent International Commission on Decommissioning
IRA	Irish Republican Army
IRB	Irish Republican Brotherhood
LVF	Loyalist Volunteer Force
NIO	Northern Ireland Office
NIPB	Northern Ireland Partnership Board
NIWC	Northern Ireland Women's Coalition
PA	Press Association
PUP	Progressive Unionist Party
RUC	Royal Ulster Constabulary
SDLP	Social Democratic and Labour Party
UDA	Ulster Defence Association
UDP	Ulster Democratic Party
UFF	Ulster Freedom Fighters
UKUP	United Kingdom Unionist Party
UUP	Ulster Unionist Party
UUUC	United Ulster Unionist Council
UVF	Ulster Volunteer Force

CHAPTER ONE

Introduction: From Sunningdale to Belfast, 1973–98*

Stefan Wolff

The conflict in Northern Ireland is caused by incompatible conceptions of national belonging and the means to realise them. These two different conceptions are the idea of a united Ireland, pursued by Nationalists and Republicans, and the idea of continued strong constitutional links between the province and Great Britain within the United Kingdom, desired by Unionists and Loyalists. Historically, these two traditions have been associated with two different religions – Catholicism and Protestantism. These labels have played a significant role in the conflict as they have made possible the systematic pursuit of discrimination and segregation. Yet, this has not made the conflict an ethnoreligious one. The same holds true for the issue of language. Although less significant, the equality and preservation of Gaelic and Ulster Scots has mobilised some sections of the population in Northern Ireland, yet overall, the conflict is not ethnolinguistic in its nature either. Similar cases could be made for other dimensions of this conflict, such as class, culture and ideology. What they all have in common is that they have polarised Northern Irish society for decades, leaving too little room for cross-cutting cleavages, and eventually aligning all these various dimensions of the conflict behind two fundamentally different conceptions of national belonging.

Defining the Northern Ireland conflict thus as an ethnonational one has important implications for its analysis and for the analysis of attempts to settle it. Causes for failure and success in conflict management and settlement need to be sought at more than one level. While the situation in Northern Ireland itself is of great significance, it must not be seen in isolation from the political processes in the United Kingdom and the Republic of Ireland. Increasingly over the past two decades, factors in

---

* In this introduction I draw freely on my earlier published and unpublished work on Northern Ireland. For a more detailed comparative analysis of the Sunningdale and Good Friday Agreements, see Wolff (2001); for a more comprehensive treatment of the conflict as a whole, see Wolff (2002). Particular thanks are due to Brendan O'Leary.

the international context have become more and more important as well
– international connections of paramilitary groups, the influence of dias-
poras, and the consequences of European integration. The dynamics at
and between these four levels (Northern Ireland, Republic of Ireland,
United Kingdom, international context) can explain why the various
conflict management and settlement attempts that have been made since
the 1960s have faced extreme difficulties during the negotiation and
implementation stages and often never even reached the stage where
they could have proven their operability. This has only changed with the
Good Friday Agreement concluded in April 1998. Several years on, it
appears that, despite numerous difficulties facing its supporters, the
Agreement provides sufficient stability and flexibility to allow a political
process to take place in Northern Ireland that is regarded by the vast
majority of the population as representative of their interests.

In this introductory chapter, I will analyse over thirty years of unsuccessful conflict management in Northern Ireland that preceded the
conclusion of the Good Friday Agreement. Following a brief exploration
of the debate about the nature of the Northern Ireland conflict and the
solution it requires, I will trace the various attempts to settle the conflict
from the Sunningdale Agreement of 1973 to the Anglo-Irish Agreement
of 1985, and finally to the Good Friday Agreement itself. This will make
it possible to assess the reasons for the success so far of the Good Friday
Agreement and its future prospects, and to frame the subsequent discussions of individual dimensions of Northern Irish politics and society
and the impact the Agreement has had on them.

The Conflict about the Conflict and its Solutions[1]

Explanations of the Northern Ireland conflict vary widely between and
within the two principal communities in Northern Ireland. Generally, a
line can be drawn between external and internal accounts. The two
external explanations are the Nationalist, and especially Republican,
contention that the involvement of the British state into what is essentially described as internal Irish affairs is the major cause of the conflict;
the alternative Unionist and Loyalist versions are that the Republic of
Ireland in upholding its constitutional claim to the whole of Ireland in
Articles 2 and 3 of its 1937 constitution unnecessarily fuelled the existing tensions and encouraged the Nationalist/Republican tradition to
strive for Irish reunification.[2]

1 An overview of the various interpretations of the Northern Ireland conflict is McGarry and
   O'Leary (1996).
2 As part of the Good Friday Agreement, the Irish Constitution has been modified in this
   respect.

Internal explanations, in contrast, see the roots of the conflict in a variety of factors within Northern Ireland itself by focusing on the implications of economic, religious and/or cultural conditions in the province. Economically, deprivation and systematic discrimination of Catholics in Northern Ireland is the most common argument to account for the conflict, alongside suggestions of economic opportunism of those who actually profit from the ongoing conflict. As an explanatory concept, religion is either seen as a phenomenon that deepens and aligns already existing social divides, making positive intercommunal relationships virtually impossible, or the religious fanaticism of certain sections within each community is interpreted as the driving force behind the conflict policies of each community. Cultural accounts, finally, treat the conflict either as inherited, that is, simply as the tradition of being in conflict with the other community and/or the authorities, or as an ethnocentric clash of two fundamentally different cultures.

As a consequence of this conflict about the conflict, proposed solutions have differed widely. They range from full integration of Northern Ireland into Great Britain, to devolution, independence, repartition, and eventually to Irish unification, with a variety of different models for each of the major proposals.

Integration into Great Britain, defined as direct government by Westminster, is an idea mostly supported by various streams within the Unionist community and based on an understanding of the conflict as caused by the 'Irish dimension'. Full integration, in one version, aims at making Northern Ireland part of the United Kingdom such that it would neither be treated any differently from any other part of the country, nor would it have separate, or independent, or different institutions.[3] Supporters of electoral integration propose a slightly different model, according to which the main British political parties should expand into Northern Ireland to create a party-political 'normality' above sectarian divisions and thus eliminate or at least gradually realign Northern Irish political parties on other issues. Both of these models of integration suggested a modification of the system of direct rule, which, at the time of its introduction in 1972, was only supposed to be temporary, but then lasted for almost three decades. However, there is a third group of integrationists who argued that, instead of changing this system, it should have simply been made permanent.

In contrast to the various types of integration, which were supported almost exclusively by Unionists, the idea of devolving powers held by the Westminster government has been favoured, in its various forms, and each of them with different degrees of support, by sections of both

---

3   This solution is no longer a real option since devolution in Scotland and Wales has created a constitutionally different situation for the whole of the United Kingdom.

communities. While a return to simple majority rule, as it existed between 1921 and 1972, was, and still is, favoured among significant sections of the Unionist community, notably the Democratic Unionist Party (DUP) and some parts of the Ulster Unionist Party (UUP), this proposal enjoys no support from within the Nationalist camp. Majority rule with safeguards, such as a Bill of Rights and an election system based on proportional representation (PR), is a more moderate approach that tries to take account of the historic concerns of the minority community. However, any significant support for such a solution has always been confined to Unionism. Another proposal for a devolutionist arrangement, supported by the explicitly cross-communal Alliance Party of Northern Ireland, and to some extent by sections of the UUP, was power sharing, giving political representatives from both communities the opportunity to be involved in the executive and legislative branches of a new system of government in Northern Ireland. While the moderate Nationalist community, primarily the Social Democratic and Labour Party (SDLP), supported the idea of power sharing, they wanted it to be qualified by some measure of executive and legislative involvement of the Republic of Ireland, which was unacceptable to Unionists before the 1990s.

Between suggestions for integration into Britain and Irish reunification stand proposals for repartition along the major demographic divides in the West and Southwest of the province, the independence of Northern Ireland from both Britain and the Republic of Ireland, and joint authority of both states over Northern Ireland. With the exception of joint authority, which found significant support among Nationalists, none of these proposals was attractive to a majority within either of the two major traditions in Northern Ireland.

In contrast, the idea of a united Ireland has always been very popular as a long-term goal in the Nationalist community. While moderate Nationalists favour its achievement by consent and peaceful, constitutional, and democratic ways, Republican paramilitary groups tried since 1921 to force the issue through violence. While this approach is rejected by large sections of the Nationalist community, a majority of the same community is nevertheless united over the desirability of the goal of Irish unification, which, in turn, is strongly opposed by Unionists and Loyalists.

All these positions have developed and gradually changed over time. Nevertheless, they provide a general understanding about where the distinct political traditions and different parties within them come from. As such, they form the context in which the Sunningdale and Anglo-Irish Agreements were concluded, and in which eventually the Good Friday Agreement was approved.

The Failure of Sunningdale

With the Northern Ireland conflict at its early climax in 1972 and 1973, the British government published The Future of Northern Ireland: A Paper for Discussion (Northern Ireland Office 1972) shortly after the introduction of direct rule. This publication was followed by a consultation process in Northern Ireland, and, after the conclusion of the latter, constitutional proposals for the province, which were to provide a power-sharing executive and closer, formal links between Northern Ireland and the Republic of Ireland, were introduced in parliament (Northern Ireland Office 1973). After their approval in Westminster, elections to a power-sharing assembly were held on 28 June 1973. Based on an electoral system according to which between five and seven candidates were elected by proportional representation in each of the then twelve parliamentary constituencies in Northern Ireland and on a turnout of 72.5 percent, the elections returned seventy-eight representatives of eight parties to the new assembly. The official Unionists won 29.3 percent of the vote and sent twenty-four members to the assembly, followed by the SDLP with 22.1 percent and nineteen successful candidates. Together with the Alliance Party, which won 9.2 percent of the vote and eight seats, they formed a coalition government (Northern Ireland executive), initially supported by fifty-two of the seventy-eight members of the assembly, which was in favour of both the idea of power-sharing and of a Council of Ireland to be established subsequently.

Between 6 and 9 December 1973, representatives of the British and Irish governments and of the parties involved in the designated executive met at Sunningdale and discussed and agreed the setting up of the Council of Ireland. The provisions foresaw a Council of Ministers with executive, harmonising and consultative functions, consisting of an equal number of delegates from the Northern Ireland Executive and the Irish government, and a Consultative Assembly of thirty members from each of the parliaments, chosen by proportional representation on the basis of the single transferable vote system within each parliament. The Council was to have executive functions, by means of a unanimous vote in the Council of Ministers, in the fields of environment, agriculture, cooperation in trade and industry, electricity, tourism, transport, public health, sport, culture and the arts. The conference also agreed on closer cooperation in security-related matters, on inviting the Council of Ireland to draft a human rights bill, and on the possibility of a future devolution of further powers from Westminster to the Northern Ireland Assembly and the institutions of the Council of Ireland.

The initially favourable situation of apparently widespread support for these arrangements began to change dramatically early in 1974. The Westminster elections on 28 February had been turned into a referendum on the new constitutional status of the province and the more formal links with the Republic of Ireland. Opponents of any change in the status quo united in a coalition called the United Ulster Unionist Council and won 51 percent of the vote and eleven of the twelve seats in Northern Ireland, with the remaining seat going to the SDLP. Shortly afterwards, the recently established Ulster Workers' Council (UWC) called for new elections to the Northern Ireland Assembly. When a motion against power sharing and the Council of Ireland was defeated in the assembly by forty-four to twenty-eight votes on 14 May 1974, the UWC called for a general strike. The following two weeks of the strike brought Northern Ireland to an almost complete standstill. The British government failed to breakup the strike and was unwilling to negotiate a settlement with the UWC. This led to the resignation of the Northern Ireland Executive on 28 May 1974. The assembly was prorogued two days later, and direct rule was resumed.

The essential conditions for the success of power-sharing and a formal institutional involvement of the Republic of Ireland in the affairs of Northern Ireland had not been in place, and even where they had appeared to be present, they were not stable enough to endure the pressures put on them. Even though the initial elections to the Northern Ireland Assembly seemed to be a clear vote in favour of the new constitutional status, the reality of the situation in the province betrayed this superficial impression. The cooperating elites had a rather secure two-thirds majority in the assembly, but their influence and control over their (former) electorate on the outside was far less permanent and stable, in particular as far as Unionists in favour of the new arrangements and the Alliance Party were concerned.[4]

To complicate the situation even further, Harold Wilson, the Labour Prime Minister, condemned the UWC strike in a television broadcast as a 'deliberate and calculated attempt to use every undemocratic and unparliamentary means for the purpose of bringing down the whole constitution of Northern Ireland'. He also accused the strikers of 'sponging on Westminster and British democracy' (cited in Buckland 1981: 172), a remark which both broadened and deepened the alienation of the Unionist community. Even after this statement on 25 May 1974, no decisive steps were taken to end the strike, either by entering into negotiations with the UWC, as Brian Faulkner, the head of the Northern Ireland Executive, demanded, or by deploying and using enough security forces, as the SDLP requested. In these circumstances the Executive as a whole lost its confidence in the willingness and ability of the British govern-

---

4   The votes both received in the 1974 Westminster elections were cut down to one-third of the results they had achieved in the 1973 assembly elections. Part of the explanation lies in the different voting systems applied in both elections – PR for the assembly and plurality rule for the Westminster elections.

ment to preserve the constitutional arrangements put in place at the beginning of the year.

The situation in the Republic of Ireland, too, did little to help ensure the success of Sunningdale. Not only was the Sunningdale Communiqué vague in its wording, in particular it lacked a guarantee by the Irish government concerning the constitutional status of Northern Ireland. This was further aggravated by a ruling of the Irish Constitutional Court on the compatibility of Article 5 of the Sunningdale Communiqué[5] with Articles 2 and 3 of the Irish Constitution on 16 January 1974. The Court declared that Article 5 was merely a statement of policy, but that any attempt to implement it might be in violation of the constitution (Boyle and Hadden 1994: 120). Realising the potential dangers for the situation in Northern Ireland, the Dail rejected a motion against partition on 25 February; and on 13 March, the then Irish Prime Minister, William Cosgrave, gave further assurances stating that 'the factual position of Northern Ireland is that it is within the United Kingdom' and that his 'government accepts this as a fact'.[6] Yet, in the eyes of Loyalists, this was too little, too late.

The effects on the situation in Northern Ireland were devastating. As neither the Northern Ireland Executive nor the British government sought clarification from the Irish government on this issue, the SDLP's interpretation of the new constitutional arrangements – that they were merely transitional on the road to Irish unity – was significantly strengthened. Correspondingly the fears within the Unionist community about the constitutional future of Northern Ireland were compounded.

In addition, the Labour government under Harold Wilson did little to assure Loyalists of its genuine desire to find a settlement acceptable to all parties. Instead, British policy statements increased Loyalist fears of a sell-out. In a speech in Newcastle-under-Lyme, the then Secretary of State for Defence, Roy Mason, acknowledged the pressure put on the government to set a date for the army to be withdrawn from Northern Ireland in order to increase the leverage on politicians in the province to seek a solution to their differences (Bell 1993: 409). Even more difficult to explain was a letter by the Secretary of State for Northern Ireland, Merlyn Rees, which was presented at an IRA press conference on 13 May 1974, in which Rees had stated, 'We have not the faintest interest to stay in Ireland and the quicker we are out the better' (cited in Bell 1993: 410).

The Sunningdale Agreement was not a treaty between two states, but an agreement reached between two states and a selected number of political parties. In order to work, it would have required substantial support

---

5   The relevant passage of Article 5 reads as follows: 'The Irish Government fully accepted and solemnly declared that there could be no change in the status of Northern Ireland until a majority of the people of Northern Ireland desired a change in that status.'
6   William Cosgrave in the Dail Debate on 13 March 1974, cited in Coogan (1995: 169).

for those partners in the Agreement who were most volatile to pressures from within their own communities: the pro-Agreement parties in both blocs who were vulnerable to outflanking by extremists. That this support for pro-Agreement politicians was not forthcoming was one of the major reasons for the failure of this early attempt to resolve the Northern Ireland conflict. In contrast to the situation two-and-a-half decades later, there was also hardly any international pressure to implement the Agreement.

The conditions accounting for the failure of Sunningdale can be listed as follows:

In Northern Ireland:
● vulnerability of the pro-Agreement parties to outflanking by extremists in both communities;
● traditional mistrust of large sections of the Unionist community towards all issues involving cross-border cooperation;
● recent high level of violent interethnic conflict;
● ability of the UWC to mobilise key sections of the Unionist community in a general strike against the Agreement;
● lack of popular and institutional support in defence of the Agreement.

In the United Kingdom:
● failure to take decisive measures in support of the pro-Agreement parties in Northern Ireland and to defeat the general strike in its early stages;
● public comments by leading government officials that fuelled anger and fear within the Unionist and Loyalist communities;
● lack of effective responses to the Irish Constitutional Court's ruling on the compatibility of the Sunningdale Agreement with Articles 2 and 3 of the Irish constitution.

In the Republic of Ireland:
● Irish Constitutional Court's ruling on the compatibility of the Sunningdale Agreement with Articles 2 and 3 of the Irish Constitution;
● lack of sufficient assurances by the Irish government to respect the constitutional status of Northern Ireland.

International context:
● lack of any pressure on, or incentives for, the conflict parties to resolve their differences through compromise.

The Anglo-Irish Agreement

After the failure of Sunningdale, the British government undertook several other initiatives. In an attempt to eliminate what was seen as the reason for the failure of Sunningdale, these initiatives were either strictly limited to Northern Ireland itself, such as the 1974/75 constitutional convention, or, when they had cross-border implications, they did not involve any Northern Irish political parties, as with the Anglo-Irish Intergovernmental Council set up in 1981. Yet, none of these initiatives were any more successful in resolving the conflict than Sunningdale had been.

Between 1982 and 1984, another attempt was made by reintroducing devolution. A scheme of 'rolling devolution' involving an assembly and a committee-style executive was proposed. The devolution of powers to elected representatives in Northern Ireland was supposed to be gradual and subject to a 70 percent majority in favour in the assembly to be elected. As there was no adequate recognition of the Nationalist tradition in Northern Ireland, both Sinn Féin and the SDLP participated in the 1982 elections on an abstentionist platform and subsequently boycotted the assembly (Cunningham 1991: 150).

In 1983 the Fianna Fail, Fine Gael and Labour parties of the Republic of Ireland met with the Northern Irish SDLP in Dublin at the so-called New Ireland Forum to discuss the future of Northern Ireland from their viewpoint. Invitations had also been issued to all the Unionist parties, yet these decided to boycott the Forum. Eleven public meetings were held in the period up to February 1984. In September 1983 delegates from the Forum visited Northern Ireland and in January 1984 the United Kingdom. In conclusion, the Forum produced a report (New Ireland Forum 1984) in which the members gave their analysis of the problem, examined the situation in Northern Ireland, and presented three potential solutions to the conflict – a unitary Irish state, a federal or confederate Irish state, and joint British-Irish authority over Northern Ireland. While this report represented a determinedly Nationalist interpretation of the conflict and its possible solutions, it nevertheless signalled to the British government that there was a certain basis for negotiation and compromise.[7]

Given this and the British desire to involve the Republic of Ireland in the responsibility of running the province amidst the continuously serious security situation, as well as the growing Irish interest to stabilise the situation in the North and to prevent a spill-over of violence and/or Republican influence, a new and joint approach to the conflict seemed

7   See Gerard Murray's more detailed examination of the importance of the New Ireland Forum
    for the current peace process in Chapter 3 below.

possible. Furthermore, both governments faced a growing appeal of Republican ideology within the Nationalist community, in particular after the hunger strikes of the early 1980s. Based on these considerations, both governments decided to enter into negotiations, which resulted in the Anglo-Irish Agreement of 1985.

The Agreement dealt with a variety of issues, including an Intergovernmental Conference, a human rights bill for Northern Ireland, security and judicial policies, and cross-border cooperation on economic, social and cultural matters. The British attempt to address concerns of the Nationalist community was apparent, but as the implementation of the Agreement did not produce any dramatic or even particularly noticeable results, the reward for Britain alienating the Unionist community was not forthcoming as expected. Although the influence of Sinn Féin within the Nationalist camp decreased towards the end of the 1980s, activities of the IRA increased, facilitated by a shipment of weapons and equipment from Libya. However, the declining electoral appeal of Sinn Féin set in motion a rethinking process among the leadership of the party. Eventually, the party moved away from its unqualified support for, or at least tolerance of, Republican violence to become one of the participants in the peace process(es) of the 1990s that finally brought about the Good Friday Agreement in 1998. At the same time, strong Unionist opposition to the Anglo-Irish Agreement failed to secure one of the central objectives of the British government, namely to strengthen moderate Unionism in the form of the UUP and marginalise the extremists of and within the DUP. Similarly unsatisfactory were the workings of the Intergovernmental Conference, acknowledged in the official 1989 review, the hoped-for improvement in the security situation, and the envisaged cross-border cooperation.[8]

The attitudes towards the Anglo-Irish Agreement also revealed the persistently deep divisions within Northern Irish society. In a survey of January 1988, 55.1 percent of those who declared themselves as Protestants voiced their opposition to the Anglo-Irish Agreement, compared with 7.9 percent of those describing themselves as Catholics. Only 8.7 percent of Protestants opted more or less in favour of the Agreement, as compared to 31.8 percent of Catholics who did so. Asked in the same survey for the biggest problem in Northern Ireland, only 8.6 percent of Catholics, but 29.5 percent of Protestants, pointed to the Anglo-Irish Agreement (Hamilton 1990).

8   According to statistics produced by the Royal Ulster Constabulary (RUC), the three years prior to the Anglo-Irish Agreement produced 195 deaths, 2,342 injuries, 716 shooting incidents, 607 explosions, and 1708 armed robberies. The respective figures for 1986–1988 are: 247 deaths (+27%), 3,661 injuries (+56%), 1,132 shootings (+58%), 661 explosions(+9%), and 2,253 armed robberies (+31%). This increase was not necessarily a direct effect of the Anglo-Irish Agreement as O'Leary and McGarry (1996: 270–3) have shown.

Although the Anglo-Irish Agreement had by no means failed as badly as Sunningdale, it also did not produce a significant breakthrough in the political stalemate in Northern Ireland. In some respects, such as the increasing alienation of parts of the Unionist community, it even worsened the situation and prevented major progress for years to come. Although the stalemate continued, it did so on a different level. The Agreement had shown that solutions were possible to which the two governments and a significant part of the Nationalist community could agree. This had a positive long-term effect on the opportunities to reduce the level of violent conflict and to increase the chances of achieving an inclusive agreement for the future of Northern Ireland, because it made uncompromising, hard-line Unionism less credible as a strategy to preserve Northern Ireland's link with Great Britain and, similarly, indicated that there was overwhelming support for constitutional, nonviolent politics within the Nationalist community, the latter finding its expression in the poor electoral performance of Sinn Féin in the late 1980s, early 1990s. The limited success that the Anglo-Irish Agreement had in the short term was mostly a consequence of its being reached and implemented at intergovernmental level. This being a recognition of the situation in the mid-1980s, in which cross-communal agreement was virtually impossible, the British and Irish governments also had to accept that no stable and durable solution would be possible without the involvement and consent of the parties representing the two traditions in Northern Ireland.

Conditions accounting for the limited success of the Anglo-Irish Agreement can be listed as follows:

In Northern Ireland:
- exclusion of the political parties in Northern Ireland from the formal negotiation process;
- no opportunity for the people of Northern Ireland to approve, or reject, the Agreement;
- disappointment among Nationalists and Republicans about the lack of visible improvements in their situation;
- increased hard-line Republican resistance to British policy;
- radicalisation of the Unionist community in opposition to the 'Irish' dimension of the Agreement;
- continued high levels of violent interethnic conflict.

In the United Kingdom:
- deliberate attempt to address concerns of the Nationalist community, even at the price of alienating sections within the Unionist community;
- failure to deliver on key aspects of the Agreement, such as the Intergovernmental Conference, cross-border cooperation, and an improved security situation.

In the Republic of Ireland:
- upholding of the constitutional claim to Northern Ireland and its perception by Unionists as a threat to a nonnegotiable aspect of their identity;
- failure to deliver on key aspects of the Agreement, such as the Intergovernmental Conference, cross-border cooperation, and an improved security situation.

International context:
- lack of any pressure on the conflict parties to resolve their differences through compromise;
- support of the IRA through Libyan arms shipments.

From the Framework Documents to the Good Friday Agreement

By 1994, the situation in Northern Ireland had changed significantly. Following a Joint Declaration by the British and Irish Prime Ministers in 1993, a number of confidence-building measures were introduced, leading to cease-fires by the major paramilitary organisations that did not cover a specified period of time (as they had in the past), but seemed, if not permanent, at least longer-term. In addition, the British government had entered into official and formal talks with representatives of the paramilitary organisations of both communities, and Sinn Féin was heading back into the political process, being recognised as a necessary partner by both governments. However, both governments also realised that the causes of conflict in Northern Ireland had not been removed and that a more comprehensive settlement was necessary to achieve this. Thus, they developed A New Framework for Agreement, which proposed structures for British-Irish (or, Northern Ireland – Republic of Ireland) and East-West (British-Irish) institutions and sought to integrate the earlier suspended talks with the political parties in Northern Ireland with a new effort of peacemaking (O'Leary 1995: 867). Both governments recognised that a settlement would not be possible without significant and substantial compromise from all conflict parties and reaffirmed the basic positions of the Joint Declaration – the principles of self-determination and consent, peaceful and democratic means as the only acceptable political strategies and tactics, and the recognition of the fundamental 'rights and identities of both traditions'. In addition, the British government proposed its own ideas for a possible solution of the conflict within Northern Ireland in a document called A Framework for Accountable Government in Northern Ireland.

Throughout 1995, contacts continued between the British government and Sinn Féin, but no major progress was achieved. Part of the reason for this lack of progress was the British insistence that the decommissioning of paramilitary weapons precede Sinn Féin's admission to formal multiparty talks. The Conservative government under John Major set this precondition after the negative response Unionists gave to the Framework Documents, but it also reflected the wider problems of the government and its decreasing majority in Westminster (O'Leary 1997: 672).

The end of the IRA cease-fire in February 1996 and the resumption of (Republican) violence across Northern Ireland and in England proved to be a major setback. Despite this, the British and Irish governments announced the beginning of all-party talks, following elections to them in May, for June 1996. Although Sinn Féin polled a record 15.5 percent of the vote in these elections, the party was not allowed to take its seats at the negotiation table, because IRA violence continued and the party did not sign up to the Mitchell Principles of nonviolence.[9] The multiparty talks commenced as planned but did not bring about any significant results in their first year.

The election of a Labour government in May 1997, the emphasis Labour put on reaching a settlement in Northern Ireland, and the perception, primarily among the Nationalist community, that there was a new approach in Northern Ireland policies offered new opportunities. In July 1997, the IRA renewed its cease-fire. After Sinn Féin had signed up to the Mitchell Principles, the party was allowed into the peace talks at Stormont. This, however, resulted in the DUP and the United Kingdom Unionist Party (UKUP) walking out. After more than half a year of intensive negotiations with several setbacks,[10] eight political parties in Northern Ireland and the British and Irish governments agreed on what has become known as the Good Friday Agreement.

---

9 Section III, Article 20 of the so-called Mitchell Report spells out the following principles to which parties participating in the talks should commit: 'a. To democratic and exclusively peaceful means of resolving political issues; b. To the total disarmament of all paramilitary organisations; c. To agree that such disarmament must be verifiable to the satisfaction of an independent commission; d. To renounce for themselves, and to oppose any effort by others, to use force, or threaten to use force, to influence the course or the outcome of all-party negotiations; e. To agree to abide by the terms of any agreement reached in all-party negotiations and to resort to democratic and exclusively peaceful methods in trying to alter any aspect of that outcome with which they may disagree; and, f. To urge that "punishment" killings and beatings stop and to take effective steps to prevent such actions' (Mitchell et al. 1996).

10 For a more detailed analysis of the negotiation process see Stephen Farry's chapter below.

The Good Friday Agreement – A Way to a Lasting Settlement?

The Good Friday Agreement, which eventually found the consent of all parties involved in the talks process on 10 April 1998, is accompanied by a declaration of support from the two governments, in which they commit themselves to recognising and implementing the will of the majority of the people in Northern Ireland regarding the constitutional status of the province and to upholding the right of all people in Northern Ireland to have dual citizenship of the United Kingdom and the Republic of Ireland. At the same time as the Good Friday Agreement was concluded, a new agreement between the two governments replaced the old Anglo-Irish Agreement. In Article 1, the same commitments are made as in the declaration of support; Article 2 confirms the will of both governments to support and implement the Good Friday Agreement where this falls under their jurisdictional competence, and Article 3 lays down the procedures for phasing out the 1985 Anglo-Irish Agreement. Article 4 describes the conditions for the new Agreement to enter into force as the enacting of British legislation in accordance with the Constitutional Issues section of the Good Friday Agreement, the amendment of the Irish Constitution and its approval in a referendum (also in accordance with the Constitutional Issues section of the Good Friday Agreement), and the establishment of the institutions outlined in the Good Friday Agreement.

The Agreement itself deals with three main areas – democratic institutions in Northern Ireland (Strand One of the negotiations), a British-Irish Ministerial Council (Strand Two of the negotiations), and the British-Irish Council, the British-Irish Intergovernmental Conference, and Rights, Safeguards, and Equality of Opportunity (Strand Three of the negotiations).

Concerning Strand One of the negotiations, the establishment of a 108-member-strong Assembly was agreed. This assembly is elected by the single transferable vote system from existing Westminster constituencies. It will initially exercise full legislative and executive authority over the powers currently held by the six Northern Ireland Government Departments. Subject to later developments, the Assembly could take on responsibility for other matters in accordance with the Agreement. Among the safeguards to ensure that all sections of the community can participate in the work of the Assembly, and to protect them in their rights and identities, are the allocation of Committee Chairs, Ministers and Committee membership in proportion to party strength in the Assembly; the subordination of legislation to the European Convention on Human Rights (ECHR) and any future Bill of Rights for Northern Ireland over Assembly legislation; arrangements to ensure that key decisions are taken on a cross-community basis;[11] and the creation of an Equality Commission. Crucial for the operation of the Assembly is that its members register their identity as Nationalist, Unionist or Other to have a measurement of community support in place for decisions taken according to the cross-community consent procedures.

According to the Agreement, a Committee for each of the main executive functions of the Northern Ireland Administration is established. Chairs and Deputy Chairs of these Committees are allocated proportionally according to the d'Hondt system, while ensuring membership in the Committees in proportion to party representation in the Assembly. The responsibility of the Committees includes scrutiny, policy development, consultation and legislation initiation functions with respect to the Departments with which they are associated, and will have a role in initiation of legislation. Their powers include considering and advising on Departmental budgets and Annual Plans in the context of the overall budget allocation; approving relevant secondary legislation and taking the Committee stage of relevant primary legislation; and initiating enquiries and making reports. In addition to these permanent Committees, the Assembly has the right to appoint special committees as required.

Executive authority on behalf of the Assembly rests with the First Minister and his or her deputy and up to ten Ministers with departmental responsibilities. Following the joint election of the First Minister and Deputy First Minister, the posts of Ministers are allocated to parties based on the d'Hondt system based on the strength of each party in the assembly. An Executive Committee, comprising all Ministers and the First and Deputy First Minister, is to handle all issues which cut across the responsibilities of two or more Ministers to formulate a consistent policy on the respective issue. Ministers have full executive authority in their respective departmental areas within a policy framework agreed by the Executive Committee and endorsed by the Assembly. In the early hours of 18 December 1998, the pro-Agreement parties at Stormont reached a compromise on a list of departments for the government: agriculture and rural development; enterprise, trade and investment (to include tourism); health, social care and public safety; finance and personnel; education, advanced education, training and employment; the environment; regional development; social development; culture, arts and leisure. This was a significant step forward on the way to full implementation of the Good Friday Agreement.

11 There are two such mechanisms: parallel consent (i.e., more than 50 percent of members present and voting in each designation) and weighted majority (i.e., sixty percent of members present and voting, including at least forty per cent of each of the Nationalist and Unionist designations present and voting). Key decisions requiring either of these procedures include the election of the Chair and Deputy Chair of the Assembly, the First Minister and Deputy First Minister, standing orders and budget allocations. There is also the possibility that these procedures can be requested by a petition of concern brought by at least thirty of the 108 members of the Assembly.

Concerning legislation, which can be initiated by an individual, a Committee or a Minister, the Assembly can pass primary legislation for Northern Ireland in all areas where it has devolved powers. The passing of legislation is subject to decisions by simple majority of members voting (except for decisions that require cross-community support) to detailed scrutiny and approval in the relevant Departmental Committee, and to coordination with Westminster legislation. Any disputes over legislative competence will be decided by the Courts. In its relations with other institutions, the Assembly has to ensure cross-community participation.

As there are a number of powers which will not be devolved to the Assembly, the Secretary of State for Northern Ireland retains a role in the political process, including the Northern Ireland Office (NIO) matters not devolved to the Assembly, the approval and laying before the Westminster Parliament of any Assembly legislation, and to represent Northern Ireland interests in the United Kingdom. The Parliament in Westminster will continue to be responsible, among other things, for legislation on nondevolved issues and for legislation necessary to ensure the United Kingdom's international obligations in relation to Northern Ireland.

The Agreement also establishes a consultative Civic Forum comprising, among others, representatives of the business, trade union and voluntary sectors and acting as a consultative mechanism on social, economic and cultural issues.

With respect to Strand Two, which dealt with North-South relations, agreement was reached on the establishment of a North-South Ministerial Council to institutionalise formal relationships between the executive organs of Northern Ireland and the Republic of Ireland (for more details, see O'Leary 1999: 80–2). Its responsibilities include consultation, cooperation and implementation of decisions on issues of mutual concern. All decisions of the Council have to be by agreement between the two sides.

Council meetings are to be held in three different formats – in plenary format twice a year, with the Northern Ireland delegation being led by the First Minister and Deputy First Minister and the Irish government led by the Taoiseach; in specific formats with the delegations being represented by the respective Minister; and in other appropriate formats to consider institutional and cross-sector matters and to resolve any issues of discontent. Even though the Council and the delegates represented on it have the authority to take decisions on all matters within their competence, implementation is subject to approval by both parliaments.

As a prerequisite for the formal devolution of powers to the Northern Ireland Assembly, inaugural meetings had to take place of the Assembly, the British-Irish Council and the British-Irish Ministerial Council in their transitional forms. With a delay of more than one month (the original deadline had been 31 October 1998) the parties in Northern Ireland agreed six implementation bodies for the British-Irish Ministerial Council by 18 December 1998 – inland waterways, food safety, trade and business development, special EU programmes, the Irish and Ulster Scots languages, and agricultural and marine matters. Areas of functional cooperation were determined as selected aspects of transport, agriculture, education, health, environment and tourism. A change in the arrangements regulating the operation of the North-South Council is possible in the future by agreement of the governments of Great Britain and Northern Ireland and the endorsement of their respective parliaments. Further tasks for the Council relate to representing Irish interests at the European level, developing a form of interparliamentary cooperation and establishing a consultative forum comprising representatives of civil society.

According to the agenda of the talks process, Strand Three dealt with three different issues – the establishment of a British-Irish Council, the creation of a British-Irish Intergovernmental Conference, and the broad field of rights, safeguards and equality of opportunity in Northern Ireland.

The British-Irish Council was to be established in relation to a new British-Irish Agreement to deal with the totality of relationships among the peoples of 'these islands', and was thus to bring together within a formal institutional framework representatives of the British and Irish governments, of the devolved institutions in Northern Ireland, Scotland and Wales and of territorial and political units in the British Isles. The format of meeting is similar to that of the North-South Council. Issues with which the British-Irish Council is to deal include transport links, agriculture, environment, culture, health, education and the European Union. Common policies can be agreed by the members of the British-Irish Council without being binding for all of the regions represented in it. Further arrangements of the operational procedures of the British-Irish Council and changes to existing ones are subject to negotiations and consensual agreement among the representatives within it.

In addition to the British-Irish Council, a British-Irish Intergovernmental Conference will be established according to a new Anglo-Irish Agreement subsuming both the Anglo-Irish Intergovernmental Council and the Intergovernmental Conference established under the 1985 Agreement. The task of the Conference is to promote broad and substantial bilateral cooperation between the United Kingdom and the Republic of Ireland. As part of this, the Conference also deals with non-devolved matters of the affairs of Northern Ireland, including security, rights, justice, prisons and policing.

The third area – rights, safeguards and equality of opportunity – covers a wide variety of different matters and sets out a framework for the implementation of new policies in the areas of human rights, reconciliation, economic, social and cultural issues, decommissioning of paramilitary weapons, security, policing and justice, and prisoners, including the necessary changes in United Kingdom and Irish legislation, the creation of new institutions in Northern Ireland, the set-up of a commission on policing and of a joint committee of representatives of the Human Rights Commissions in the Republic of Ireland and in Northern Ireland, and a review of the criminal justice system.

Despite the apparent comprehensiveness of the Good Friday Agreement and its endorsement by overwhelming majorities in referenda in Northern Ireland and the Republic of Ireland, the question remains whether it provides an effective framework for a permanent resolution of the conflict. In order to answer this question, it is useful to compare the Good Friday Agreement with previous settlement attempts, both in terms of their content and the context of their implementation.

Starting with the first of these issues, a comparison between the Sunningdale Agreement, the Anglo-Irish Agreement and the Good Friday Agreement reveals that there is a core of issues dealt with by all three or at least two of these agreements in a similar manner (see Table 1.1).

Table 1.1: Agreements on and in Northern Ireland, 1973–1998

	Sunningdale Agreement	Anglo-Irish Agreement	Good Friday Agreement
Signatories	United Kingdom, Republic of Ireland, Unionist Party, SDLP, Alliance	United Kingdom, Republic of Ireland	United Kingdom, Republic of Ireland, UUP, UDP, PUP, NIWC, Labour, Alliance, Sinn Féin, SDLP
Consent principle	X	X	X
Self-determination	O	O	X
Reform of the policing system	X	X	X
Early release of prisoners	X	(X)	X
Bill of Rights	X	X	X
Abandonment of violence	X	X	X
Security cooperation X	X	X	
Cross-border cooperation	X	X	X
Recognition of both identities	O	X	X
Intergovernmental cooperation	X	X	X
Institutional role for the Republic of Ireland	X	X	X
Cooperation between Unionists and Nationalists required	(X)	X	X
Inter-island cooperation	O	(X)	X
Devolution of powers	X	X	X

Key: X–issue addressed; (X)–issue implicitly addressed; O–issue not addressed.

It is, however, worth noting that a number of significant changes have occurred primarily in the context (as opposed to the content) of the Good Friday Agreement compared with the two previous agreements. The improved prospects for a stable settlement in 1998 were largely accepted as being the result of increasing conflict weariness among the wider population in Northern Ireland, of greater pragmatism among the political elites in the province as well as in London and Dublin, and of American involvement in the peace process. In the past three years, however, many of these advantages seem to have faded away or even been reversed, which raises the question whether the reasons for this must be sought in the Good Friday Agreement itself, in the way in which it has been implemented, and/or in the process of post-agreement peace-building. I will return to this question in my conclusion.

The first difference between the situation in 1998 and in 1974 and 1985 lies in the degree of participation in the negotiation of the Good Friday Agreement, which has been far higher than during any previous settlement attempt, and crucially comprised representatives of paramilitary organisations alongside the mainstream constitutional parties and the British and Irish governments. With the exception of the DUP and another marginal Unionist party, the United Kingdom Unionist Party, all major political players have been involved in the original negotiations and continued to participate in the first review in 1999. In a second round of review talks in 2001, sponsored by the British and Irish governments, the political representatives of the Loyalist paramilitary organisations left the negotiations early amidst increasing levels of Loyalist violence in Northern Ireland. At the same time, Republican violence has increased, chiefly through the increased activities of the so-called Real IRA, a group that emerged in October 1997 from a split within the IRA. This split effectively provided the Real IRA with sufficient skills and resources to wage its own terrorist campaign on the British mainland and in Northern Ireland. By August 2001, over twenty explosions, booby traps and shootings in Northern Ireland and six attacks in London and one in Birmingham have been attributed to the Real IRA.

A second difference concerns the comprehensiveness and detail of the arrangements. Here the Good Friday Agreement, as it is based on an inclusive negotiation process, addresses the greatest number of issues and lays down in great detail for most of these issues the operational procedures for their implementation. Two key issues, however, were kept rather vague – decommissioning and the reform of the policing system. At the time, this seemed the only way forward in order to secure a deal, but has given parties on both sides a lot of room to politicise these two issues for a variety of other purposes. In particular, the link established between decommissioning and the stability of the new institutions (on the part of Unionists) and between decommissioning and the wider area of security sector reform (on the part of Republicans) has contributed not just to the many implementation impasses the Good Friday Agreement has seen since 1998, but also to increased doubts about the overall prospects for a sustainable peace process.

A third difference is the character of the implementation process. Only the Good Friday Agreement was proposed to the people in the Republic of Ireland and in Northern Ireland in a referendum, while all previous agreements were implemented merely by government decree, thus giving the people a sense of imposition. The majority with which the Good Friday Agreement was endorsed by the population north and south of the border and across the communities in Northern Ireland had been unprecedented in the history of the conflict. However, recent developments have shown that this majority, particularly among Unionists, has faded away under the strains to which the Agreement has been, and continues to be, subjected.

Fourth, since the beginning of the final round of the negotiation process in the autumn of 1997, the major paramilitary organisations on both sides have upheld their cease-fires, and levels of organised intercommunal violence have dropped dramatically. Without doubt, the beginning of decommissioning of the IRA's arsenal in October 2001 has given a boost to what appeared to have become a peace process beyond rescue. However, there can equally be no doubt that persisting tensions between and within the two communities in Northern Ireland have escalated into violence. Rioting has accompanied the annual marching season and has been triggered by what often seem minor events.[12] The Loyalist turf wars of summer 2000 and a noticeable increase in sectarian violence in 2001, too, underline the volatility of the situation in Northern Ireland. This is increasingly interpreted as a failure of the Good Friday Agreement to deliver on key aspects of security and contributes to an overall sense of gloom and doom, particularly among those Unionists who had initially supported the new institutions.

Fifth, there is the question of what alternative arrangements would be put in place in case the Good Friday Agreement fails. A comparison with the situation that existed after Sunningdale reveals that the incentives for both communities to find a modus vivendi within the Agreement structure are more compelling than they were before. The failure of Sunningdale meant the reintroduction of direct rule, an outcome that many in the Unionist community preferred to power-sharing. A failure of the Good Friday Agreement, however, will mean most likely that the United Kingdom and the Republic of Ireland will move towards shared sovereignty over Northern Ireland. Clearly, this is not an outcome that Unionists would prefer. Nationalists, however, would also lose out, as the influence of both communities on the decision-making process in Northern Ireland would decrease to a level well below to what they have achieved now. In particular, Sinn Féin, unless the party substantially increases its representation in the Irish parliament, would loose an unprecedented power base.

12 See Dominic Bryan's chapter in this volume.

Finally, the international context, especially the involvement of the United States, has been a critical factor in the success of the Good Friday Agreement to date. The international mediation of the talks process and the simultaneous and subsequent American pressure on, and incentives for, all parties in the process to come to an agreement and to implement it has played a significant role in the maintenance of the peace process. The vital role of former US Senator George Mitchell in brokering the Belfast Agreement in 1998 and in overcoming the decommissioning impasse in 1999, as well as the support from the European Union, must not be underestimated in their importance. The early endorsement of the post-Agreement peace process in the form of the award of the Nobel Peace Prize to John Hume and David Trimble was similarly significant. It assisted in encouraging the pursuit of a long-term and stable peace in Northern Ireland and in putting the spotlight on the developments in the province in which the major protagonists seemed unwilling to contemplate failure in their efforts to seek accommodation. However, with the change in administration in Washington, official US involvement has been less high-profile than before, meaning that an important lever of influence over both Unionists/Loyalists and Nationalists/Republicans might have been lost. In all fairness to the new American administration, President George W. Bush announced on 15 March 2001, that Richard N. Haass, the Director of Policy Planning at the State Department, would take responsibility for US support of the Northern Ireland peace process. On 16 May 2001, the Secretary of State, in consultation with the Attorney-General and the Secretary of the Treasury, decided to designate the Republican paramilitary group Real IRA (including its aliases '32 County Sovereignty Movement' and 'Irish Republican Prisoners Welfare Association') as a 'Foreign Terrorist Organization', which makes it illegal for persons in the United States or subject to US jurisdiction to provide any material support to this group and requires U.S. financial institutions to block any of the group's assets. It is now also possible to deny entry visas to the USA for members or representatives of the group. The President himself expressed his commitment to help with the implementation of the Good Friday Agreement at a press conference on 19 July 2001, in London, saying that 'if there's anything that I can help to do to bring peace to the region, I will do so' (Transcript 2001). In a statement released on 1 August 2001, the President commented on the two governments' proposal to rescue the Good Friday Agreement from the imminent institutional collapse brought on by the resignation of David Trimble as First Minister by stating his 'strong support for the package of proposals their governments released to the political party leaders in Northern Ireland' (White House 2001). It is also obvious that increased American pressure (both from the Bush administration and the Irish American community) after both the terrorist attacks on the US on 11

September 2001 and the arrest of three alleged IRA members in Colombia (suspected of training Marxist guerrillas in explosives and urban terrorism) in August have played a major part in bringing about the beginning of IRA decommissioning.

Both communities have attached great significance to the Good Friday Agreement, or, more precisely, to their specific interpretation of it, thus creating an unprecedented level of public symbolism related to its implementation. This in turn has generated a sense of entitlement to have one's particular vision of the Good Friday Agreement implemented, which can quickly turn into deep resentment if that is not possible. At the same time, the public expression of both entitlement and resentment add to the continuing strain on intercommunal relations as well as on the often still difficult relations between the communities' elites and the two governments involved. The core problem underlying this tension is the fact that, while the opportunity structures for both communities have been altered by the Good Friday Agreement, their interests have remained fundamentally the same; that is, the ethnonational nature of the conflict has not been transformed yet, even though the means with which each community pursues its goals have changed. The public discourse on what exactly the Good Friday Agreement means has thus also become a discourse not just about the legitimacy of the new institutions, but also of the old elites that will have to work within them (or not).

The conditions accounting for the possibility and likely success of the Good Friday Agreement can be listed as follows:

In Northern Ireland:
- inclusion of all parties in the negotiation process based on a prior election;
- opportunity for the people of Northern Ireland to approve the Agreement;
- protection mechanisms built into the Agreement to address concerns of both communities;
- cease-fires of all major paramilitary organisations considerably reducing the level of violent interethnic conflict.

In the United Kingdom:
- change in government, fresh and more determined approach to achieve an inclusive settlement;
- pressure on all sections of the communities in Northern Ireland to compromise;
- greater degree of flexibility on key issues, such as Sinn Féin participation in the negotiation process, decommissioning, early release of prisoners etc.;
- negotiation of a new Anglo-Irish Agreement;
- reiteration that any change in the constitutional future of Northern Ireland was subject to the approval of the people of Northern Ireland;

- close cooperation with the government of the Republic of Ireland and the international chairmanship of the talks.

In the Republic of Ireland:
- preparedness to withdraw the constitutional claim to Northern Ireland;
- pressure, particularly on Sinn Féin and the IRA, to appreciate the opportunity presented by the multiparty negotiations in 1997–8;
- active steps to address concerns of the Unionist community in Northern Ireland;
- close cooperation with the government of the United Kingdom and the international chairmanship of the talks;
- opportunity for the citizens of the Republic of Ireland to approve the Agreement.

International context:
- international, particularly American, involvement in the talks process, including official and unofficial pressure on both communities to come to a settlement and on the IRA to maintain its cease-fire and begin decommissioning.

In summary, and as the following contributions to this volume will make clear, the conflict in Northern Ireland in all its different aspects and dimensions and in its dependence on factors that can be influenced only to a limited degree by the political actors in Belfast, London and Dublin is not certain, but is also not unlikely, to be resolved within and by the institutional framework set out in the Good Friday Agreement. The reason for this uncertainty is that the Good Friday Agreement, as any other agreement reached before, is dependent upon cooperation and compromise between two communities that have fundamentally different political aspirations and identities. These, of course, may change over time, provided opportunities and incentives for such change exist.

References

Bell, J. B. 1993. *The Irish Troubles. A Generation of Violence, 1967–1992*. Dublin.
Boyle, K. and Hadden, T. 1994. *Northern Ireland. The Choice*. London.
Buckland, P. 1981. *A History of Northern Ireland*. Dublin.
Coogan, T. P. 1995. *The Troubles. Ireland's Ordeal 1966–1995 and the Search for Peace*. London.
Cunningham, M. J. 1991. *British Government Policy in Northern Ireland, 1969–1989. Its Nature and Execution*. Manchester.
Hamilton, A. 1990. *Violence and Communities*. Coleraine.
McGarry, J. and O'Leary, B. 1996. *Explaining Northern Ireland: Broken Images*. Oxford.

Mitchell, G. J., de Chastelain, J., Holkeri, H. 1996. *Report of the International Body on Arms Decommissioning 24 January 1996*. Belfast.

New Ireland Forum. 1984. *Report*. Dublin.

Northern Ireland Office. 1972. *The Future of Northern Ireland: A Paper for Discussion*. London and Belfast.

————1973. *Northern Ireland Constitutional Proposals*. London and Belfast.

O'Leary, B. 1995. 'Afterword: What is Framed in the Framework Documents', in *Ethnic and Racial Studies*, vol. 18, no. 4, October 1995, pp. 862–72.

————1997. 'The Conservative Stewardship of Northern Ireland, 1979–1997: Sound-Bottomed Contradiction or Slow Learning?', in *Political Studies*, vol. 45, 1997, pp. 663–76.

————1999. 'The Nature of the British–Irish Agreement', in *New Left Review* no. 233, 1999, pp. 66–96.

O'Leary, B. and McGarry, J. 1996. *The Politics of Antagonism*. London.

The White House, Office of the Press Secretary. 2001. 'Statement by the President on Northern Ireland'. http://www.usembassy.org.uk/ni154.html

Transcript of the News Conference held by Prime Minister Tony Blair and President George W. Bush. 19 July 2001. http://europe.cnn.com/2001/WORLD/europe/07/23/bush.blair.transcript/index.html

Wolff, S. 2001. 'Context and Content: Sunningdale and Belfast Compared', in *Interpretations of the Good Friday Agreement*, ed. Rick Wilford. Oxford.

————2002. *Disputed Territories: The Transnational Dynamics of Ethnic Conflict Settlement*. Oxford.

CHAPTER TWO

The Morning After: An Alliance Perspective on the Agreement[1]

Stephen Farry[2]

In the spring of 1998, the Good Friday Agreement was treated with almost biblical reverence by virtually all of its supporters and almost irrational hysteria by its opponents. The major strength of the Agreement continues to lie in its creation of a set of political institutions with cross-community legitimacy within a deeply divided society. Similarly, the weakness in the position of the Agreement's opponents remains their failure to articulate any alternative that is remotely capable of achieving such crucial cross-community consent.

Several years on, it is possible to view the Agreement and its implementation from a clearer and more critical perspective. Over the past four years, several deficiencies and flaws in the Agreement have come into much clearer focus. Indeed, there is a paradox of the Agreement and its implementation in that while the intensity of the conflict in Northern Ireland has been reduced, divisions have become even more clearly defined and entrenched.

The Agreement is necessary to provide legitimate institutions of governance within a deeply divided society. However, unless those divisions are at the same time ameliorated, the Agreement will remain upon weak foundations. There is no teleological inevitability to the Agreement contributing to peace and stability in Northern Ireland, let alone the creation of a shared and nonsectarian society. By itself, the Agreement only amounts to conflict management. Strategies must be developed and sustained in order to move from conflict management through conflict transformation to conflict resolution if the new dispensation is to prove durable.

While the persistence of deep divisions, accompanied by a lack of overarching loyalties and a sense of common interests, provide longer-term threats to the durability of the Agreement, continued wrangling over the

1 The author thanks Steven Alexander, Kathy Ayers, David Ford, Allan Leonard and Wendy Watt for their comments.
2 The author writes in a private capacity. His views do not necessarily express the official position or policy of the Alliance Party of which he is the General Secretary.

implementation, particularly regarding the issues of decommissioning, the stability of the institutions, policing reform and security normalisation (demilitarisation) have posed more immediate threats to its survival.

In terms of public opinion, the repeated crises over the Agreement, in which attempts to find a breakthrough often become regarded as a series of sectarian trade-offs that are perceived to favour one side over the other, and the increasing challenges to the rule of law have led to an erosion of cross-community support. This drop in support has been most marked in the crucial moderate Unionist constituency. The Agreement, which was initially regarded on all sides of the community as a win-win scenario, is now largely seen in zero-sum terms, with Nationalists the winners and Unionists the losers on almost every issue.

At the time of writing, the decision of the IRA to commence actual decommissioning, plus the intervention of the Alliance Party in temporarily re-designating three of its Assembly Members in order to secure the re-election of David Trimble as First Minister, has bought considerable space for the process. However, one of the side-effects of increased community polarisation is that the more extreme Unionist and Nationalist parties have overtaken or are on the brink of overtaking their more moderate rivals. If such an outcome did occur in future Assembly elections, it would not only challenge the more rigid forms of consociationalism exhibited in the Agreement, but renders as irrelevant the more flexible, centre orientated forms of power-sharing that had featured in other peace initiatives prior to this Agreement. Both reform of the institutions, and action to address to the underlying divisions in society, are required if the Agreement is to have a long-term future.

Background

At its heart, the multiparty talks merged two processes that had previously been separated: the political process, i.e., the process of attaining sufficient cross-community consensus among the various parties over the institutions of governance for Northern Ireland, and the peace process, i.e., the process of achieving and consolidating cessations of violence from paramilitary organisations.

Until the current process, the dominant approach to peacemaking had been based upon the idea of building a political process, and then using that as a platform to create and consolidate peace. The political process would begin within the political centre and work outwards in an attempt to include as many political strands as possible, while fending off those on the extremes who refused to compromise. In theory, if sufficient cross-community consensus could be created, this would go a considerable way to undermine the political legitimacy of paramilitary organisations.

Accordingly, it would then be possible to deal with any remnants of terrorism through a security approach alone.

This approach was reflected in the short-lived power-sharing Executive and Assembly of 1973–4. This initiative failed through lack of Unionist support.[3] It is a moot point whether this system could have been successful if Unionists had backed it. However, such a system would have avoided many of the contradictions apparent both within the multiparty talks and the Agreement itself. Yet, doubts can legitimately be raised regarding whether the system could have undermined politically the paramilitary organisations. We may never know. Nevertheless, Donald Horowitz argues persuasively that the wrong lessons were learnt from the failure of the Sunningdale Initiative. He suggests that parties abandoned the concept of a government across the moderate middle and assumed that any government had to be all-inclusive and fully consociational, but rather should have seen Sunningdale as simply an experiment ahead of its time. Horowitz states: 'The fact that the 1973–74 government was merely a coalition of the middle and thus insufficiently inclusive was not the source of its disintegration. Had the government been more inclusive, it might actually have fallen sooner. Consociational guarantees would not have saved it' (Horowitz 2001).

The Alliance Agenda

The liberal, cross-community Alliance Party recognised that the problems in Northern Ireland were related to its deep ethnonationalist divisions. While these divisions do have some basis in fact, they have been largely constructed and exaggerated.[4] This is what Michael Ignatieff calls 'the narcissism of minor difference' (Ignatieff 1998: 34).

These divisions were further constructed into the narrow constraints of the separate 'communities' of Unionists and Nationalists. This approach not only denies the existence of significant pluralism and cross-cutting cleavages, not least from those in mixed marriages or from a mixed background, but excluded ethnic minorities from the mainstream of society. In the absence of any substantial sense of common overarching loyalties, centripetal forces predominated over centrifugal ones.

---

3 The loss of support for Unionist leader, Brian Faulkner, the election of eleven anti-Sunningdale MPs out of a total of twelve from Northern Ireland in the 1974 General Election, and the Ulster Workers' Strike (May 1974) were all contributing factors.

4 The people of the land that is Northern Ireland perhaps have more in common with each other than the peoples outside of Northern Ireland with whom they claim to share an affinity.

These differences are played out in various arenas, including competition for political and territorial control, the dispute over the constitutional status of Northern Ireland, and through cultural conflict. Terrorism, or political violence, is simply the most extreme manifestation of these divisions.

A security response to the problems of Northern Ireland could at best achieve a short-lived stability, but at a price of substantial infringement of individual human rights. Therefore any solution had to be political. The long-term priority had to be to promote shared institutions that could transcend traditional divisions. In the short term, there was first a need to create political institutions that could pass the cross-community test of legitimacy.[5]

The Alliance Party advocated four main planks to be addressed in the Talks. First, it was committed to devolution. It argued that Northern Ireland was a distinct region within both the UK and the European Union. The party dismissed the possibility of majority rule, except in the long-term aspirational circumstances where divisions had been sufficiently transcended and a recognisable liberal democracy was in place. Therefore, the Assembly had to function on the basis of power-sharing. The Party preference was for a flexible system under which a voluntary coalition Executive would be sustained by a weighted majority in the Assembly, similar to the Sunningdale approach (Sisk 1996).

Second, the Party wanted to see accountable North–South structures. These would not only provide a means to address many of the social and economic dislocations, arising from a border within a small island, but would also serve to provide some institutional expression to the aspirations of Irish Nationalists.

Third, Alliance argued that the Principle of Consent be further entrenched through universal acceptance by both governments and the other parties. It was necessary to grant the people of Northern Ireland alone the right to determine their own constitutional status.

Fourth, the Party believed that every individual citizen should feel comfortable within Northern Ireland. Accordingly, it was important that human rights and equality provisions were integral to the Agreement. Alliance urged both the British and Irish governments to incorporate the European Convention on Human Rights into their domestic law.

---

5 The major problem with the Stormont regime was that it relied upon a narrow majority of legitimacy that was based more or less exclusively within the Unionist section of the population; it was an ethnic rather than a liberal democracy. Furthermore, no strategies were pursued, with the possible exception of the policies of Terence O'Neill during the 1960s, to try to expand this base. If anything, they were dismissed as a threat to the state. The Unionist reaction to the Civil Rights movement, and the vitriolic rejection of O'Neill's policies by Paisley, can be seen in this light.

The Multiparty Talks[6]

The multiparty talks did not become energised until Senator George Mitchell, the principal Chair, imposed a deadline of 9 April 1998 for the conclusion of negotiations. A draft Agreement, from the Joint Chairs, had been expected in the penultimate week. However, behind-the-scenes disputes between the governments delayed its release to the parties until the beginning of the final week, producing substantial anxiety among the participants. This paper seemed to have been drafted by London- and Dublin-based civil servants, who appeared to be uninformed of the deliberations between the party delegations that had been occurring since January.[7]

Four days of frantic talks ensued. The draft Agreement was modified through a number of parallel processes. Greatest attention was devoted to Strand Two (the North-South relationship), with the Ulster Unionists negotiating with the British and Irish Prime Ministers, and the Nationalist parties virtually excluded. Strand One (the internal governance of Northern Ireland) was largely negotiated between the UUP and SDLP delegations. The 'peace' aspects to the Agreement, that is, the terms for decommissioning and the release of politically motivated prisoners – the main concerns of Sinn Féin, the PUP and the UDP – were largely agreed between those parties and the governments.[8]

The revised draft Agreement was finally presented to all the participating parties at dawn on Good Friday, on what was essentially a 'take it or leave it' basis. Most of the parties, including Alliance, quickly made their acceptance of the document clear. Two parties held out: Sinn Féin and the Ulster Unionists. The support of Sinn Féin was not technically necessary to proceed; it was hoped that at least acquiescence would be forthcoming. With a rejection, the minimum sufficient consensus would still have been possible, though this would have run counter to the inclusive approach that underpinned the Talks.

The support of the Ulster Unionists was fundamental. They were particularly unhappy at the terms relating to decommissioning and the release of prisoners. UUP Leader David Trimble's request to British Prime Minister Tony Blair for amendments was rebuffed, as this risked opening up the entire document to renegotiation. The UUP delegation was split down the middle over acceptance of the document. It took a letter from Blair setting out his understanding of what had been agreed to

6   For more details see Mitchell (1999).

7   This paper was reluctantly tabled by Mitchell, who, from reading between the lines of his covering letter, appreciated that it would not be a runner, capable of gaining cross-community support.

8   This is particularly ironic, given that approximately the first eighteen months of the Talks had been taken up with these issues.

in the decommissioning section, and the personal intervention of US President Bill Clinton, to persuade enough Unionists reluctantly to accept the Agreement.

Alliance played several roles during these negotiations. First, the party was most closely associated with the advocacy of many of the concepts within the Agreement, including power-sharing, integrated education and mixed housing, and a formal role for civic society. Second, given the cross-community nature of the party, Alliance acted not only to serve the interests of its own immediate constituency, but also to look out for solutions that could gain acceptance by both Unionists and Nationalists.[9] The party had to fight hard for the right of Assembly members to designate themselves as something different from Unionists and Nationalists. Alliance was very uncomfortable with the proposal for the use of designations and the associated voting system, as it would institutionalise divisions, undermine the emergence of greater pluralism and deter any realignment of politics along socioeconomic grounds. Alliance was prepared to tolerate this for the greater good, and hoped that the flaw could be addressed in the context of a Review into the Agreement and its operation that was to be held within four years. However, the creation of designations on the basis of only two traditions was unacceptable. It took considerable lobbying at Prime Ministerial level for the space for 'Others' to be created.

Third, Alliance was forced into playing the role of de facto policeman of the Talks. The Talks combined two kinds of political parties that had to be reconciled. The main parties were more or less constitutional in nature, in that they officially spurned the use of violence.[10] Other parties – Sinn Féin, the PUP and the UDP – were clearly associated with paramilitaries.[11]

While there was a clear desire on the part of both governments to consolidate the cease-fires at the same time as agreeing cross-community political institutions, it was not appropriate to negotiate a deal in Northern Ireland that essentially represented the balance of forces at the end of hostilities. The Mitchell Principles had been drafted to ensure that the use of violence did not alter the course of negotiations. Parties signed up to the use of democratic and exclusively nonviolent means. The application of undetermined sanctions by the British and Irish governments was

---

9   It is in this context that the warning from the then Alliance Leader, John Alderdice, on the morning of the final Tuesday of the multiparty talks that the Prime Minister had to hurry to Belfast if he wanted an Agreement, should be regarded. It prevented David Trimble from being portrayed as a typical rejectionist Unionist, and demonstrated that there were genuine problems with the text.

10   However, in practice, some had had associations with violent individuals or organisations.

11   The latter two had little democratic mandate, and were present in the multiparty talks essentially to represent Loyalist paramilitaries.

envisaged for those parties declared in breach of these Principles. The dilemma facing the governments and other parties was that a desire to maintain an all-inclusive process could conflict with the need to maintain the rule of law and primacy of democracy in the face of violent actions by paramilitaries.

Throughout the Talks, Republican and Loyalist paramilitaries pushed this approach to its limits. Both sides continued to engage in so-called 'punishment attacks' against those within their own communities that they accused of some criminal or antisocial behaviour. These activities showed no respect for due process under the law or for international human rights standards. Although 'punishment attacks' were referred to within the Mitchell Principles, they were not challenged through any formal political sanction.

Alliance tabled indictments against other parties on two occasions. In September 1996, the Party indicted the UUP, DUP, PUP and UDP for threatening massive civil unrest in order to get their way over the marching dispute at Drumcree during July. The governments dismissed these charges. The de facto threshold of the acceptable level of violence was eventually reached in January 1998, when the Chief Constable of the RUC confirmed that the UDA had been responsible for the sectarian killings of some Catholics. With the culpability of the UDA exposed, the position of their political wing, the UDP, within the Talks became untenable. Nevertheless, it took an Alliance indictment before the governments suspended the UDP for six weeks from the Talks. Subsequently, the Chief Constable declared that the IRA had also been involved in a number of murders, and the governments had little alternative but to suspend Sinn Féin from the Talks, albeit for a shorter period of two weeks.

These actions had an important effect in asserting the primacy of the rule of law, at least for a short period. However, there was still a wider problem in that minimum standards of behaviour implicitly accepted by the government for a cease-fire – a cessation of military operations (i.e., against the security forces, economic targets and people on the 'other side') – were not conducive to the impartial maintenance of the rule of law.

Assessment of the Agreement[12]

The Agreement constitutes an honourable accommodation between competing traditions within Northern Ireland, and the governments of the United Kingdom and the Republic of Ireland. It can be broken down

12 This section draws on Farry and Neeson (1999).

into political compromises over constitutional and institutional issues, and the peace compromises regarding the consolidation of the cease-fires.

A frequent charge made against the Agreement is that it was a product of violence – that it was an attempt to buy off paramilitaries in order to avoid further violence. In reality, Northern Ireland had been moving towards a political agreement over many years in order to create a set of constitutional and institutional arrangements that could be backed by the overwhelming number of people. What was different with these Talks was the participation of parties associated with paramilitarism. While neither the paramilitaries nor the British state defeated each other, the presence of a cease-fire and acceptance of the Mitchell Principles were preconditions for entry into negotiations. The peace aspects of the Agreement, such as the timetable for decommissioning and the early release of politically motivated prisoners, reflected steps to consolidate the cease-fires. These were difficult aspects for many people to accept, but the electorate backed the Agreement despite certain reservations.

While the North-South arrangements proved to be the most difficult element of the Agreement to negotiate, perhaps as a consequence of the effort that was put into this aspect during the final days of the Talks, they have been relatively uncontroversial in implementation.[13]

By contrast, Strand One was accepted with less controversy at the time, but has been much more problematic in implementation. In a broad sense, it is conceptually sound in that it delivers a power-sharing regional government to Northern Ireland, but there are a number of flaws in the specifics.

The use of designations, and the related voting system, constitutes institutionalised sectarianism (The Agreement, Strand One, paragraphs. 5–6). Those who do not wish to associate with either Unionism or Nationalism are relegated to the derogatory category of 'Others', with their votes carrying less weight. This is not just an issue for the members themselves but also for the voters who put them there. The system arguably runs contrary to the Statutory Equality Duty (Section 75 of the Northern Ireland Act 1998) and international human rights standards.[14] This approach provides a powerful deterrent to cross-community politics, and blocks the realignment of politics. Furthermore, the inflexibility

13 Read in conjunction with Nationalist acceptance of the Principle of Consent and its immediate implications, the North-South structures reflect modern developments in European and international law on the treatment of minorities, in terms of giving such individuals equal treatment within existing borders but allowing them to develop special relationships with kin across international borders.

14 For example, the European Framework Convention on the Protection of National Minorities (Council of Europe 1993). The United Kingdom has ratified this instrument, but not incorporated it into its domestic law.

of the voting system creates a hostage to fortune in that a significant group of members on either side could easily paralyse the Assembly. For example, on most 'cross-community' divisions, 40% of both designated Unionists and designated Nationalists, and 60% of all Assembly members present and voting must vote for a measure for it to be passed. However, for the election of the First and Deputy First Minister, the hurdle rises, with the requirement being 50% of both designated Unionists and designated Nationalists, and 50% overall.

In almost every democracy, like-minded parties, or those at least prepared to cooperate together, form a voluntary coalition that has either simple or weighted majority support within the legislature. The Agreement does not provide for such a government operating on the basis of collective responsibility. Instead, it institutes a government in which parties are allocated portfolios on the basis of their comparative strength in the Assembly, irrespective of their compatability. This approach could lead to a Balkanised Executive, in which Ministers exercise considerable authority in their own area of responsibility, with little sense of working to fulfil a common set of interests or to address cross-cutting issues.

Some checks and balances, however, do exist: Ministers cannot act in breach of the law, equality or human rights provisions; their decisions are open to judicial review;[15] and they can be removed from office for breach of the Pledge of Office, provided there is a successful cross-community vote in the Assembly.[16] While there is a requirement upon Ministers to agree upon an annual programme of government and a budget, the Agreement is unclear on what happens when they are unable to, or fail to, do so. In fact, it is difficult, if not impossible, to remove the entire Executive from office. With no real alternative coalition, it is likely that the same parties and personalities would regularly be in office. This risks breeding complacency or possibly corruption; it is not a good environment for policy innovation or economic efficiency. There is also the potential for anti-system parties to benefit from any popular disillusionment that results. Donald Horowitz (2001: 16–19) has commented: 'The architects of the Agreement abandoned the concept of a government across the moderate middle and instead opted for an all-inclusive government that coopted rather than marginalised the extremes. Through

15 This has been strengthened through the Equality Duty, and the Human Rights Act (1998) which gives the courts the power to strike down secondary legislation (including all acts of a devolved assembly) or executive decisions that run contrary to the European Convention on Human Rights.

16 The Agreement, Strand One, Annex A. Grounds for this amount to association with the use of violence, or failing to fulfil their duties of office. As the latter should arguably include attending meetings of the Executive and the North-South Ministerial Council, it is arguable that DUP Ministers have clearly been in breach, given their failure to attend Executive and North-South ministerial meetings.

its maximalist approach, the system violates Riker's Law of Minimum-Winning Coalition, which finds the optimum trade-off between breadth and cohesion. Furthermore, there are few incentives for the development of either cross-community politics or a political realignment along socioeconomic lines'. At the same time as they opted for this broad-based government, these architects tried to skew the balance of power in favour of a strong UUP-SDLP axis, in the process tacitly acknowledging the limitations in their system, but inadvertently creating the context, through institutionalised ethno-nationalist politics, where the extremes would overtake the moderates.

Another feature of the Agreement is constructive ambiguity. While it may be useful for the purposes of finding consensus, that is, for parties to settle for a common set of words but with different understandings of their meanings, problems are inevitable when it comes to implementation.

Overall the Agreement was sold to Unionists as a means to solidify the union of Northern Ireland with Great Britain, while Nationalists were told that it would be a way-station on the road to a united Ireland. Furthermore, different understandings of its constitutional implications have been exhibited. Unionists believe that in return for agreeing to share power with, and grant equality to, Nationalists, the latter in turn recognised Northern Ireland's full place within the United Kingdom. For Nationalists, Northern Ireland has become an almost sui generis entity, something that is not quite part of the United Kingdom but not yet part of a united Ireland.

The specific element of the Agreement carrying the greatest ambiguity is decommissioning. Despite the language of the Agreement, it was the understanding of the other parties that the IRA and others had in fact signed up to decommissioning by May 2000. By contrast, Republicans argued that they, like all the other parties, had a similar obligation to encourage decommissioning. In addition, the UUP had a different version of the Agreement, appending the letter from Blair to their text. Part of the problem lay in the formal absence of the IRA from the negotiations. Both governments and all of the other parties regarded Sinn Féin, the PUP and the UDP as proxies for the IRA, UVF and UDA, respectively. The Talks were structured in order to include all these parties for precisely that reason. However, they each maintained a public fiction that they had no formal links to their related paramilitary organisation, and could not make commitments for them.

Long-Term Threats to the Agreement

The principal route to the creation of lasting peace and stability lies in addressing the deep divisions in Northern Ireland society. To be successful in the long run, the Agreement will have to go some way to reducing sectarianism and communal segregation. However, much of the Agreement is based on the institutionalised assumption of 'two communities', separate but equal, and living in peaceful coexistence. Through the absence of a clear vision of a united Northern Ireland, and even the outline of a policy programme to promote sharing over separation, the Agreement remains on weak foundations that contain the seeds of its potential destruction. Skilful conflict management is no substitute for genuine conflict resolution. This strategy only has to slip once for separate communities, with no overarching loyalties or cross-cutting cleavages, to go their own separate ways. At the worst extreme, this separation could amount to the territorial partition of Northern Ireland, with associated ethnic cleansing on a par with Bosnia.

The Agreement sets out a rigid form of consociational rather than liberal democracy. The lessons from political science are that the more flexible and successful forms of consociational democracy tend to come in those societies where divisions have become relatively unimportant over time, and where significant cross-cutting cleavages exist.[17] By contrast, in societies where divisions have been deeper, consociational structures have been more rigid, and have generally failed or stalled.[18] In addition, consociational democracies work more effectively when there is some sense of overarching loyalty.

On paper, Northern Ireland fails both these tests. During 'the Troubles', the trend was for politics to become increasingly corporatised along ethnonationalist lines. The Agreement institutionalised this trend, and unsurprisingly divisions have become more acute since it came into existence. During the peace process, an inordinate emphasis upon the political extremes as the key players in delivering an inclusive process further undermined the political centre. Furthermore, although the parties have agreed common rules to determine the constitutional status of Northern Ireland, there is no consensus over outcome. Both Unionists and Nationalists believe that their aspirations can be achieved under the Agreement. These competing claims to self-determination continue to polarise Northern Ireland, and reinforce voting along ethnonationalist lines.

---

17 For example, Austria, the Netherlands and Switzerland. Indeed, in the first two cases, consociational measures have become unnecessary.
18 Examples include Cyprus, Lebanon and post-Dayton Bosnia. In Belgium, as the linguistic divisions become more entrenched, the ultimate survival of the state is increasingly in question.

Problematic Implementation

The Agreement was overwhelmingly endorsed by 71 percent of the people of Northern Ireland in a referendum. Yet, while there was a clear majority of Protestants, there was at best only 50 percent support among Unionists. By contrast, over 95 percent of those describing themselves as Nationalists or Republicans backed the Agreement. Either the Agreement was out of equilibrium or had been poorly sold to and by Unionists. Nationalists, essentially, regarded the Agreement as part of a wider process, leading to a united or 'agreed' Ireland; even unreconstructed Republicans could rationalise the acceptance of Northern Ireland as a tactical move. By contrast, Unionists mostly saw the Agreement as a settlement. For many, despite the presence of a plausible alternative, it was a step too far, and they rejected it. Pro-Agreement Unionists were half-hearted and accepted it with little enthusiasm.

Four issues have dominated the squabbles over the implementation: decommissioning, policing reform, security normalisation/demilitarisation, and the stability of the institutions. It had been hoped that the gap of understanding over decommissioning would gradually close with the implementation of the Agreement. However, it was blown wide open through the Ulster Unionists' linkage of progress on decommissioning with the formation of the Executive. This linkage between decommissioning and the Executive did not lead to progress on either, but rather paralysis on both. However, given the practical reality that the Ulster Unionists were central to any power-sharing arrangements, the two governments reluctantly accepted that such linkage existed.

From March 1999 onwards, a series of political initiatives led by the British and Irish governments, including the Hillsborough Declaration (April 1999) and the Way Forward document (July 1999) attempted to resolve the deadlock. The Mitchell Review (September–November 1999) seemingly broke the deadlock. The UUP essentially agreed to jump first into the Executive in exchange for the IRA entering into dialogue with the Independent International Commission on Decommissioning (IICD) on the understanding that a start to decommissioning would follow shortly thereafter. In order to achieve the consent of his governing Party Council, David Trimble unilaterally imposed a deadline of the end of January 2000 for the beginning of actual decommissioning. This effectively negated the voluntary aspect of decommissioning which was so important to the Republican movement in selling this measure to their supporters.

The process sleepwalked into crisis at the end of January. With Trimble facing another meeting of his Council to review progress, he was faced with the choice of either walking away from the Executive or being sacked by his own party. Republicans came under immense pressure, both domestically and internationally, to decommission. In the face of an

imminent resignation of Trimble and the other UUP Ministers, the suspension of the Executive became the only viable option for the incoming
Secretary of state, Peter Mandelson.

A prolonged, or even permanent, suspension of the institutions would
provide the clearest threat to the survival of the Agreement. The atmosphere within the political process was not conducive to a swift
resumption of normal business. Unionists were not prepared to counte-
nance the restoration of the political institutions in the absence of
sufficient progress on decommissioning. Republicans were insistent that
there would not be an appropriate context for decommissioning unless
the political institutions were restored. None of the outstanding problems on the Agreement were particularly intractable as there were no
major issues of principle at stake; peacemakers could readily provide for-
mulae or sequences of moves to provide for the full implementation of
the Agreement. However, the problem was one of lack of mutual trust
and confidence among the parties. To make matters worse, the spirit of
compromise and accommodation which had made the Good Friday
Agreement possible had evaporated, with the parties abandoning any
notion of a common vision in favour of exclusivist demands for the
implementation of their definition of the Agreement.

At the beginning of May 2000, the British and Irish governments
finally achieved a major breakthrough. In return for the agreement of the
IRA to reengage with the IICD and, more significantly, to permit inspections of some of their arms dumps as part of a wider process leading to
weapons being placed beyond use, the Unionists agreed to the restoration of the political institutions. This offer from Republicans did not yet
constitute decommissioning in the view of most parties, including the
governments, but did buy the process some time.

Nonetheless, the Agreement once again lurched into crisis in the
autumn of 2000, as the Ulster Unionists lost a crucial by-election in the
parliamentary constituency of South Antrim. The DUP victory drove
anti-Agreement forces within the UUP to call another meeting of the
Ulster Unionist Council. At this meeting, Trimble appeased those elements by refusing to allow Sinn Féin ministers to attend North–South
Ministerial meetings, and threatened further action if no further progress
was made on decommissioning. At the same time, Republicans broke off
contacts with the IICD and further arms inspections, accusing the British
government of bad faith in not normalising the security situation more
quickly. Efforts at 'demilitarisation' are hampered by the growing security
threat from dissident Republicans, and the gradual deterioration in the
Loyalist ceasefires. Finally, policing reform was stalling badly at a time
when the rule of law across Northern Ireland was clearly deteriorating.

During the multiparty talks, no serious effort was made to address the
particularly divisive issue of the policing of Northern Ireland. Instead,

the matter was referred to a commission. Unionists regarded the RUC as their force, not only to provide law and order, but to defend their version of the state, while Nationalists dismissed the RUC as a discredited service, and refused to work with it politically. The RUC did make a crucial contribution in preventing Northern Ireland slipping into total chaos during 'the Troubles'. However, it was unrepresentative of the community and has had its reputation marred by the abuses committed by some individual officers.

Chris Patten and his fellow Commissioners reported in September 1999. Alliance (despite strong reservations concerning 50:50 communal recruitment quotas) and the SDLP largely welcomed the report, while Unionists and Republicans rejected it. Attempts by the British government to facilitate greater Unionist acceptance of change during the legislative phase alienated the SDLP from policing reforms. The SDLP, in effect, placed a rigorous insistence of the literal implementation of Patten above the need to compromise and maintain broad-based support for the Agreement; their absolutist position stood in contrast to their demands that others compromise on other outstanding areas of the Agreement. The continued wrangling over the issue delayed policing reform and, in particular, fresh recruitment, at a time of growing law and order problems on the streets.

No progress was made on the remaining issues in the run-up to the June 2001 Westminster and local government elections. Particularly, with the moderate pro-Agreement parties unable to demonstrate their ability to collectively implement the Agreement, it was clear that there would be a significant swing to the extremes of both Unionism and Nationalism. As predicted, both Sinn Féin and the DUP made considerable gains in seats and votes at the expense of the SDLP and Ulster Unionists respectively. For the first time, Sinn Féin overtook the SDLP to become the largest Nationalist party, and the DUP came perilously close to this on the Unionist side. It was clear that if similar results were to be repeated in subsequent Assembly elections, then even the version of power-sharing envisaged in the Agreement could become unsustainable. Despite the inclusive nature of those arrangements, there was an underlying assumption that a strong UUP–SDLP axis would control the Executive from the offices of First Minister and Deputy First Minister. The prospects of the DUP, or indeed the UUP, and Sinn Féin successfully cooperating together in the common interest are particularly bleak.

Putting the unity of his party ahead of the wider interests of the process, David Trimble had gone into the elections threatening to resign as of 1 July 2001 in the absence of sufficient progress on decommissioning. When this came into effect, there was a six-week window of opportunity to resolve the outstanding difficulties before the Secretary of State would be required to again suspend the institutions or to call fresh elections to the Assembly. Attempts to overcome the deadlock through spiriting the parties away to an English stately home, Weston Park, were inconclusive. The joint package from the two governments that sought to provide a way through the outstanding issues was subsequently presented to the parties on a 'take it or leave it' basis. Controversially, it included new provisions for dealing with paramilitaries 'on the run' from outstanding prosecutions that, in practice, constituted a general amnesty for all terrorist offences committed prior to 1998. No party unequivocally accepted the document. Faced with the unenviable choices of fresh elections or a prolonged suspension, the Secretary of State used a legal loophole in the Agreement legislation to impose a limited 24-hour suspension of the institutions that created another six-week window of opportunity. In the run-up to this suspension, the IRA agreed modalities for decommissioning with the IICD, but fell short of providing a timetable for actual decommissioning. However, this offer was subsequently withdrawn in protest at the suspension. Seemingly, by not moving a little further, it appeared that Republicans had missed an historic opportunity to move the process further.

The subsequent six-week period did not see any significant progress or attempts to resolve the outstanding issues. However, the belated decision of the SDLP, and reluctantly of both the main Unionist parties, to sign up to the Police Board finally allowed the government to move forward on policing reform. Once again, the Secretary of State instituted a tactical one-day suspension, which was this time presented as the last opportunity to resolve the outstanding issues. At the end of that period, either the parties would have worked through the difficulties sufficiently or decided collectively to exclude Sinn Féin from the Executive for failure to deliver decommissioning, or the governments would suspend the institutions and launch a Review, or hold new elections to the Assembly. However, the Ulster Unionists curtailed this process, despite the poor history of unilateral ultimatums, and tabled their own motion of exclusion, ironically using the support of the PUP in order to achieve the necessary threshold of signatures. Trimble withdrew the UUP Ministers when the motion was inevitably defeated.

Nevertheless, the collapse of the process was avoided by an act of decommissioning by the IRA. The discovery of three Republican activists in the FARC rebel-held territory in Colombia in suspicious circumstances, and the resultant questions over the intentions of the IRA, and the changed attitude of the US Administration and even traditional Irish-American supporters, in the wake of the Al-Qaeda terrorist attacks against the USA, were the new external factors that seemed to provide the necessary momentum. This act was sufficient for the Ulster Unionists to seek to return to the NI Executive and for the British government to begin to implement the Weston Park package.

Since the creation of the Agreement, it was clear that the voting system for the Assembly was a hostage to fortune and that a crisis would be inevitable. The balance of forces between pro- and anti-Agreement Unionists in the Assembly was very tight, and difficulties in the re-election of David Trimble and Mark Durkan, the successor to John Hume as the leader of the SDLP, as First and Deputy First Minister could be expected. In the first election, despite over 70% of MLAs supporting this ticket, two Ulster Unionist MLAs voted against their own leader, blocking the election of David Trimble, and throwing the future of the Assembly into crisis. The choices facing the Government seemed to be either another suspension or elections.

Instead, over a weekend of high drama, the new Alliance leader, David Ford, agreed that three Alliance MLAs would redesignate as 'Unionists' for one week in order to facilitate the election of the top two posts. In return, the UUP and SDLP agreed to propose a temporary change in Assembly Standing Orders to allow this to happen, and the Government agreed to a Review into Strand One of the Agreement, specifically the voting system. This limited Review ultimately proved unsuccessful, as the UUP and SDLP rejected Alliance proposals for the use of a two-thirds weighted-majority, unencumbered by designations, either by itself or as a third mechanism for cross-community votes.

The problem with the voting system remains. There is some prospect that a more broad-based Review may be held before the Assembly elections due on 1 May 2003 that may address this problem. However, if it is not fixed by that stage, it is likely that when Sinn Fein overtake the SDLP, and DUP possibly overtake the UUP in numbers of Assembly seats that the system will once again stall.

Problems with Implementation: Analysis

It is no understatement to say that the implementation of the Agreement has not proceeded according to plan. A number of interrelated problems have contributed to this unfortunate situation.

The deep divisions within the Ulster Unionist Party and the half-hearted support among its pro-Agreement elements
David Trimble and the pro-Agreement Unionists have failed consistently to sell the Agreement in a positive manner to their own constituency. Instead, their commitment, particularly to power-sharing, has at times seemed half-hearted. While the UUP Assembly Party is on the whole supportive of the leadership, the danger of losing any members to anti-Agreement forces minimises room for manoeuvre. Grassroots divisions within the party are more evenly balanced. Trimble's leadership and the commitment of the Party to the Agreement have been tested through a series of meetings of the governing Council where pro-Agreement forces have managed only to eke out narrow victories, frequently through resorting to messy compromises to buy more time.

The failure of pro-Agreement parties to articulate and defend sa hared vision of the future not least through accommodating each others' concerns

Few, if any, of the outstanding issues relating to the implementation of the Agreement are particularly intractable. There are few matters of principle at stake; all the pro-Agreement parties nominally support the goals of decommissioning, stabilising the institutions, police reform and security normalisation. The problems have been ones of interpretation, sequencing, and who is responsible for action. The ability of parties to abandon exclusivist demands and interpretations in order to facilitate progress has been disappointing.

The inability of the paramilitaries to provide sufficient confidence in the durability of their cease-fires, through the decommissioning of weapons and the ending of violence

Depending upon one's opinion, Northern Ireland is either already a democracy or aspires to be. In any event, the existence of political parties associated with paramilitary wings is clearly at odds with the democratic ideal. Accordingly, there is a clear need for both Republican and Loyalist paramilitaries to demonstrate the bona fides of their cease-fires. This could be established through statements permanently renouncing the use of violence and/or visible demonstrations that all activities are ceasing. In addition, it could have been achieved through the symbolic handover of weapons.

With perhaps fatal consequences, the Unionists chose the latter as a precondition for progress at every stage in the process. When decommissioning did not occur, faced with the choice of either stalling the process or fudging the issue, the governments chose to push the blockage further down the pipe, with the consequence that Unionists became more disillusioned, and Republicans simply ratcheted up the price in terms of expected concessions from the governments in order to make it happen.

It was only belatedly that Republicans sought to provide some confidence through a substantial act of decommissioning. However, it remains to be seen whether that one act will be followed up with further acts, or whether Loyalists will reciprocate. If not, it is likely that pressure will once again build for follow-up action with the associated threats to the stability of the institutions.

The perception of a moral vacuum in the implementation of the Agreement in light of the inability of the authorities adequately to address the growing threats to the rule of law

Although the Agreement provides the means for exerting the primacy of democracy and the rule of law, threats to law and order, perhaps somewhat paradoxically, have persisted and metamorphosed since the

Agreement. First, there remains a continued terrorist threat from both dissident Republicans and Loyalists. Second, those organisations officially 'on cease-fire' have continued to engage in a range of activities. These include the continuation of so-called 'punishment attacks' and even murders of people on their own perceived side of the community, such as rivals in territorial turf-wars or alleged drug-dealers. However, in 2001, paramilitary activities escalated into a number of attacks on the security forces, and blatant sectarian murders and pipebomb attacks. Paramilitarism is becoming institutionalised, and is reflected in an increased drug-dealing and racketeering activity, shows of strength, and the marking out of territory through flags and kerbstone painting. Third, in relation to continuing disputes regarding parades, particularly the now annual stand-off at Drumcree, the Orange Order and Loyalists have blocked roads and engaged in confrontations with the police.

The response of authorities to these threats has been sporadic and half-hearted. In particular, steps to declare paramilitary organisations to be in breach of their cease-fires could be costly in that they would undermine the inclusive philosophy that has underpinned the peace process and could risk increased violence from those sources. In the face of inaction from the governments, the paramilitaries have increased the severity of their activities to the point that they challenge even the narrow definitions of cease-fires.

However, the threshold of acceptable levels of violence cannot be drawn so high without consequences upon public opinion. Many people had supported the Agreement despite strong reservations and distaste over the early release of paramilitary prisoners. On top of this, the failure of the authorities to address continued paramilitary activity and successfully to pursue prosecutions has contributed to a perception that there is a moral vacuum at the heart of the implementation of the Agreement, with the reality of what organisations are engaged in sectarian violence being downplayed for reasons of political expediency.[19]

The institutionalisation of sectarianism in the Agreement, and the policy failure to sufficiently tackle sectarianism and communal segregation
Finally, the institutionalisation of ethnic division within the Agreement has had immediate consequences on the peace process. The entrenchment of group identity has reinforced divisions, and fuelled intercommunal conflict. In a sense, peace has become the pursuit of war by other means. As sectarianism and segregation have increased in the aftermath of the Agreement, the response of the authorities has been

19 The governments' proposal for a de facto amnesty risks reinforcing this perception. Through forgoing prosecutions totally rather than even seeking nominal convictions followed by immediate release, the governments could in effect recognise that the paramilitaries were fighting legitimate 'wars'.

pitiful. In particular, the Executive in its first Programme of government gave virtually no attention to the promotion of communal integration. The effects of increased polarisation when played out through the ballot box is contributing to the destabilisation of the institutions.

The Future

Despite some recent progress, the future of the Agreement remains uncertain. There is a clear need for radical thinking on how to create and maintain cross-community, politically legitimate and effective institutions, but also on how to tackle the deeper problems of sectarianism and segregation.

In essence, the platform provided by the Agreement must be used to create an alternative vision of a shared, nonsectarian Northern Ireland with a more united community than that of separate but equal communities.

A number of steps need to be taken.[20] First, it is conceptually important to move from talking in terms of 'two communities', and to talk about one community - united in diversity. Cultural differences should be celebrated within a common civic and multicultural space. Such pluralism should provide greater cross-cutting cleavages to strengthen the political institutions. The institutionalism of the 'two communities' approach should be reversed within public policy.[21]

Second, communal integration should be encouraged in order to combat segregation. Policies to support integrated education and mixed housing should be stressed. All policies should be appraised for their impact upon sharing over separation.

Third, the public and private manifestations of sectarianism and other forms of intolerance should be addressed. This includes the very public displays of paramilitarism that tend to 'ghettoise' parts of Northern Ireland and intensify social exclusion.

Fourth, the human rights of every individual should be upheld and equality of opportunity guaranteed to give every citizen a stake in Northern Ireland's peace and stability. Similarly, continued improvements in Northern Ireland's economy and the quality of public services are integral.

---

20 These themes are developed in Alliance Party (2000).

21 The most immediate danger here is the remit given to the Northern Ireland Human Rights Commission in furnishing advice to the Secretary of State regarding a Bill of Rights (additional to the European Convention on Human Rights) to 'reflect the ethos and identities of both communities' (The Agreement, Rights, Safeguards and Equality of Opportunity, Human Rights, United Kingdom Legislation, paragraph 4).

Fifth, given the competing claims to self-determination, it could be hoped that loyalty to the Good Friday Agreement would be sufficient to overcome the centrifugal forces. However, it will also be necessary to develop Northern Ireland as a coherent region within a decentralising British Isles and an emerging federal Europe of the regions. Northern Ireland and European identities should be celebrated to emphasise what the people hold in common rather than what divides them. In addition, it is to be hoped that with borders breaking down around the world, old-fashioned, absolutist concepts of sovereignty will also break down in Ireland.

Finally, reforms should be made to the Agreement, within the context of a comprehensive Review, to remove designations, to reform the voting system to create greater incentives for the development of cross-community politics, and to introduce genuine collective responsibility into the Executive. Fundamentally, top-down power-sharing should be complemented with bottom-up reconciliation within the community.

In the event that the institutions of the Agreement do at some point collapse, the political initiative would return to the British and Irish governments. The immediate prospects of a return to power-sharing devolution would be bleak, particularly in the context of a political balance of power (mirroring the situation in the final days of Weimar Germany) that is not conducive to producing a critical mass of parties working towards a shared interest. Nevertheless, the sobering reality for Unionists and Loyalists, Nationalists and Republicans is that if another attempt is made to negotiate a multiparty Agreement, then the self-same issues that bedevilled the implementation of the Good Friday Agreement are likely to reemerge awaiting a solution. Eventually, perhaps ten or twenty years from now, the parties may find acceptable a set of arrangements that today they could not accept or even contemplate.

References

Alliance Party. 1998. *Governing with Consent*. Belfast.
———2000. *Centre Forward: Alliance Leading the Way*. http://www.allianceparty.org
Farry, S. and Neeson, S. 1999. 'Beyond the Band-Aid Approach: An Alliance Party Perspective upon the Belfast Agreement', in *Fordham International Law Journal*, vol. 22, no. 4 (April 1999), pp. 1221–49.
Horowitz, D. 2001. 'The Northern Ireland Agreement: Consociational, Maximalist, and Risky', in *Northern Ireland and the Divided World*, ed. J. McGarry. Oxford.
Ignatieff, M. 1998. *The Warrior's Honour*. London.
Mitchell, G. 1999. *Making Peace*. London.
Sisk, T.D. 1996. *Power-Sharing and International Mediation in Ethnic Conflicts*. Washington, DC.

CHAPTER THREE

The Good Friday Agreement: An SDLP Analysis of the Northern Ireland Conflict[1]

Gerard Murray

National Democratic Party: SDLP Principles

Prior to the formation of the National Democratic Party (NDP) in 1965 there was no structured or coherent party organisation to represent the politics of Catholics in Northern Ireland. The earliest thinking of the SDLP on the constitutional issue can be traced back to elements of NDP policy. From the outset the NDP rejected the stance of the former Nationalist Party by facing up to the reality that the island of Ireland was partitioned. What was articulated by the NDP was an active political voice that demanded democracy in Northern Ireland society. The party represented a new view of 'classic Nationalism' which had been demonstrated by the Civil Rights movement in the late 1960s.[2] The NDP delineated a revisionist form of thinking in terms of traditional sterile concepts of Nationalism. From its origins the NDP argued from a pragmatic premise that partition had not been imposed on the Irish people but rather grew out of the political divisions in the island. Significantly, the NDP moved away from the inactive politics of the Nationalist Party, who adopted the traditional Nationalist position that Britain was the cause of division in Ireland, and basically refused to take an active role in the politics of the Northern Ireland state. However, the NDP still wanted to end partition, but only by agreement (Caraher 1994).[3]

1 This chapter is based on material to be published in Murray and Tonge (2002). I acknowledge the support of the Nuffield Foundation, and the Economic and Social Research Council (R000222668) for funding this research.
2 See Todd (1999) for an analysis of tensions in classic and liberal Nationalism in the SDLP and Sinn Féin.
3 Caraher, a senior strategist of the SDLP in the early years of the party, was also a former member of the NDP.

The NDP wanted to form an alternative government to the Unionist-dominated administration at Stormont. In effect, the NDP had the potential to function as a successful opposition based in the British system of politics. But the NDP found that the nature of majority rule politics in Northern Ireland, and in particular the parochialism in the province, made the party's task of creating a socialist rather than a pan-Catholic party virtually impossible (McAllister 1975: 363). The NDP also injected the consent principle into the revisionist Nationalist debate by stating that it 'would negotiate for reunification only if the majority of the people in the North wanted it'.[4] As soon as the SDLP was formed in August 1970, the NDP dissolved itself at a special conference in October 1970. At that conference a resolution was passed that NDP members should join the recently formed SDLP.

SDLP Early Documentation: Good Friday Agreement – Themes

The first detailed SDLP document argued that a solution to the Northern Ireland conflict would not be viable unless it recognised the interdependence of both parts of the island. In reference to Unionist intransigence, the SDLP paper acknowledged that 'Unionists have a right to equal consideration where the future of sic the country is concerned. What is challenged is the right of the Unionist Party to claim more than equality' (Murray 1998: 17). The document set out that the British and Irish governments should pass legislation establishing a 'Supreme Council of Ireland' composed of members from the Northern Ireland Commission and from the Republic. Part of the remit of this Supreme Council would be to identify cross-border programmes for economic development, and other areas of cooperation between both parts of the island.

The SDLP issued a policy document, Towards a New Ireland, on 20 September 1972, immediately before the Darlington Conference. This was a three-day congress for Northern Ireland parties to attempt to reach agreement on an acceptable form of government for Northern Ireland. However, aware that militant Republicans might think that they were signalling tacit support to British internment policy, the SDLP turned down the offer from the Secretary of State, William Whitelaw, to take part in the Darlington discussions formally (Murray 1998: 17). The careful timing of the publication of Towards a New Ireland, however, compensated somewhat for the party's absence at the talks. An analysis of the document demonstrates that SDLP policy was centred on attaining Irish unity through the establishment of an interim settlement, with evolving cross-border harmonisation functions. The proposals were, in principle, acknowledging that Northern Ireland should no

---

4   NDP Attitude to Northern Ireland, NDP File, Northern Ireland Political Collection, Linenhall Library, Belfast.

longer be part of the United Kingdom. Instead, Northern Ireland would come under the joint control of the United Kingdom and Irish Republic (as it was called at that time). Again, in Towards a New Ireland, as in earlier SDLP documents, Britain was asked to take on the role of encouraging Irish unity. The consent principle referring to all the people of Ireland was an integral part of the document.

Ben Caraher, a key SDLP strategist in the 1970s, was disappointed with Towards A New Ireland because it was a condominium for a United Ireland. The thinking behind Caraher's own views on what a condominium might be was not dissimilar to the Good Friday Agreement. The institutions Caraher was proposing to draw up for the SDLP were not designed as part of a mechanism to construct a United Ireland. Caraher recalled: 'My condominium was intended to be stronger than joint sovereignty. It was not a preparation for anything, but was intended to be an actual solution there and then. It left the door open for a United Ireland if there was an agreement' (Caraher 1994). The transition from a revisionist stance on the constitutional issue on Irish unity within the SDLP in 1972 to that of a more Nationalist position was largely attributable to the strong Nationalist sentiments unleashed after the killing of thirteen civilians in Derry/Londonderry on Bloody Sunday, 30 January 1972.

Controversial aspects of the Northern Ireland conflict remained. A call for an 'amnesty for all those convicted or charged with "political" offences since 13th August 1969' was included in an unpublished SDLP document entitled SDLP Towards A New Ireland, written just before the publication of Towards A New Ireland in 1972 (Public Records Office Northern Ireland PRONI, D 3072/1088). In any imminent discussions for a political settlement the SDLP paper firstly recommended a wide range of reform measures to develop community relations in Northern Ireland in the context of continuation of direct rule. Secondly, it stressed the importance of 'increasing cooperation between Northern Ireland and the Republic of Ireland in economic and cultural affairs'.

In the SDLP submission to Merlyn Rees's Constitutional Convention of 1975–6 there were suggestions to reform the Royal Ulster Constabulary (RUC). The measures which the SDLP felt should be included were the 'civilianisation' of the RUC, accompanied by the establishment of a new image, and professional service for policing. The section on policing reiterated the SDLP argument that a successful police force was dependent on a society's institutions to retain the support of the majority of its people. Ironically, the lukewarm SDLP support for the RUC was one of the major reasons the United Ulster Unionist Council (UUUC) cited in the main body of the Convention Report as a reason why they could not accept power-sharing in government with the SDLP (Northern Ireland Constitution Report, paragraph 94). The SDLP also promoted the concept of a double referendum in Northern Ireland and the Republic of Ireland to endorse any political settlement.

SDLP Proposals

The late 1970s in Northern Ireland were difficult for the SDLP. At Sunningdale the British government appeared conciliatory, but later abandoned the principles of power-sharing and an Irish dimension. Despite these setbacks, the SDLP championed the essential principles of power-sharing and an Irish dimension as 'nonnegotiable' in an overall political settlement taking place in Northern Ireland. The SDLP did not advocate 'indefinite direct rule', but asked for the British government to work with the Irish government and the people of Northern Ireland to bring about necessary change in Northern Ireland (PRONI D 3072/4/74/34). From 1979 on, the SDLP advocated an Anglo-Irish strategy involving both governments. This meant, firstly, that the problems of Northern Ireland should only be solved by joint Anglo-Irish action taken as part of a clearly agreed programme between both governments; secondly, that the British government should drop its unconditional guarantee to the Unionist population; and thirdly, that the Irish government should spell out what it meant in practical terms by Irish unity, regarding social and economic changes. These issues became the key concerns of SDLP strategy from the beginning of the 1980s.

The SDLP support for the Sunningdale Agreement was based on the fact that the government White Paper of 1973 (Northern Ireland Office 1973) included the key SDLP principles of power-sharing not only at executive level but for all sectors of society in Northern Ireland. The SDLP maintained a premise that guaranteed the Unionist population no change in the constitutional status of Northern Ireland in the United Kingdom without the consent of the majority of the Northern Ireland population. This premise was not the main source of SDLP grievance with the British government. The focus of SDLP grievance throughout its history was that the British government was unwilling to take a responsible role in resolving the conflict in an impartial manner which addressed Nationalist or minority interests in the province. The party opposed a British government position that only promised to sustain a guarantee of membership in the United Kingdom to the Unionist population.

The SDLP also maintained the premise that correct administration of matters in Northern Ireland implied a democratic system of government that took into consideration two different communities in the province who held different political affiliations. The British government, by continually upholding the Unionist guarantee, was in effect governing Northern Ireland in a partisan manner. To govern Northern Ireland simply as another region of the United Kingdom was to abdicate responsibility of what the conflict was really about. This was the problem that the SDLP was able to make the British government eventually address through the Anglo-Irish Agreement, and more fully through the Good Friday Agreement. Prior to the signing of the Anglo-Irish Agreement, the British government resolutely refrained from any attempt to become actively involved in addressing the core dimensions of the Northern Ireland conflict. By deviating from responsible government and exercising a policy of containment in Northern Ireland (New Ireland Forum 1984) the minimalist administration of the province, in effect, upheld Unionist interests. The SDLP initiated and promoted power-sharing and the development of an Irish dimension during the most problematic days of the Northern Ireland troubles, when the basis for a political settlement seemed nonexistent.

The SDLP definition of power-sharing in 1976 was synonymous with the term 'partnership' and currently remains at the heart of the Good Friday Agreement. The 1976 definition of power-sharing included: (1) the sharing of government responsibility at executive level by representation of the two traditions within the province (Strand One: Democratic Institutions in Northern Ireland of the Good Friday Agreement); and, (2) political cooperation between the two parts of the island 'as a focus of loyalty for that part of the Northern people that considered itself Irish' (Strand Two: North-South Ministerial Council of the Good Friday Agreement). The principle of majority consent was a vital part of the SDLP definition of power-sharing, which addressed the Unionist concern over their Britishness (Murray 1998: 50).

New Ireland Forum: A Key to the Good Friday Agreement

One underlying SDLP motive for the New Ireland Forum negotiations (published as The New Ireland Forum Report in May 1984) was to articulate a coherent constitutional Nationalist argument to resolve the Northern Ireland conflict. Another motivating factor for the SDLP was to captivate the attention of the British by engaging with the Irish government on making a partnership framework to resolve the intractable Northern Ireland problem. The Forum was a successful SDLP exercise in that it produced an analysis of the Northern Ireland conflict which was accepted by the three main political parties in the Republic, an analysis which in due course led to a consensus view for resolving the conflict on the constitutional Nationalist side of the equation. Despite Margaret Thatcher's legendary 'out, out, out' response to the New Ireland Forum Report, a response which predicted bleak prospects for Anglo-Irish developments in Northern Ireland, nevertheless, in a relatively short period the Anglo-Irish Agreement was signed on 15 November 1985. The New Ireland Forum Report was, in fact, a formative text providing the impetus for the two governments to set up the necessary framework to bring about a political settlement to the Northern Ireland conflict. While the framework was initially validated through the Anglo-Irish Agreement, in due course more detailed plans from the Forum Report were incorporated in the Good Friday Agreement.

The New Ireland Forum Report largely reflected SDLP thinking both on the background and the way to resolve the Northern Ireland conflict. Specific sections of Chapter Five, 'Framework for a New Ireland: Present Realities and Future Requirements', represent the SDLP analysis of the Northern Ireland conflict. The text refers to the existing structures which have failed 'to recognise and accommodate the identity of Northern Nationalists [and which have] resulted in deep and growing alienation on their part from the system of political authority' (New Ireland Forum 1984). By maintaining the conflict within the confines of the borders of Northern Ireland, the conflict over the question of Nationalist and Unionist identities remained irreconcilable. Hence the SDLP argued for a three-stranded approach to the question, reflecting the existence of the Nationalist community in Northern Ireland.

Commenting on British policy in Northern Ireland the Forum Report (New Ireland Forum 1984) stated that, 'the basic approach of British policy has created negative consequences. It has shown a disregard of the identity and ethos of Nationalists. In effect, it has underwritten the supremacy in Northern Ireland of the Unionist identity. Before there can be fundamental progress Britain must reassess its position and responsibility.' The Forum Report noted, 'attempts from any quarter to impose a particular solution through violence must be rejected along with the proponents of such method. It must be recognised that the New Ireland which the Forum seeks can only come about through agreement, and must have a democratic basis.' It continued to discuss the need for wider negotiations: 'Agreement means that the political arrangements for a new and sovereign Ireland would have to be freely negotiated and agreed to by the people of the North and by the people of the South.' The report also pointed out, 'the validity of both the Nationalist and Unionist identities in Ireland and the democratic rights of every citizen on this island must be accepted; both of these identities must have equally satisfactory, secure and durable, political, administrative and symbolic expression and protection.' To reach a satisfactory solution, the report indicated, 'new arrangements must provide structures and institutions including security structures with which both Nationalists and Unionists can identify on the basis of political consensus; such arrangements must overcome alienation in Northern Ireland and strengthen stability and security for all the people of Ireland.'

The Good Friday Agreement: The SDLP Principles

From the outset, the SDLP were protagonists of British Civil Rights for the Nationalist community in Northern Ireland. This was, in essence, about persuading the British government to adopt an agenda to promote 'inclusion and equality of opportunity' for the Nationalist community in Northern Ireland. The SDLP has been committed to political progress and moderation for at least thirty years of 'the Troubles': they have tried to move Republicans and Unionists from entrenched positions. The Good Friday Agreement has contained the essence of SDLP strategy for the last twenty-eight years. Since their formation in 1970 the SDLP sought to create partnership government in Northern Ireland with moderate Unionists. The whole concept of cross-border cooperation through a Ministerial Council of Ireland and the principle of power-sharing between Unionists and Nationalists in Northern Ireland were set out, as noted above, in unpublished documents in 1971. The SDLP argued in these discussion documents for almost exactly the same principles which were set out in the Good Friday Agreement.

Overall the SDLP were not disappointed with the Agreement. The key points the party sought were contained in the document in a significant way. These were to establish balanced institutions in Northern Ireland requiring cross-community involvement and North–South bodies with significant remit. The SDLP has articulated for Nationalists in Northern Ireland that the creation of a single Irish state is not likely to be achieved in the foreseeable future. They recognised back in 1971 that while a Socialist Republic of thirty-two counties was the ultimate aim of the party, it was not an attainable short-term objective. What was needed were new political structures which addressed the realities of partition. Rather than seeking unrealistic demands for British withdrawal and Irish unity, the SDLP articulated in their unpublished 1971 documents that it was the people of Ireland that had to be united. Therefore, political frameworks had to reflect this new reality, based on what became known as the three-stranded approach: cooperative relations between the two communities in Northern Ireland; between North and South; and between the peoples of Britian and Ireland.

Cross-border institutions, from the SDLP viewpoint, have the potential for moving towards Irish unity, but only in terms of democracy, so that the people on the island of Ireland can decide its political fate at some future point. At this moment in history, the SDLP has consciously decided that a unitary republic is not an attainable goal. The party is focused on maximising strong executive functions for proposed cross-border bodies. In essence, the party has adopted the views reflected by Ben Caraher (as noted above) that a final agreement between all the parties to the conflict would have no other open-ended agenda. If demographic change in Northern Ireland dictates reunification at some future point, the British government has committed itself to set the necessary legislation in place for withdrawal to take place.

Nationalists who still aspire to a united Ireland have demonstrated by their strong support of the Good Friday Agreement that if you ultimately want a United Ireland, then you have to settle for less and start building trust with Unionist counterparts. Sinn Féin are settling for terms that fall a long way short of their original objective of British withdrawal and coercion of Protestants into a United Ireland. Unionist consent is still required for the foreseeable future for any change in Northern Ireland's position within the UK.

The constitutional policy of the SDLP prior to the signing of the Good Friday Agreement was not dissimilar to Tony Blair's current Northern Ireland policy. This was expressed at the Royal Ulster Agricultural Show in May 1997, when the Prime Minister spoke of his commitment to the negotiation of a settlement based on consent, a commitment which eventually became reality in the Good Friday Agreement. In that speech Tony Blair stated: 'My agenda is not a United Ireland – I wonder just how many see it as a realistic possibility in the foreseeable future. Northern Ireland will remain part of the United Kingdom as long as a majoritywish' (*Irish Times*, 16 May 1997). Since this speech, and the subsequent signing of the Good Friday Agreement on 10 April 1998, not only have the principles of consent and self-determination which have to be negotiated by the majority in Northern Ireland been supported by the SDLP, but they are now endorsed by Sinn Féin.

Two years after the Agreement, the BBC Northern Ireland poll taken by the programme 'Hearts and Minds' on attitudes towards the Good Friday Agreement reveals overall optimism in the SDLP. While 70.7 percent of SDLP voters believed the armed struggle of the Republican movement was over, only 54.9 percent of the UUP members disagreed.[5] The 1998 Northern Ireland Life and Times Survey conducted by Queen's University, Belfast and the University of Ulster portrays the SDLP as a moderate Nationalist party in relation to the constitution of Northern Ireland. Fewer than 47 percent of the SDLP voters polled believed Northern Ireland should reunify with the rest of Ireland. This contrasts with the views of 78 percent of Sinn Féin members. This difference of opinion between SDLP and Sinn Féin voters is further reinforced when over 66 percent of SDLP voters polled supported majority consensus (namely that they could happily accept the reality if the majority of people in Northern Ireland never voted to become part of a united Ireland), with only 29 percent of Sinn Féin supporters in the poll accepting such a position. However, in terms of the equality agenda, it is significant that SDLP members polled only 36.2 percent when asked if they believed they were treated equally with Protestants. The SDLP vote was nevertheless higher than the 14.7 percent of Sinn Féin members polled on this issue.

5   'Hearts and Minds' Poll conducted for BBC Northern Ireland by Price Waterhouse Coopers on 9 May 2000.

Table 3.1: The Political Identity of the SDLP

	Strongly agree%	Agree %	Neither %	Disagree %	Strongly disagree %	Other %	Missing %
Q15: The SDLP is a Nationalist Party	31.6	55.9	7.4	2.3	2.1	–	0.8
Q16: The SDLP is a European Party	39.4	49.2	7.6	1.7	–	0.4	1.7
Q17: The SDLP is a Social Democratic Party	32.4	56.3	9.5	0.6	0.4	0.2	0.8
Q18: The SDLP is a Socialist Party	9.7	40.7	24.6	16.7	3.2	0.2	4.9
Q19: The SDLP is a Catholic Party	7.2	31.1	24.2	29.5	7.0	–	0.9
Q42: SDLP should promote distinct European identity	22.7	50.6	18.9	4.7	1.5	0.4	1.1
Q43: Confusion over SDLP political identity	5.1	26.9%	18.4	37.5	10.2	0.4	1.5

It is specifically in the sphere of employment opportunities that 76 percent of the SDLP participants in the poll believed Protestants fared better than their Catholic counterparts. There is evidently a higher degree of satisfaction from the Good Friday Agreement among SDLP supporters than from the Sinn Féin constituency. Generally the SDLP is optimistic about the long-term chances of peace prevailing in Northern Ireland because 92.2 percent of party supporters back the position that the chances of peace in Northern Ireland are better now than they were five years ago. In the search for peace, slightly over half of the SDLP voters, 53.3 percent of those polled, believed that David Trimble was helpful in the search for peace, compared to only 33.3 percent of Sinn Féin supporters polled. In relation to the RUC only 20.4 percent of SDLP supporters polled believed the RUC should be disbanded, while 67 percent of Sinn Féin members thought it should be dissolved. Nevertheless, 63.4 percent of SDLP supporters polled believed the RUC should be reformed but not disbanded, compared to only 26.5 percent of Sinn Féin supporters taking a similar position.[6]

What is interesting in Table 3.2[7] is the overwhelming support at the core of SDLP membership to uphold the principle of power-sharing more than the principle of Irish Unity. The level of support for this position is at around 70 percent for those members joining the party from 1981 onwards, and 63.1 percent for those joining the party between 1970 and 1980. However, this position is endorsed marginally in Table 3.3 with over 50.5 percent who agree that the Good Friday Agreement plus power-sharing is the best constitutional solution to resolve the Northern Ireland problem. This is not to underestimate the near 50:50 scenario of SDLP members recording the importance of Irish Unity within the party. What is to be disputed in this type of exercise is the interpretation of meaning in relation to a United Ireland. Does it mean a traditional Socialist Irish Republic of thirty-two counties, or is it really what the SDLP term an 'agreed Ireland'? One can only assume that with the revision of Irish Nationalism that has taken place since the formation of the SDLP in August 1970 that the latter, an 'agreed Ireland', is the case. This position can be further endorsed in Table 3.1 when over 87.5 percent of party members identified the party as a Nationalist party with a slightly higher number of 88.6 percent identifying the party as a European party. In essence: the party has developed a practical basis by which to promote Irish unity within the overall context of European integration.

Table 3.2: Power-sharing versus Irish Unity
(N = 528)

Q23: Power-sharing more important than Irish unity to SDLP	1970–80 %	1981–90 %	1991–99 %
1. Strongly agree	22.0	27.5	21.8
2. Agree	41.1	42.2	49.0
3. Neither agree/disagree	16.3	8.3	15.0
4. Disagree	15.8	17.4	9.7
5. Strongly disagree	3.8	1.8	2.9
6. Missing	1.0	2.8	1.5

6   The 1998 Northern Ireland Life and Times Survey is a joint project between Queen's University, Belfast and the University of Ulster. The Centre for Social Research at Queen's University, Belfast, provided these statistics for this survey as weighted figures in relation to the SDLP and Sinn Féin.

7   Data in Tables 3.1 to 3.5 inclusive are provided from a survey of the SDLP membership as part of an ESRC Project (R000222668) based at the University of Salford. I would like to acknowledge the invaluable assistance of Kerstin Hinds, Edinburgh, for collating the data for this article.

The SDLP was the first Northern Ireland political party, and for that matter the first constitutional party in the whole of Ireland, to set out in policy documents an accurate analysis of the crux of what the reality of the Northern Ireland conflict was about. The party clearly formulated in its analysis the reality that the dispute was largely over two different sets of national identities and allegiances. Catholics had traditionally been alienated from the institutions of the Northern Ireland state. The Good Friday Agreement put in place and implemented the SDLP's main principle of partnership government in Northern Ireland. The agreement was a major coup for the SDLP in so far as its long-advocated analysis of the Northern Ireland conflict is now, for all practical purposes, enshrined within the Good Friday Agreement. What is more significant is the fact that it is endorsed by the British and Irish governments with the strong international support of the United States. Erstwhile arch-enemies, the UUP and Sinn Féin, are now part of the power-sharing administration at Stormont and they are putting into practice the first step of SDLP policy, in what Hume called the 'healing process'.[8]

Table 3.3: Constitutional Issues

	Strongly agree	Agree %	Neither %	Disagree %	Strongly disagree %	Other %	Missing %
Q20: United Ireland the best solution N = 528	20.5	29.5	25.8	16.9	2.8	–	4.5
Q21: Joint British-Irish sovereignty the best solution N = 524	6.7	27.9	21.6	27.1	9.0	0.2	7.6
Q22: Good Friday Agreement plus power-sharing the best solution N = 528	41.1	39.4	11.2	4.0	1.3	–	3.0
Q24: Northern Ireland remaining in UK the best solution N = 528	1.5	6.3	18.5	34.9	36.6	0.4	1.7

8   First stated by John Hume in 1964.

Throughout the negotiations leading to the Good Friday Agreement, Sinn Féin were completely against an Assembly being devolved under Strand One of the talks process, fearing that Northern Ireland would be further integrated as a region of the United Kingdom, thus allowing the majority rule principle to come to the fore (Ruane and Todd 1999: 10). In elections since the hunger strike era of the early 1980s, Sinn Féin has benefited from Nationalist and Republican perceptions of grievances, particularly in the institutional framework of prison and media prohibition. The oblivious stance conventionally held by the British government towards the legitimacy of a Nationalist sense of culture, and allegiance to the Republic of Ireland, have assisted their cause. Republicans have accepted the former SDLP position of British equality within Northern Ireland as an interim measure on the path to Irish Unity. However, 'if it turns out that, despite all the provisions of the Agreement, Northern Ireland does not and cannot function in an egalitarian manner, the question of its constitutional legitimacy and legitimacy as a political entity will again come sharply into question. Indeed for many Republicans, these issues have never disappeared' (Ruane and Todd 1999: 21).

The Good Friday Agreement: The Future of the SDLP

The Good Friday Agreement is the culmination of SDLP influence. They developed an ideology of Southern constitutional Nationalism over many years. The ideology manifested itself in the New Ireland Forum Report in May 1984. The British government implemented their analysis of the Northern Ireland conflict as outlined through the New Ireland Forum Report. Despite the reluctance of mainstream Unionists and Republicans to accept these principles, they nevertheless formed the basis of a consensus when different parties endorsed the Good Friday Agreement. The Good Friday Agreement is a demonstration of SDLP resilience in its efforts to bring about an arrangement which included their core principles of power-sharing and partnership government. Not only had the party to convince the British government through the eventual international pressure of the White House, but it had also to educate the main constitutional parties in the Republic of Ireland of the necessity to include these two core principles as part of an overall political settlement in Northern Ireland.

The SDLP see the Good Friday Agreement as the acme of an Anglo-Irish process created at the 1980 Haughey-Thatcher summit (Farren 1996). While the Good Friday Agreement epitomises the SDLP principles and philosophy, nevertheless the reality is that, following the 2001 general election, the party is now no longer the largest Nationalist party in Northern Ireland because Sinn Féin has four MPs to the SDLP's three. The SDLP rested on its laurels as a consequence of its excellent result in the 1998 Assembly elections. The party failed to address Sinn Féin's ability to overtake it as the main Nationalist party in Northern Ireland. It is evident that the main tenets of Sinn Féin policy to overtake the SDLP as the chief political representatives for the minority community in Northern Ireland can be traced back to references in An Phoblacht/Republican News during 1983, clearly stating that objective.[9] This 1983 Sinn Fein goal was finally attained in the 2001 General Election.

There are various factors contributing to Sinn Féin's success. Firstly, one cannot underestimate Sinn Féin's fundraising potential over that of the SDLP. The US Department of Justice recorded the collection of US$2.484 million from October 1995 to August 1999 for Sinn Féin in America (*Irish Times*, 5 December 2000). The figures supplied by Friends of Sinn Féin make the party the biggest recipient of US funding in the whole of Ireland.

Secondly, one of the major difficulties for the SDLP is the age factor in the top echelons of the party. Table 3.5 illustrates that 56.4 percent of the SDLP membership is over the age of 55. Even more alarming is that 30.1 percent of SDLP membership is above the age of 65. Nevertheless, it is significant, as Table 3.4 shows that the party had its highest intake of new members (26.9 percent) between 1996 and 1999. This rise in new membership was a consequence of the peace process.

Table 3.4: Year of Joining the SDLP (N = 528)

Year	Valid
1970–4	27.1
1975–80	12.5
1981–5	12.3
1986–90	8.3
1991–5	12.1
1996–9	26.9

Table 3.5: Age of SDLP Members (N = 528)

Age	Valid percent %
15–24	3.4
25–34	6.8
35–44	13.4
45–54	19.9
55–64	26.3
65+	30.1

9   An Phoblacht/Republican News, 28 April 1983, 15 May 1983 and 17 November 1983.

Thirdly, Sydney Elliott identified a significant turning point among SDLP voters in 1993. The percentage of SDLP transfer votes to Sinn Féin rose to almost 53 percent compared to 22.2 percent in 1992; 34 percent in 1985, and 32 percent in 1989. Middle-class Nationalists are now willing to support Sinn Féin whose transfer votes traditionally went to the Alliance Party (*Belfast Telegraph*, 17 March 1997).

The SDLP made a serious error of judgement when their former leader, John Hume, did not step down as leader following the prominent electoral position of the party after the 1998 Assembly elections. Mark Durkan as the new SDLP leader would then have come into the political limelight with his party vote at its highest since the formation of the organisation in 1970. The SDLP's political gamble of always monitoring Sinn Fein's position to sensitive issues such as policing and decommissioning did not pay off, as the 2001 general election results clearly demonstrate. Instead the party should have sent out better signs of reconciliation to Unionists, by specifically addressing the decommissioning issue, and also by putting forward members to the new policing board prior to the 2001 general election.

Time will tell whether the Good Friday Agreement, which is a compromise arrangement between two irreconcilable nationalisms, and which is based on an SDLP analysis of the Northern Ireland conflict, will succeed. One can never predict the fragility of Northern Ireland politics. If the negative forces prevail, then who knows whether the SDLP will take a place in the history books and become subsumed by the more belligerent politics of Sinn Fein?

References

Caraher, B. 1994. Interview with the author conducted on 28 September 1994.

Farren, S. 1996. 'The Northern Ireland Peace Process: The View from the SDLP, a Nationalist Approach to an Agreed Peace', in *The Oxford International Review*, Spring Issue, 1996, pp. 41–6.

Joint Statement of the SDLP Executive Committee and Assembly Party, 3 September 1974, PRONI D 3072/4/74/34.

McAllister, I. 1975. 'Political Opposition in Northern Ireland: The National Democratic Party, 1965–70', in *Economic and Social Review*, VI/3, 1975, p. 363.

Murray, G. and Tonge, J. 2002. *From Alienation to Participation in Northern Ireland: The SDLP and Sinn Féin 1970–1999*. London.

Murray, G. 1998. *John Hume and the SDLP*. Dublin.

New Ireland Forum. 1984. *Report*. Dublin.

Northern Ireland Office. 1973. *Northern Ireland Constitutional Proposals*. London and Belfast.

Ruane, J. and Todd, J. 1999. 'The Belfast Agreement: Context, Content, Consequences', in *After the Good Friday Agreement: Analysing Political Change in Northern Ireland*, ed. J. Ruane and J. Todd. Dublin, pp. 1–29.

Todd, J. 1999. 'Nationalism, Republicanism and the Good Friday Agreement', in *After the Good Friday Agreement: Analysing Political Change in Northern Ireland*, ed. J. Ruane and J. Todd. Dublin, pp. 49–70.

CHAPTER FOUR

Sinn Féin: Beyond and within Containment

Peter Shirlow

Thirty years of sustained political violence in Northern Ireland and the near collapse of the Northern Ireland Assembly over the issue of decommissioning have created considerable cynicism about the feasibility of securing a fixed and sustainable cessation of ethnosectarian violence. The repercussions of sectarianised ethnic affiliation, the continued spatial and ideological segregation of the population by religion and political identity, and the difficulties of Sinn Féin in taking up executive ministerial posts within the Northern Ireland Assembly have combined to ensure that the politics of Northern Ireland are still nurtured by a binary opposition between the pro-Union and pro-Irish reunification sections of the population.

As a result of the decommissioning débâcle, the continuation of violence, and the initial failure to create a Northern Ireland Assembly with executive powers, much media and public attention has been centred rather superficially around present events while the realities of how the peace process came into being have been largely obscured. Moreover, and within the Unionist community in particular, there has been a tendency to concentrate on the negative aspects of Republicanism, such as the IRA's cease-fire breaking and the issue of decommissioning, rather than the pursuit of a positive exploration of how Sinn Féin began their journey towards a 'path to peace'. As a result of such negative commentary, Sinn Féin remains more politically marginalised than any other political party in Northern Ireland. This marginalisation not only threatens the whole rationale of the peace process, but also leads to dissent within the Republican movement itself. This article outlines the nature of this political containment through exploring the political realities of peace-building in Northern Ireland.

The process of peace-building for Sinn Féin, was initially centred upon internal political rethinking and reformulation as opposed to consensus building with the British state and pro-Union political parties.

Undoubtedly, the immediate strategies being employed by Sinn Féin and the IRA have undergone a transition, not in terms of desire or motivation, but in terms of procedure and political operation (Bean 1995). This has been accepted throughout Northern Ireland's political camps, including pro-Union academics such as Hazelkorn and Patterson (1995) and Aughey (1995) who have asserted that Sinn Féin members have been dynamic agents in the momentum for political renegotiation. Confirmation of an alteration in Sinn Féin's political deliberations has also emerged from more ardent Republican groups, such as Republican Sinn Féin, the 32 County Sovereignty Committee, and the Irish Republican Socialist Party, all of whom have accused Sinn Féin of a protracted and unwavering corrosion of Republican principles (O'Bradaigh 1996).

Prominent Republicans, such as Bernadette McAliskey, Anthony McIntyre and Social Democrats, have critically asserted that the Sinn Féin leadership is moving towards the advocation of a Nationalist consensus which plays down the Republican ethos of unconditionally ending the partition of Ireland. In particular, Republican critics castigate Sinn Féin for endorsing a partitionist Northern Ireland Assembly. For Sinn Féin, the adoption of constitutional politics is seen not as an endorsement of partition but as a medium- to short-term approach aimed at engaging in dialogue and a united Ireland by other means.

This contribution charts the logic of Sinn Féin's political transformation through investigating the development of new political relationships between Sinn Féin, the majority pro-Irish reunification party in Northern Ireland, the SDLP, and the government of the Republic of Ireland. It is asserted that Sinn Féin has absorbed a mode of political legitimacy, which is being executed via the reinvention of the wording of 'peace' and the abstraction of Republican-Nationalist unity. Recent shifts in Sinn Féin's strategy are not based upon a radical departure in ideological intent but instead are centred upon a transition underpinned by a range of internal and external influences, political blockages and the self-identified adoption of political pragmatism (Ryan 1995; Smith 1995).

The Politics of Competing Identities

Through highlighting the pertinence of the identity dimension, in relation to dominatory modes of sociocultural and political activity, it is contended that Sinn Féin's endeavour to distance and protect itself and its electorate from their 'powerlessness' and containment has fundamental consequences in relation to the reproduction of unsymmetrical relations of power. As noted by Stedman-Jones (1983), the interpretation of sociocultural conflict should not reproduce the assumption that conflictual communities retain a rational linguistic expression such that there is a direct reflection in language of their essential interests. But instead it should be acknowledged that:

> Language disrupts any simple notion of the determination of consciousness by social being because it is itself part of social being. We cannot therefore decode political language to reach a primal and material expression of interest since it is the discursive structure of political language which conceives and defines interest itself. (Stedman-Jones 1983: 21f.)

Clearly, Stedman-Jones's definition of how interests and communal devotion are culturally reproduced is identifiable within any society in which markedly contested interpretations of the political predicament, and how it is circumscribed, engenders conflict in its own terms. As contended by Finlayson (1997), it is the constitution of these different discursive structures that makes for the political problem. Acknowledging this, in any arena of conflict, results in a displacement of our fascination with the sociohistorical roots and class dimensions of sectarian division as it permits a concern with how politics fashions the cognition and understanding of interests centred around an inflexible knowledge of community conformity and devotion.

Moreover, language, discourse and dialogue, their definition and mobilisation, create chains of equivalence which enclose subjects within not only ethnosectarian but at times entirely self-referential and self-sustained notions of identity, practice and collective devotion. Crucially, radical and violent discourses attempt to embody the very identity of the movement, the mass itself, and the community whose interests it represents.

The incisive point to be comprehended is the constitutive nature of such discursive processes. Foucault's work has been persuasive in explaining the vinculum between the fabrication of the social and discursivity (Foucault 1972, 1979). For Foucault, discourse analysis is concerned with the variable 'discursive formations' which permit specific assertions and remarks to be made while others are excluded. A discursive formation is 'a set of rules'; that is to say, the code by which objects, subject positions and strategies are moulded, forged and reproduced. Foucault is not simply concerned with written or spoken words but with discourse in its most commodious sense and with the articulatory social practice of discourse. As noted by Foucault (1972: 46):

> These rules define not the dumb existence of a reality, nor the canonical use of vocabulary, but the ordering of objects. 'Words and things' is the entirely serious title of a problem; it is the ironic title of a work that modifies its own form, displaces its own data, and reveals, at the end of the day, a quite different task. A task that consists of no longer-treating discourse as groups of signs...but as practices that systematically form the objects of which they speak.

Clearly, ideology and discourse constrain and engender the process of entrapment that exists within ethically defined imaginings of community.

These allegories and mythic representations are themselves the consequence of discursively fabricated categorisations of belonging, as they are the effect of political processes rather than, as is usually accepted, the root of such processes in Northern Ireland.

As such the analysis offered in this chapter upholds Foucault's concern with the analysis of localised power relations and the attainable nature of resistance towards those specific power relations. Moreover, the critique conferred appraises how modes of resistance and domination operate in terms of political shifts, vocation and deterrence.

Achieving a Mandate for War and then Peace

Re-formed during the political unease and escalation of sectarian violence in the early 1970s, the IRA and Sinn Féin had initially little in the way of a cultivated political strategy, other than an instantaneous desire to use military means so as to dislodge the British state from Northern Ireland (Bishop and Mallie 1988; Burton 1978; Burton and Carlen 1979; Campbell 1994; Clark 1987). The failure to remove the British state due both to its military ability and its use of counter-insurgency tactics meant that by the late 1970s the IRA was forced to adopt what became known as the 'long war' strategy. The 'long war' evolved as a battle of attrition, aimed especially at the economic infrastructure of Northern Ireland. During this time, Sinn Féin continued to be a junior partner of the IRA, and was primarily a propaganda instrument which provided ideological maintenance for the ongoing 'long war' campaign (Sluka 1989; Todd 1990).

The 1981 Hunger Strike campaign indicated the ability of Sinn Féin to gain widespread electoral support. The twin strategy of military warfare and electoral support that was established became euphemistically known as the 'armalite and ballot box strategy'. This strategy had two central objectives. First, the use of electoral politics was intended to deliver Sinn Féin as the dominant voice within Irish Nationalism in Northern Ireland through challenging and incapacitating the political leverage of the SDLP. Second, in achieving a wider political mandate, the IRA, assuming that they now retained legitimacy via political support, accentuated their campaign of violence (Rolston 1989 and 1996).

Originally, this twin political and military strategy was comparatively successful. Sinn Féin achieved electoral gains in the early 1980s, reaching a high point in the 1983 Westminster elections when they accrued 43 percent of the Nationalist vote and as such engaged the prospect of becoming the dominant voice of Northern-based Irish Nationalism. However, in the longer term the ability to progress beyond its new-found support base proved both finite and unendurable, especially within the

Republic of Ireland. During the late 1980s it became indisputable that in electoral terms violence was largely counter-productive, particularly if such violence was viewed as either 'intemperate', 'excessive' or 'wrongful' (McClelland and Dowd 1992; McDonald 1995; McGarry and O'Leary 1995; McThomas 1992; Munck 1992). The impact of the peace process upon Sinn Féin has proven to be a positive experience given that in the Westminster election of 2001 they achieved, for the first time, a majority (52 percent) of pro-reunification votes.

Among certain Sinn Féin strategists there was uncomfortableness with the use of intense violence. This apprehension was accompanied by a recognition that the proclaimed 'long war' strategy, which supposed that violence must proceed until the departure of the British state, meant that the IRA became a reproductive agent in the cause of war (Sluka 1989). It was acknowledged that violence was discouraging those whose consent, as envisaged by both the British and Irish states, was essential in order to advance significant political alteration (Munck 1998).

In addition, as political strategies reached a glass ceiling, the upsurge in Loyalist violence, which was partly a reaction to Republican violence, indicated that the twin strategy merely perpetuated and reproduced violence. Moreover, by the late 1980s the IRA was finding it increasingly difficult to find recruits and many of its members were unwilling to perpetuate an armed campaign which would continually result in the imprisonment and possible death of members of their own community. However, the fact that Sinn Féin's electoral support had grown and that the IRA was in military terms undefeated meant that the British state could not ignore or marginalise this section of the Republican community in the manner that it had wished (Shirlow and McGovern 1998).

Even more important was the recognition that the Unionist population would not engage with Sinn Féin nor recognise their political mandate without a cessation of political violence (Todd 1990). Thus, prominent Republicans realised that 'real' political progress would not be achieved without a recognition that their activities aided the creation of the dismal space within which ethnosectarianism operated. Moreover, it became an increasingly palpable reality in certain Sinn Féin quarters that the political situation was escalating to a civil war instead of the intended anti-imperialist battle.

These realities, combined with the British state's insistence in the Anglo-Irish Agreement of 1985 that it would support Irish unification through consent, indicated to some members of Sinn Féin that it could conceivably adopt a political plan of Irish reunification through persuasion and conversion of the Unionist community (Shirlow and McGovern 1998). Not only was violence counter-productive in that it granted subsistence to Unionist intransigence, but it also procreated Irish state opposition to Republicanism, obstructed the utility of socioeconomic provision, precluded much-needed investment in deprived areas and encouraged Loyalist requital and reprisal (O'Doherty 1998).

New political procedures appearing within the extended Nationalist community rebounded other political alterations including the endorsement of joint-authority as a model of self-determination and a cognisant recognition, as stated by John Hume as then leader of the SDLP, that the British state was no longer the primary barricade to Irish unity. These factors promoted ideological flexibility and sociopolitical alterations which conceived more pluralist Nationalist interests and aspirations. Even more essential was the critique endorsed by constitutional Nationalists that conflict was a causal and increasingly consequential factor which maintained militarisation and prevented cross-community communication and dialogue (O'Hearn et al. 1999).

By the late 1980s and early 1990s the British state's qualification that it would constitute a united Ireland through acquiescence displayed a previously unwitnessed preparedness to alter territorial adjustment. This preparedness disputed the Republican contestation that Britain had combative or militaristic purposes in its aspiration to uphold a Unionist veto over Northern Ireland's future constitutional status. Given these seismic shifts in constitutional politics and other realities, the mandate which, somewhat ironically, was won to wage war was now shifted towards a mandate for building peace.

Old Adversaries and New Tentative Friends

In order for Sinn Féin to break out of containment it required the political and symbolic support of the wider Nationalist community. However, building relationships with the SDLP and the Irish state had to proceed on a deliberate but slow path. Undoubtedly, the adoption of a new-fashioned political procedure was influenced by a desire to avoid political fragmentation and the development of inter-Republican feuding, as had been the case when the (Provisional) IRA split from the Official Irish Republican Army in the mid-1970s.

A split within the Sinn Féin/IRA movement did occur in 1986 over the issue of abstentionism within the Republic of Ireland. Dissidents within Sinn Féin were solidified in the dispute over the elaboration and eventual acceptance of an electoral strategy in the Republic of Ireland, which rejected the principle of nonrecognition of the Irish state, and led to pro-abstention dissenters forming Republican Sinn Féin. The subsequent endorsement of the Irish state's legitimacy provided the Sinn Féin leadership with the opportunity to embark upon open negotiation with it.

This 'battle for fresh allies' led to the formation of a broad and loose alliance of pro-Nationalist groups and parties including Sinn Féin, the SDLP, the Irish government and the significant Irish-American lobby (Shirlow and McGovern 1998; Todd 1990). Sinn Féin thus became connected to a wider pro-Irish unification community even though many of its constituent members promoted alternative ideological positions.

A broad Nationalist position did emerge, centring on the acceptance by both Sinn Féin and the SDLP that the doctrine of national self-determination was essential to any peace process. In order to maintain this new alliance, Sinn Féin had to remove its social radicalism, revolutionary rhetoric and traditional, and at times violent, hostility to the SDLP. Dialogue between the two party leaders, Gerry Adams and John Hume, continued, and from 1991 protracted secret negotiations between Sinn Féin/IRA and the British government took place. While suspicion and distrust continued to characterise these contacts the Sinn Féin/IRA leadership gradually became convinced that the resolve of the British state to remain in Northern Ireland was sufficiently inconclusive as to suggest that gradual disengagement could be achieved – but only if the IRA halted their campaign of violence (McCann 1999).

As Gerry Adams (1995) reiterated in *Free Ireland*, this new strategy rested upon fundamental proposals, all notable for their concentration on the actions and attitudes of the London and Dublin governments. For example, the British state was called upon to recognise the right to self-determination of the Irish people, and, as a consequence, 'to change its current policy to one of ending partition' (Adams 1995: 2). Similarly, because 'the future of Unionists lies in this all-Ireland context ... the British government has a responsibility to influence Unionist attitudes' (ibid.: 4). Britain should, in other words, 'join the ranks of the persuaders' (ibid.).

A changing discourse thus emerged, reflecting different tactical approaches. This strategic shift centred on the imperatives of alternative avenues of political pressure and a reorientation of Sinn Féin ideology as a form of 'mobilised social consciousness'. The process also saw the reformation of a broad Nationalist agenda and the symbolic reintegration of the ideologically 'ghettoised' Republican communities of Northern Ireland into the wider Irish 'nation'. For Sinn Féin these new alliances were centred upon shared concepts of nation, community and justice.

Of particular importance to Sinn Féin was the interaction between community and nation and the 'imagined community' of the Irish people in the process of designing new political strategies and activities (Shirlow and McGovern 1998). The emphasis upon the national and local is also tied to removing political isolationism and self-imposed territorial strictures of containment, and the reintegration of the 'lost' Republican communities of Northern Ireland into the wider 'family' of a 'reinvigorated' nation.

The symbols of the 'nation' under the new strategy continued as the means used to 'mythologise' the necessarily tight-knit 'resistance community', and help maintain political and cultural cohesion (Hillyard 1993). Despite a wider political strategy, a celebration and utilisation of localised identity, solidarity and community networks are still intrinsic to Republicanism. Sinn Féin spokespersons continually emphasise the process of consultation and discussion within the wider 'Republican family' set in its territorial base. In his description of the peace process, Adams (1995: 41) reflected on the importance of ongoing community solidarity:

> Nationalists, and more particularly Republican communities or those which were deemed to be so, were equally subjected to insults (by responses to the Hume/Adams Initiative). Nationalist West Belfast had long been a target for such odium; however it was also a community which refused to take things lying down. The community was enjoying its own local revitalisation process, and the creativity, resilience and aspirations of its people were reflected in a thriving range of enterprises.

The process of de-ghettoisation of Republicanism is heralding a slow thaw in the sense of separation to which such differences bore witness. For this process to take place, however, it was first necessary to establish a discourse which could recombine community and nation, and relate both to the new 'unarmed strategy'. This need to break out of containment therefore implied a form of semiotic struggle: to redefine the political agenda, and the role of Republicans therein (Porter and O'Hearn 1995).

Discourses of Peace and Quasi-Deliverance

In the move towards a peace strategy a first priority for Sinn Féin was to question and undermine the legitimacy of British counter-insurgency strategies employed in Northern Ireland. Most significantly this priority involved a confrontation over the use of language. Taking possession of the language of peace in order to redefine the meaning of the conflict was central to the new strategy and opened up a new communicative dimension. The adoption of the word 'peace', in 1987, by Sinn Féin was a conscious act aimed at breaking out of the containment strategy undertaken by the British and Irish states. As noted by Adams (1995: 31):

> For too long Republicans had permitted others to hijack the word 'Peace'... They needed to be confronted on their stance... This required Republican political initiative and a Sinn Féin offensive in the battle of ideas.

The roots of legitimacy had become embedded in the language of insurgency and counter-insurgency used in the propaganda war between Sinn Féin/IRA and the British and Irish states. The ability to establish a dominant discourse, a 'truth', which marginalises the 'truths' and delegitimises the actions of others is a vital means by which the modern state operates as a major locus of power (Feldman 1991; Foucault 1972, 1979; Giddens 1985; Walter 1969). Establishing 'a truth' as 'the truth' means taking possession of certain discourses central to political identity through establishing a prevalent conviction that the system conforms to the rectitude of equity, equivalence and autonomy (Burton and Carlen 1979; Held 1989). In its emerging analysis Sinn Féin recognised that discourses become weapons of attack and defence in the relations of power and knowledge (Foucault 1972, 1979).

In developing a peace discourse, Sinn Féin also had to recognise that the British policy of containment had a variety of dimensions operating at a variety of levels (O'Dowd et al. 1980). It was designed to limit the impact of the conflict by restricting it geographically to certain urban working-class and border areas. Containment also operated at the ideological level through the official discourse which 'criminalised' the 'terrorist'. In this discourse armed opposition to the state, or incidents of political violence were denuded of their political context and were defined rather as 'criminal' acts. This was facilitated by the establishment of a system of 'prohibited words' (Foucault 1972, 1979). Undoubtedly, 'peace' was one such prohibited word which could never be used legitimately by Sinn Féin/IRA.

The control of language provided the British state and media with an opportunity to define 'Republican' and 'Loyalist' communities as deviant, criminal and outside the bounds of the normative values which governed wider society. This process not only legitimised the use of force against deviant individuals and communities but it was furthermore designed to undermine the collective psychological security of such communities and their desire to resist. This process, alternatively identified by Burton (1978) as 'felon-setting', ultimately removed the use of certain ideas, discourses and even words from people within those communities.

Precisely to escape from the ghettoisation and containment – both physical and political – imposed upon 'Republican' communities, the words 'peace', along with 'freedom' and 'justice', were taken up and expounded in a deliberate policy by Sinn Féin from the late 1980s onward to repossess certain discourses which had become synonymous with the British state. This reflected a change in direction on the part of the movement in that the aim was no longer simply to hold on to the support of those within, nor to maintain the hegemony of Sinn Féin in the areas where they held sway, but to expand beyond: to combat containment by establishing links with other groups and other bodies of opinion.

In real terms the strategy endorsed created not only a significant growth in Sinn Féin's mandate but also created the first meaningful cross-community dialogue within Northern Ireland. The establishment

of the Northern Ireland Forum ultimately provided, redefined and created new political realities within Northern Ireland.

New Realities: Old Problems

Among Sinn Féin activists there was a general acceptance that new political avenues could only be explored through maintaining a communal
solidarity which was devoted to a more politicised strategy. The problem
for Sinn Féin activists was to convince their supporters that the cease-fire
did not equate with surrender or political oblivion (Shirlow and McGovern 1998), but instead was to be portrayed as a political coup which indicated the potency and durability of the Republican cause (O'Hearn et al.
1999). The symbols which portrayed the importance of these procedural
shifts were centred around the notion that Republicanism was a politically influential discourse which truly represented secularism, egalitari-
anism and ultimately democracy.

Sinn Féin activists have striven to delineate the cease-fire as a decisive
political shift which warranted a future in which Sinn Féin would have a
fundamental impact upon Irish politics. As many Sinn Féin activists have
stated privately, post-cease-fire rhetoric is grounded in a realisation that
Sinn Féin voters must continually be reminded that their political perspective is going to be taken seriously in impending negotiations and
constitutional change. However, being unequivocally accepted into the
political mainstream has been a major problem for Sinn Féin.

The near collapse of the Northern Ireland Assembly has come about
because of the link between Sinn Féin and the IRA. For Unionists in parties such as the Northern Ireland Unionist Party, the UKUP and the
DUP there has always been a reluctance to engage with Sinn Féin. These
parties display the strongest feeling that Sinn Féin and the IRA are the
same organisation and as such the placing of Sinn Féin in the Executive
of the Northern Ireland Assembly is envisaged as an unacceptable victory
of the IRA. For the UUP, the PUP and the UDP there is a desire for Sinn
Féin to be in the Executive but only if the IRA decommissions. In overall terms, the refusal of Unionist parties to endorse Sinn Féin's place
within the Executive leads to a direct form of containment, which rejects
Sinn Féin's political mandate and in so doing misconstrues the nature
and depth of political shifts and ideological morphology within Sinn
Féin.

However, it is also evident that the desire for disarmament of the IRA
leads to division within the wider Republican community. Seemingly,
Sinn Féin is caught in a 'Catch-22' situation. If they encourage the IRA
to decommission they will lose some Republican support, and if they do
not, they will fail to gain the 'real' power and influence which they
promised their electorate. As such Sinn Féin are internally imprisoned in

that they must maintain a balancing act which can at one and the same time be offensive to one tradition ('theological' Republicanism) while opening the door to other nonmilitaristic interpretations and strategies.

Undoubtedly, for Republican dissenters the pursuit of decommissioning is seen as an unacceptable disavowal of the armed struggle and the legitimacy of the IRA. Prominent members of the IRA have made it clear to the Sinn Féin leadership that they will not accept Sinn Féin spokespersons condemning violent activities such as knee-capping and punishment beatings. As an IRA activist noted when interviewed by me in July 1990: 'The criticism of the (P)IRA for undertaking policing of our communities is an inappropriate mode of censure. It is as if they (Sinn Féin) have gone over to the other side.'

Consequently, it is evident that within Sinn Féin there are varying degrees of support for the IRA. Undoubtedly, for those who are devoted to the IRA it is clear that any criticism of military activity by Sinn Féin merely contributes to the isolation of the IRA in public and political discourse. In addition, the questioning of IRA activity by certain members of Sinn Féin is seen by other Sinn Féin activists as a continuation of the British state's desire to isolate, divide and defeat the Republican movement. Moreover, for many Sinn Féin activists the pursuit of decommissioning will undoubtedly lead to a diminution of the Republican movement's power base. As noted by Antony McIntyre (1997): 'If the IRA were to cease to exist the British would not care how many Nationalists voted Sinn Féin. They know that Republicans without armed struggle are like birds without wings – unable to go anywhere.'[1]

For pro-IRA dissenters, the Sinn Féin leadership has discursively felt compelled to gradually nudge the Republican project away from its traditional objective of a united Ireland regardless of Unionist consent, and dangerously, others would say deliberately, towards the partitionist fudge position of unity by consent. Behind this criticism of the Sinn Féin strategy lies the supposition that the British state for its part does not care if Ireland is united, only that it should be so with the consent of the Unionist community. This, it is argued, is not out of a respect for the democratic wishes of the Unionists but is the logic of a permanent structural acquiescence to the Unionist strategy of threat and majoritarianism.

Ultimately, Republican critics argue that all Sinn Féin has achieved via its peace strategy has been permission to enter all-party talks and a mode of political operation where they can argue for a united Ireland without the remotest possibility of securing it without gaining Unionist consent – a mode of consent which dissenters see as unachievable. Clearly, for those within the Republican movement who are beginning to criticise the unarmed strategy, Sinn Féin is acknowledged as having entered a political process within which peace and dialogue will be controlled

---

1   Anthony McIntrye is an ex-IRA prisoner and strong opponent of Sinn Féin's political strategy.

through the use of force by the majority community and the adoption of the consent principle by both the Irish and British states.

Republican leaders are as intelligent as the Republican base. And significant sections of that base are in no doubt that all-party blather can lead only to what Tony Blair has said it would – no end to partition; no British declaration of intent to withdraw; and no united Ireland. Stripped of those elements the outcome can have no identifiable Republican content.

It is obvious, given the difficulties of Sinn Féin in gaining access to ministerial posts due to Unionist intransigence over decommissioning, that dissenters can assert that Republicans have been reduced to the function of renegotiating the future of partition in Ireland. For sceptical Republicans Sinn Féin's fronting of traditional goals, such as the termination of British rule, remains a purely discursive exercise (Smith 1995). One of the most acute fears among Republican dissenters is that Sinn Féin will hurl Republicanism out of its own ideological orbit and into the arid sterility of constitutional Nationalism.

For dissenters it is clear that given the deletion of Articles 2 and 3 of the Irish constitution (the territorial claim over Northern Ireland), the return of a Northern Ireland Assembly, Sinn Féin's abandonment of its traditional policy of abstentionism, reliance on British government-appointed commissions on equality and human rights issues as well as on the future of policing, and the implicit recognition of the principle of Unionist consent on the constitutional question, that Sinn Féin can go no further without explicit and noticeable acceptance of its mandate by Unionists. As noted previously, the acceptance of significant ideological shifts in Sinn Féin's philosophy, however, is for Unionists inadmissible without the decommissioning of IRA weapons.

For Unionists, ideological intent is deemed less offensive than the holding of weaponry and the threat of violence. At this point, the decommissioning issue falls firmly behind the semantic representations and struggle over the meaning of violence, defence and violent power. Unionists see the IRA as unnecessary given both the shifts in political practice in recent years and Unionist fears that Republicans constantly mobilise the threat of violence to gain political concessions from both the Irish and British states. In response, many Republicans do not just suspect, but are convinced, that the decommissioning 'albatross' is and has been utilised by Unionists and British 'securocrats' as a means of continuing the war of attrition by other means. In addition, for many the decommissioning of Republican weapons leaves Republican communities unprotected from future state and Loyalist violence.

After several years of political progress and alterations in the nature of political representation and dialogue it is now evident that Sinn Féin is caught between the demands of Unionism, the British and Irish states and the expectations of many of their own patrons. For the Sinn Féin leadership, who have launched an unprecedented assault on the belief system of the Republican base, it is apparent that for many Republicans decommissioning without administrative power is an unacceptable step too far. Seemingly, for Unionists it is the most important step yet to be completed. In many ways, the IRA as an organisation is undoubtedly the strongest and most evocative symbol of Republican resistance and belief. As a natural consequence of partition, the IRA continues to legitimate the potential for change if political strategies fail.

Given that Sinn Féin is now the largest pro-unification party in Northern Ireland and that the Good Friday Agreement has delivered ministerial posts and a recognition of civic Republicanism, it was rumoured that Sinn Féin would begin a process of decommissioning in the autumn of 2001. Without doubt the decommissioning of some weapons in October 2001 has indicated that those who are committed to retaining all weaponry have become a minority within the IRA's Army Council. Although this may be the case, it is evident that the decommissioning that took place was more to do with the influence of the White House upon the Republican leadership. The capture of three IRA men in Colombia, who, it has been suggested, were aiding the Marxist FARC organisation, and the impact of the Twin Towers attack upon the attitude towards 'terrorism' in the United States has undoubtedly fashioned the present delivery of some weapons. In this sense it is clear that the development of links with the White House has meant two things for the politics of Sinn Féin. Firstly, the support of influential members of the American political system has provided Sinn Féin with the space to move into new arenas of influence and 'respectability'. Secondly, such a move has created a new form of containment given that the White House now has the capacity to dictate the future of Sinn Féin's political direction. The central issue is that with decommissioning having now begun, it is evident that the constitutional and organisational structure of Sinn Féin and the IRA will have to endorse a political morphology based upon how Republicans effect peace, stability and political progress.

However, even with some evidence of decommissioning, Sinn Féin remains loathed, despised and held up as a symbol of Republican fascism within certain quarters. Ironically, the IRA provides Sinn Féin with an all-important power base and legitimacy which is rejected outside of the Republican movement. In many ways, Republicans are not only contained by atavistic Unionism and state violence, but also by the inability of Sinn Féin to exist in political isolation from the IRA. Thus, containment is both external and internal.

Conclusion

In terms of future political appeasement and ideological alteration, Sinn Féin has reached a symbolic dead-end. The glacially slow pace imposed on the peace process, the failure of the British government to uphold and implement the timetable of the Agreement, and the recent legislative tinkering with the Agreement, has undermined the pacificators within the Republican movement. It also strengthens the hand of those dissidents whose aim is to turn disillusionment with politics into a resumption of armed struggle. So far, the Republican dissidents do not have enough support for such a strategy.

In replacing the policy of armalites and ballot boxes with a process towards peace, persuasion and an unarmed struggle, Sinn Féin has clearly set out to create wider political relationships, and encourage the IRA to pursue a cease-fire. The general reaction from the Unionist and pro-union population is still conditioned by extreme hostility. Although Sinn Féin has undertaken much soul-searching, deliberation and political adaptation, its primary instructive arguments and unwavering aspirations remain a reunited Ireland. Moreover, the recognition that politics can be framed through alliances with past foes is probably one of the most significant developments in the body politic of Ireland since the present conflict began.

However, it should be remembered that, because of political alteration and morphology, Sinn Féin has become much more heterogeneous in terms of content, form and ideological commitment. There are those who wish to reproduce Irish Republicanism via threat, violence and intimidation, and who see Unionism as an 'unnatural aberration', a 'foreign virus' which must be expelled from the Irish body politic. Others see the link with the IRA as a tactical ploy which ensures that Sinn Féin is taken seriously in and throughout future political arbitration. In addition, there are many who have become war-weary and convinced that military approaches fail in a society within which the defeat of ideologically committed ethnic communities is impossible and infeasible. The latter group are those most likely to solidify political change and convince the IRA to continue decommissioning, which will instil confidence in the Unionist community. However, in order that this latter group can carry Sinn Féin out of both internal and external containment it is essential that Unionists do not seek the surrender or humiliation of the Republican community. Conversely, as the history of Irish Republicanism dictates, only short-term power comes from the barrel of a gun.

References

Adams, G. 1995. *Free Ireland. Towards a Lasting Peace*. Dingle.

Aughey, A. 1995. 'In Search of a New Vision', *Belfast Telegraph*, 10 August 1995.

Bean, K. 1995. 'The New Departure', in *Causeway* 6 (1995), pp. 202–13.

Bishop, P. and Mallie, E. 1988. *The Provisional IRA*. London.

Burton, F. 1978. *The Politics of Legitimacy: Struggles in a Belfast Community*. London.

Burton, F. and Carlen, P. 1979. *Official Discourse: On Discourse Analysis, Government Publications, Ideology and the State*. London.

Campbell, B. 1994. 'Voices from the Edge', in *An Glor Gafa*, vol. 4, no. 1 (1994), pp. 9–17.

Clark, L. 1987. 'Broadening the Battlefield: The H-Blocks and the Rise of Sinn Féin', in *An Glor Gafa* vol. 8, no. 1 (1987), pp. 32–42.

Feldman, A. 1991. *Formations of Violence: The Narrative of the Body and Political Terror in Northern Ireland*. Chicago.

Finlayson, A. 1997. 'Discourse and Contemporary Loyalist Identity', in *Who are the People: Unionism, Protestantism and Loyalism in Northern Ireland*, ed. P. Shirlow and M. McGovern. London.

Foucault, M. 1972. *The Archaeology of Power*. London.

———— 1979. *Discipline and Punish*. London.

Giddens, A. 1985. *The Nation State and Violence: A Contemporary Critique of Historical Materialism*. Cambridge.

Hazelkorn, E. and Patterson, H. 1995. 'The New Politics of the Irish Republic', in *New Left Review* 211 (1995), pp. 49–71.

Held, D. 1989. *Political Theory and the Modern State*. Cambridge.

Hillyard, P. 1993. *Suspect Community*. London.

McCann, E. 1999. *War and Peace in Northern Ireland*. Dublin.

McClelland, M. and Dowd, C. 1992. 'British Strategy in Ireland', in *Starry Plough* vol. 2, no. 1 (1992), pp. 10–17.

McDonald, H. 1995. 'Starting by Surrendering the Semtex', in *Northern Ireland Parliamentary Brief* 58 (1995), pp. 47–52.

McGarry, J. and O'Leary, B. 1995. *Explaining Northern Ireland*. Oxford.

McIntrye, A. 1997. 'Digging Tunnels to the Moon', *Sunday Tribune*, 1 July 1997.

McThomas, H. 1992. 'What are the British doing in Ireland', in *Starry Plough* vol. 2, no. 1 (1992), pp. 13–21.

Munck, R. 1992. 'Irish Republicanism. Containment or New Departure?', in *Terrorism's Laboratory: The Case of Northern Ireland*, ed. A. O'Day. Aldershot.

————1998. 'Irish Republicanism – a New Beginning', in *Dis/Agreeing Ireland*, ed. J. Anderson and J. Goodman. London.

O' Bradaigh, R. 1996. 'The Evil Fruit has Ripened Once More', in *Irish Reporter* 21 (1996), pp. 19-29.

O'Doherty, M. 1998. *The Trouble with Guns: Republican Strategy and the Provisional IRA*. Belfast.

O'Dowd, L., Rolston, B. and Tomlinson, M. 1980. *Northern Ireland: Between Civil Rights and Civil War*. London.

O'Hearn, D., Porter, S. and Harpur, A. 1999. 'Turning Agreement to Process. Republicanism and Change in Ireland', in *Capital and Class* vol. 69, no. 2 (1999), pp. 12-21.

Porter, S. and O'Hearn, D. 1995. 'New Left Podsnappery: The British Left and Ireland', in *New Left Review* 212 (1995), pp. 66-86.

Rolston, B. 1989. 'Alienation of Political Awareness: The Battle for the Hearts and Minds of Northern Nationalists', in *Beyond the Rhetoric: Politics, the Economy and Social Policy in Northern Ireland*, ed. P. Teague. London, pp. 58-80.

———1996. *Politics and Painting. Murals and Conflict in Northern Ireland.* New Jersey.

Ryan, M. 1995. *War and Peace in Ireland.* London.

Shirlow, P. and McGovern, M. 1998. 'Language, Discourse and Dialogue: Sinn Féin and the Irish Peace Process', in *Political Geography* vol. 17, no. 2 (1998), pp. 171-86.

Sluka, J. 1989. *Hearts and Minds, Water and Fish: Support for the IRA and INLA in a Northern Irish Ghetto.* London.

Smith, M. 1995. *Fighting for Ireland.* London.

Stedman-Jones, G. 1983. *Languages of Class: Studies in English Working Class History.* Cambridge.

Todd, J. 1990. 'Northern Irish Nationalist Political Culture', in *Irish Political Studies* 5 (1990), pp. 31-44.

Walter, E. V. 1969. *Terror and Resistance: A Study.* Oxford.

CHAPTER FIVE

Ulster Unionism after the Peace

James W. McAuley

Introduction

It is now extremely difficult to remember with any clarity the feelings of elation and political optimism of the period immediately following the signing of the Good Friday Agreement. Throughout the island of Ireland, and particularly in the North, such expressions were almost tangible. In the referenda that followed, support for the political settlement was endorsed in overwhelming terms. In Northern Ireland, the 'Yes' campaign drew support from 71 percent of the voters, while in the South 95 percent endorsed the deal.

Yet even then there were indications that not all surrounding the settlement was assured. While in Northern Ireland support was forthcoming from both sides of the political divide and the bulk of Irish Nationalists supported the deal, only a small majority of Unionists gave backing to the process. This meant from the outset that Unionism was divided over the future direction and politics of Northern Ireland, something that was directly reflected in the subsequent Assembly elections.[1]

Soon after the referendum, however, optimism rapidly withered amid events surrounding continuing conflicts involving Orange Order parades and especially circumstances around the disputed Drumcree march. Even these concerns were rapidly put on the back-boiler, however, in the light of the world's stare following the killing of twenty-eight people by a bomb planted in Omagh by the 'Real IRA' on 15 August 1998.

---

1   The party support in the new Northern Ireland Assembly was as follows: UUP (pro-Agreement Unionist) 28; SDLP (pro-Agreement Nationalist) 24; DUP (anti-Agreement Unionist) 20; Sinn Féin (pro-Agreement Nationalist) 18; Alliance (pro-Agreement) 6; UKUP (anti-Agreement Unionist); Independents (anti-Agreement Unionist) 3; PUP (pro-Agreement Unionist) 2; Women's Coalition (pro-Agreement).

Thus, when the new Northern Ireland Assembly eventually met, it was against a background of increasing political tension and conflict. Since then the peace process has stuttered and stalled and the institutions it set in place have been subject to a series of resignations by Ministers and suspensions by the Secretary of State for Northern Ireland. Those elected to the Assembly largely found themselves embroiled in such divisive issues as the future of policing and the 'flags' issue. Despite some evidence that the two blocs could operate on a day-to-day level (McAuley and Tonge 2001), the broader political Agreement finally ran aground on the issue of the decommissioning of paramilitary weapons in October 1998, where it has more or less remained until the IRA's move towards actual decommissioning in October 2001.

The broad reaction of Unionism to these contemporary events and the search for political settlement has been involved and intricate. Within party political Unionism, groupings such as the Democratic Unionist Party (DUP) and the United Kingdom Unionist Party (UKUP), declared their position early in the peace process, refusing to engage in any formal negotiations with the political representatives of Republicanism. Both have remained deliberately tangential to events since.

The Ulster Unionist Party (UUP) has been and remains deeply divided over the party's continued support for the Good Friday Agreement and the roles UUP representatives should adopt within the new political institutions. In the current phase the party leader, David Trimble, has narrowly won a key series of votes at the party's ruling Council to keep them engaged in the political process. In October 2000, for example, support for the UUP leadership was only secured after the adoption of a policy to impose sanctions on Sinn Féin, to prevent the party's representatives from attending the joint meetings of Belfast and Dublin Ministers, and to limit cooperation within the Assembly. Such injunctions were only to be lifted once there was substantial 'movement' towards IRA decommissioning. There remains within the UUP a strong anti-Agreement element, the most public face of which is represented by Jeffrey Donaldson and his followers.

There have also been responses from those political organisations representing Loyalist paramilitary organisations such as the Ulster Volunteer Force (UVF) and the Ulster Defence Association (UDA), namely the Progressive Unionist Party (PUP) and the Ulster Democratic Party (UDP) respectively. Their position has been largely supportive. Indeed, at times since the signing of the Agreement, it has only been these groupings that have been directly meshed into and fully appreciative of proceedings. The response of the PUP and particularly the UDP has, however, become increasingly segmented and marginalised.

This chapter seeks to outline and analyse some of these major ideological and political differences and contestations within Unionism in relation to the peace process. To begin to understand this, it is necessary to identify some of the key ideology and discursive tenets upon which contemporary Unionism rests. As Laclau and Mouffe argue, it is through the drawing of political boundaries and the construction of antagonistic relationships between 'friends' and 'enemies' that discourses acquire their political identity (Laclau 1994; Laclau and Mouffe 1985). The construction of such relationships and the stabilisation of political frontiers between those seen as trustworthy and those defined as untrustworthy are a core part of the fixing of identity within discursive formations. In part, this links with the work of Althusser (1971), and in particular the notion that subjects are constructed, 'hailed', or interpellated, by ideological practices so that people understand their lives in particular ways. Moreover, they live their lives as particular subjects, as 'man', 'woman', 'worker', 'unemployed', 'mother', 'father', 'black', 'white', 'Protestant', 'Catholic' and so on. Hence an imaginary identity is conveyed to social agents about the 'reality' of their way of life. Laclau and Mouffe reject what they see as Althusser's determinism, suggesting rather that there are multiple forms by which people place themselves as social actors. Individuals can hold a number of 'subject positions'. In terms of this chapter, therefore, an individual might be a 'woman', 'working class', a 'mother', as well as a 'Unionist'. There is not, however, a complete diffusion or dispersal of these identities. They are held together within more all-embracing discourses, such as Nationalism, socialism or, in this case, Unionism.

Defining Unionism

Ulster Unionism's origins in the late 1800s were based in a response to the Home Rule movement of Parnell. The fundamental argument of Unionists was that Ireland's economic and political welfare would be greatly diminished by leaving the British Empire. In this sense, Unionism in Ulster was merely part of a greater social and political movement, embracing both Ireland and Britain. Ulster Protestants and the Tory Party vehemently opposed any policy of self-government. Hence, the period from the 1880s on saw Protestant Ulster develop a coherence of organisation and increasing ideological detachment from the rest of the island. This was manifested in 1905 in the formation of the Ulster Unionist Council.

During the early part of the twentieth century, intensifying political resistance again forced Great Britain to consider the granting of some form of 'Home Rule' to Ireland, albeit in a limited form. For vastly different reasons, large sections of both the Catholic and the Protestant populations openly rejected any such ideas. Catholic resistance, led by

Sinn Féin, centred dominantly on the notion that only full independence could satisfy their political aims. Protestant Unionists, however, increasingly feared political, social and cultural dominance by a Catholic majority. Indeed, sections of Unionism threatened the secession of Northern Ireland from the rest of the Kingdom if the British government did not back down from its plans for Irish Home Rule. When the Liberal government in 1914 eventually enacted a Home Rule law, its implementation was delayed until the end of the First World War.

Two years earlier, in 1912, as the political campaign against Home Rule intensified, the Ulster Volunteer Force (UVF) appeared on the streets and a powerful group of Unionists published a book entitled, Against Home Rule. The Case for the Union (Rosenbaum 1912). It included contributions by Arthur J. Balfour, Austen Chamberlain, Thomas Sinclair and Lord Charles Beresford, as well as an introduction by Sir Edward Carson and a preface by Bonar Law. This preface clearly intended to construct a discourse of 'the other', claiming that 'Ireland is not a nation; it is two nations. It is two nations separated from each other by lines of cleavage which cut far deeper than those which separate Great Britain from Ireland as a whole' (Rosenbaum 1912: 13). Later Carson argued that those who wished 'should not be deprived against their will of the protection of British law and of the rights of British citizenship' (Rosenbaum 1912: 14). Such claims would be recognisable by Unionists today.

Subsequently, in defiance of the British government, Unionists set about defending those Northern counties in which they had a majority. The events leading up to, and immediately following, the political division of Ireland are well-documented (Bardon 1992; Foster 1998; Hennessey 1997). Political partition institutionalised sectarian social, economic and political relations in Ireland. The primary concern of the subsequent Unionist government in Northern Ireland was to protect the new state's existence. This could only be achieved by obtaining and maintaining Unionist unity. The state had been created by the effective mobilisation of popular Protestantism and the exploitation of their fears expounded by slogans such as 'Home Rule is Rome Rule'. The Unionist Party was best able to maintain control by directly associating with organisations that promoted an essentially militant Protestant ideology, primarily the Orange Order. Thus the creation of a 'Protestant State for a Protestant people', an ideology that persisted throughout devolved government until 1972, through a series of discourses that discouraged class politics and established sectarianism as the central location of social relations.

Contemporary Unionist Discourses

The dominant construction within contemporary Unionism remains that which emphasises its traditional form and discourses. This continues to be located in those expressions that legitimise Unionism as a defence of identity, as security against external and internal threats, and as the positive promotion of a 'British way of life'. In this sense such ideas continue to provide Unionists with their core values by which they make sense of the world. These discourses can be broadly addressed as those that seek to reinforce traditional Unionist perspectives and those promoting some form of social or political change (for details, see Hanna 2001).

It is, therefore, essential to identify how contemporary Unionism mobilises, or seeks to mobilise, its followers and to highlight some of the competing ideological and political alternatives. Initially, it is important to demonstrate two key discourses that have emerged: one based around perpetuity of traditional Unionist values; and a second, around a reconstruction of Unionism into a more socially aware form. These understandings act to simplify the social world, acting upon differing situations and experiences to provide an easily understood framework and set of reference points.

At one level, the shift in Unionist politics has been intricate. At another, however, it has been remarkably simplified. It is possible to suggest two major readings around which Unionism is politically mobilising. The first suggests that Unionism must strengthen its traditional form; the second, that to continue, Unionism must change to adopt a more pluralist form.

Unionist Discourses of Perpetuity

One key discourse unifying contemporary Unionists is that of betrayal by 'Britain'. There is a deeply held Unionist belief that the contemporary political settlement marks some commitment to a form of unification by stealth. That is, many Unionists perceive the entire 'peace process' as a response by the British government to a Nationalist agenda in an attempt to 'buy off terrorism'. Hence, for many Unionists, most of the initiatives to safeguard the future of the Good Friday Agreement by the British and Irish governments mark a political defeat and the undermining of the constitutional position.

Therefore, many of those who seek to reproduce a discourse of traditional values do so in reaction to what they see as a recent history of Unionist demise. This is given credence through direct reference to a continuity of events that includes the Sunningdale and Anglo-Irish

Agreements, the Joint Declaration, the Framework Proposals and the contemporary Good Friday Agreement. All these attempts at political settlement are seen as instalments of a longer process involving steps on a slippery slope to a united Ireland.[2]

Sections of Unionism continue to provide a powerful all-embracing discourse capable of forming a coherent social and political identity. Importantly, it is this that binds together a multiplicity of other potential identities involving, among others, class, nation, gender, sexual orientation, race, ethnicity, language, regional identity, lifestyle, religion and workplace. While Unionism is an identity that is capable of superimposing itself on these, it is neither fixed nor constant. It is socially constructed as a call for individuals to constitute their self around a particular identity (Gamson 1992; Gamson et al. 1992).

Unionism is capable of mobilising participants through motivating them to engage in particular forms of action and experiences (Aughey 1995; Bach 1995, 1996). Furthermore, in Northern Ireland Unionism often demands a public statement from its supporters. Unionism hence is important not only in identity formation but also in engaging its followers in activism, whether this be in voting behaviour, public meetings, rallies or other forms of public events. To be successful, Unionism in all its contemporary forms must draw on the above in some recognisable way. Furthermore, it must do so in a way that is capable of confirming these core principles and solidifying the identity of its supporters into a coherent set of politics.

In response to these competing discourses, Unionism has reacted to contemporary events in a fragmented manner. Some sections of Unionism have simply drawn directly on long-standing discourses and sought to return Unionism to the fundamentals of its doctrine and oppose what they see as a dilution of the Unionist position. This can be seen, for example, within the political discourse of the DUP, according to which the very future existence of Northern Ireland is at stake. Take the following from Peter Robinson (1999), deputy leader of the party:

> I have been in this party from its birth and there has not been a moment when we have not been in the forefront of the battle. There has not been a period where the party has not been engaged in the struggle to save the Union. We have faced difficulties and hardships and consistently contended against unfriendly odds. We have been vilified, demonised and dismissed and our obituary has been written time and time again – but we are still here, still in the midst of the fray, still contending and still unwavering.

In elections prior to the Good Friday Agreement (i.e., to the Forum and the Assembly), the DUP consistently repeated its claim that the foundations of the Union have been made insecure by the implementation of

2 See, for example, recent editions of The Orange Standard or the DUP website: http://www.dup.org.

the 'treacherous Framework Document' (DUP 1996a–d). Central to this framing is the DUP's self-image as a sentinel against Ulster's enemies. It positions its followers around a discourse of fear. As Paisley (1998) himself puts it:

> Having ignored all past warnings together with all the vindication that the so-called 'peace' process was a tactic and a fake, this perfidious and discredited Government now incredibly continues its obstinate pursuit of the selfsame agenda... Blair, Mowlam and Clinton have much in common: they are all good liars but bad actors; they are tough on talk but weak on action; they all misled the people of Northern Ireland and for their deceit and incompetence they should all be impeached for taking advantage of the public trust.

Another important representative of traditional Unionist values has been Robert McCartney. In a whole series of writings and as leader of the United Kingdom Unionist Party (UKUP), he has strongly promoted the concept of Northern Ireland as an integral part of an independent and sovereign United Kingdom within Europe (McCartney 2001). Elsewhere, McCartney has promoted a central duality in his politics (more detailed, McAuley 1997): on the one hand, he has offered important criticisms of traditional Unionism, particularly in its sectarian formation; on the other hand, however, he has consistently utilised and drawn upon traditional Unionist discourses and interpretative frames for the basis of his politics. Hence, he has articulated the clear view that the peace process is part of an orchestrated conspiracy against Unionists and the Union and a process the implementation of which 'ultimately threatens the very existence of democracy itself' (Belfast Telegraph, 9 July 1997). From within this perspective the central aim of the British government has been to promote a settlement that persuades Unionists to sacrifice their British identity (Newsletter, 23 February 1995). For McCartney, the Good Friday Agreement is merely part of a broader strategy. Both governments, albeit for differing reasons, are engaged in a slowly evolving scheme in which British identity in Northern Ireland will gradually be replaced with an Irish one. The Joint Declaration and the Framework Documents represent the medium for achieving this objective, central to which are the development of all-Ireland institutions with a dynamic for expansion. Unionists are to be persuaded to accept the inevitable greening of their cultural and political identity.

In order for the British and Irish governments to realise their joint plans, however, the continued suspension of violence is a necessary condition. The UKUP believes that huge concessions have been made to the Republican movement in return for the halting of violence. This was made clear when McCartney claimed the following on the issue of decommissioning of paramilitary arms:

> No institution of government can be properly termed democratic if it includes representatives of a minority party that is itself inextricably linked to a terrorist organisa-

tion insisting on remaining armed for the purpose of achieving political objectives similar to those of the minority party fronting it. (Belfast Telegraph, 29 July 1999)

McCartney argues, therefore, that in particular it was the IRA campaign in Britain, especially the bombs at Warrington and the Baltic Exchange in 1993, that structured the peace process and accelerated a shift in British policy from internal settlement to one of Irish unity. These bombs made the security of the British mainland an overriding political priority to which the constitutional future of Northern Ireland became entirely subordinate.

For these reasons McCartney and his supporters have been extremely reticent to engage in a process that has included the Joint Declaration, Framework Documents and the Good Friday Agreement, as they believe that the IRA has only temporarily foregone its only effective weapon of violence. They consider that the detailed political strategy of the two governments will achieve Irish unity, although economic, social and political restraints will require its phased accomplishment. The British government is more than willing to force its agenda, without the possibility of any real debate, upon this section of the British population. For McCartney (1999) this means that:

> the pro-Union majority of Northern Ireland will not be allowed to object to institutions of government that will create an Ireland that is factually, functionally, and economically united; but before formally and legally recognising what has become an established and irreversible fact, they will be asked for their consent to a state of things which they then cannot possibly change.

Such views are also clearly reflected in the policies and arguments promoted by that grouping who split away from the UKUP within the NI Assembly to form the Northern Ireland Unionist Party (NIUP). As the group's leader recently put it:

> This total capitulation to pan-nationalist demands was sold to the unionist electorate on the fraudulent basis that the Belfast Agreement would strengthen the Union. The reality is that the security forces have been weakened under this appeasement process whilst paramilitary organisations are stronger than ever, both in illegal activity and finances.... The Belfast Agreement has weakened the Union and offers nothing for unionists. Its collapse is inevitable as the vast majority of unionists reject it. The Belfast Agreement and its institutions will be brought down and I and many others will rejoice in its demise as the whole process is a corruption of democracy and the rule of law. (Boyd 2001)

The broad perspective of those promoting Unionist perpetuity can be set out as follows. The grand strategy behind the peace process is to bring about a functionally united Ireland that will ultimately render a transfer of sovereignty inevitable, through a concealed process of unification (The Irish Times, 26 January 1998). This reading of events is supported by others whose central belief is that their British identity, expressed as Unionism, is under attack.

This has been partly seen in the contested arenas over the routes to be taken by Orange Order parades and the 'rights' of Orange Lodges to march their 'traditional routes'. From a Unionist perspective the broader context may be understood if we consider the following from the official magazine of the Orange Order:

> The onslaught on Northern Ireland's British identity continues unabated, both overtly and covertly. It is an insidious campaign undertaken on different fronts, but with one common objective – the ultimate incorporation of the Province in an all-Ireland in which British, Protestant, Orange, and Unionist culture and identity would be swamped and eventually eradicated.
>
> It is the traditional enemies of Protestantism and Unionism – Irish Nationalism and Republicanism – which is spearheading this attack on Northern Ireland's loyal ethos. But it is being aided and abetted by Government policies which can only have one outcome – a weakening of Northern Ireland's position within the United Kingdom. (Orange Standard April 1999)

Here the main dynamic of the peace process and the political settlement is perceived as undermining the British ethos in Northern Ireland and as subverting Protestants from their traditional British allegiance in an attempt to transfer this to Irish Nationalism. The weakening of Orangeism is thus seen as one of the key policies implemented by the enemies of true Ulster Loyalism (Orange Standard, April 1999). The perceived drive towards 'Irishness' is seen in everything from joint initiatives between the two tourist organisations on the island, through the official position of the British Prime Minister and on to the Irish government (Paisley 1997; DUP 1999). This in turn rests on the construction of the current peace process as involving all sorts of hidden dangers to Ulster Protestants, who are engaged in 'a last battle for Ulster'. Unionists generally must guard unceasingly against the insidious propaganda and attempts to subvert their British allegiance.

This discourse emphasises a set of understood realities within Unionism. It highlights a constructed political identity within a particular form of constitutional arrangement. The concern that these arrangements are under threat has most straightforwardly been fettered by the DUP in its representation of the situation. This is that the Unionist people of Northern Ireland are being subjected to a process driven by an untrustworthy British government, the dynamic for which comes from the combined forces of Irish Nationalism and Republicanism, supported by the Irish government and the Irish lobby in the USA.

The inevitable outcome will be a united Ireland unless Unionists can be awoken to the dangers. The core of the DUP project continues to frame the conflict in this way and to construct discourses that reemphasise and reinforce the central fears of many Unionists. Such discourses are not party-specific in their appeal and are capable of arousing and mobilising across several of the factions of the Unionist party political bloc.

Unionist Discourses of Transformation

Not all Unionists, however, have adopted the discourse and politics of perpetuity that so dominates the DUP and the UKUP/NIUP grouping. Sections of working-class Loyalism, in particular in the period immediately after the Good Friday Agreement, began to critically examine their historical and cultural identity in a meaningful way. This has been directly reflected politically in the rise of the smaller Loyalist parties, such as the UDP and especially the PUP. This experience needs to be understood in the changing context of dramatic economic decline, political disarticulation and ideological disintegration within Unionism. The period of the peace process has opened up much deliberation within Loyalist working-class communities, one possible reading of which suggests a marginalisation of sectarianism as a fundamental organising principle.

Both the UDP and the PUP have remained highly critical of traditional Unionism and in particular of the political leadership of Ian Paisley. Furthermore, as the UDP and PUP attracted almost 10 percent of the overall Unionist vote in the 1996 Forum election, and the PUP was successful in gaining representation to the Northern Ireland Assembly, there is some evidence of electoral support for the positions constructed by these groupings.

At the fore of this attempt to restructure Unionism has been the PUP. In recent years, its leadership has stated its commitment to maintaining and strengthening Northern Ireland's constitutional position within the United Kingdom. It has repeatedly claimed that it will actively work by all democratic means to ensure that there will be no constitutional changes that diminish the constitutional position of Northern Ireland as an integral part of the United Kingdom or that dilute democratic structures and procedures within Northern Ireland. The party's recent manifestos have also supported the right of any individual or group to seek constitutional change by 'democratic, legitimate and peaceful means' and spoken of the rights and aspirations of all those who abide by the law regardless of religious, cultural, national or political inclinations. They have also declared that there can never be a return to 'the awful political and social abuses of the past and Stormont' (PUP 1996a, b).

Factors such as the above have served to expose inconsistencies in the relationships between key sections of the Protestant working class and the state. Importantly, from this section of Unionism there has been a growing awareness of the consequences of a rapidly changing historical, social and economic context. This has been illustrated in the recording of a series of public political meetings and the development of ex-paramilitary prisoner, community and resident groups in Loyalist districts throughout the 1990s. Members of these groupings have consistently raised issues of what 'traditional' Unionism had done for the Loyalist working class (more details, Ballymacarrett Think Tank 1999a, b; Hall 1993, 1995, 2000; Shankill Think Tank 1995, 1998).

For a short time at least, the Loyalist political parties and that which became known as 'New Loyalism' effectively harnessed views such as those expressed above. In this sense New Loyalism provided focal points for increasingly coherent social, economic and political challenges within Unionism for confronting some of the dominant discourses within Unionism. While these processes have loosened the bonds and shifted the interpretative frames within Loyalism, they have not meant that such groupings have weakened their commitment to the Union. The position of the Loyalist working class should be seen in the context of the rene-gotiations of ideological boundaries within which they seek to express their identity as Unionists.

In the presence of rapidly changing social conditions, the expression of a more secular and class-based politics has become possible for some. The attempt by sections of the PUP in particular to establish the primacy of class as a reference point within Unionism is a potential move towards the secularisation of Unionist politics. While the processes involved are still in their rudimentary stages and often subject to changeable politics on the streets, there are indications of serious investigations of their identity and politics from within core sections of Loyalism.

The political momentum for the development of the Loyalist parties has, however, been steadily undermined throughout the period of the peace process. Support for the political project was adversely affected by the Loyalist feud between the UVF and UDA/UFF in the summer and autumn of 2000, during which seven people were killed. Further, the most recent period has seen steadily increasing sectarian tensions and violence involving at least some sections of Loyalist paramilitary organi-sations. Given this situation, it is proving increasingly difficult for New Loyalism to present itself as having made a clean break with its past. As a result the wider appeal of the PUP has been severely curtailed and the UDP have all but ceased to exist as a coherent political entity.

Nonetheless, these shifting contours of Unionist identity and the processes set in motion by the Loyalist parties are extremely important. As several commentators and Unionist politicians have noted, there are widespread feelings from within the Protestant working class that they are in decline, increasingly subject to forces of rapid economic, political, cultural and psychological retreat (Dunn and Morgan 1994, 1997). The hegemonic construction of a British identity by Ulster Loyalism, has not only traditionally included, but also absorbed, a multitude of other key identities, such as gender, geographical location, sexual preference, class identity, and so on. These have been organised into a collective political will through an all-embracing discourse. New Loyalism may continue to provide a dynamic to begin to separate these key identities, and to reformulate its central components. This may yet form the basis for the creation of alternative discourses and locations of identity within Unionism, beyond those examined below.

Locations of Unionist Identity

A common and useful starting point for examining Unionism's ideological identity is provided by Jennifer Todd (1987, 1994). She argues that Unionist ideology is essentially an umbrella category under which two distinct groups exist. The first, Ulster Loyalism, sees itself primarily as a self-contained cultural community with a secondary political allegiance to the British state. The other strand is an Ulster British tradition, which defines itself as being an integral part of Greater Britain with a secondary regional patriotism for Northern Ireland.

It is possible to conceive of each of these different positions resting on three wider formulations of Unionist identity, each of which has a different ideological and sometimes geographical location. These can roughly be identified as Ulster in Britain, Britain in Ulster, and Ulster in Ireland.

For those who identify with 'Ulster in Britain', the basic political unit of relevance is, or at least should be, 'Ulster' (Northern Ireland) and the will of the Ulster people. Despite day-to-day differences between the UDP and DUP and increased antagonism throughout the period of the peace process, this can be seen in the positioning of large sections of both the DUP and the UDP. It can be readily detected in the following statement on identity from an active DUP member:

> My fundamental loyalty is to Northern Ireland. Now most often that means I give my loyalty to Westminster and the Crown ... But there's no way I'm going to be loyal to a government that threatens our position ... you can't be loyal to someone who's out to destroy your country.[3]

For both DUP and UDP their position within the United Kingdom and relationship to the UK government is conditional (for more details, see McMichael 1999; Miller 1978; UDP 1996a, b). In the case of the DUP this attachment is stronger; with the UDP, it is weaker, reflecting perhaps their previous commitment to an independent Northern Irish State.

The DUP's position rests on traditional Unionist notions that there exist two distinct peoples on the island of Ireland. As Peter Robinson (1999) of the DUP argues, the 'whole history of Ulster has ... shown marked differences from that of the rest of the island'. Hence, within DUP discourse, for example, the large-scale emigration of people from

3 This is one of a series of interviews with Unionist political representatives, conducted by the author throughout August and September 1998.

England and Scotland to Ulster in seventeenth century marked a turning point, assimilating Ulster's original inhabitants into a new social framework. This culminated in the Act of Union of 1800. As a result of the advantages brought about by the Union, Ulster people extended their industrial expertise. They entered into the spirit of the Union and the stability that it created laid the foundation of those British loyalties that are to this day the most powerful force in Ulster life (Robinson 1999).

The position taken by the PUP and the majority within the UUP differs significantly from that outlined above. Both of these groupings see politics and society in Northern Ireland simply as an extension, albeit in a different and distinct cultural setting, of 'mainland' UK politics. Both remain highly integrationist in outlook and policy. The UUP councillor, Michael McGimpsey, in what Cochrane (1997: 37) calls a perfect illustration of the 'Ulster British tradition', illustrates this ideological perspective:

> As I see it, I'm an Irish Unionist. I'm Irish, that's my race if you like. My identity is British, because that is the way I have been brought up, and I identify with Britain and there are historical bonds, psychological bonds, emotional bonds, all the rest of it you know. I'm not so much anti-united Ireland as I am pro-Union with Britain, and I would be quite prepared to take a united Ireland tomorrow, if somehow the whole of Ireland could have some form of Union grafted on.

This focal point was also highlighted in an interview with one of the leading figures in the PUP, Billy Hutchinson. At one point he expressed his own identity as follows, revealing not his own construction of politics but the basis for the construction of a particular form of working-class Loyalist identity:

> I am Irish and I don't see any conflict between that and asserting that I am British. ... I am Irish, culturally speaking... My Britishness is rooted in my sense of belonging to the wider British working class and its struggles and it is from the British working class movement that we take our political philosophy and perspective.... Hence, the political consciousness of our working class base has a much stronger East–West dimension than a North–South one. (Hutchinson 1994: 3)

These positions reflect a much wider concern about the nature of Unionism and whether the best way of guaranteeing the Union is through full integration or by way of devolved administration.[4] The respective merits of 'Devolution' and 'Integration' have been a highly contested and divisive issue, both ideologically and politically, for some time, and particularly within the UUP. Much of the internal political debate has evolved around whether the new Northern Irish elected body should have the right to make its own laws and legislation. Beyond that, most integrationists believe that the contesting of elections in Northern Ireland should allow for those elected in Northern Ireland to play their part in the UK national political scene.

It is important to note that in its origins Unionism was not necessarily a promotion of 'Britishness' at all. Indeed, it was quite legitimate to be Irish

---

4   Supporters of integration are themselves divided between electoral and administrative integrationists.

and Unionist. The Irish dimension to Unionism and to Unionists in Northern Ireland continues to create a dilemma of aligning their sense of 'Irishness' within an identity now almost exclusively symbolised as British. This notion of 'Ulster in Ireland' is now by far the least developed location within Unionism. Nonetheless, it is important to consider how the processes initiated by the closer workings of the UK and Irish governments may alter the ideological character and political conduct of contemporary Unionism.

Within the Unionist community, some citizens already experience reasonably close contact with the Irish Republic. A fraction of middle-class Unionism, for example, is reasonably accustomed to dealing throughout Irish society through their professional and business lives. This group is unlikely to have difficulty integrating culturally or socially within a unitary Irish state. It may even be that economic integration would offer this section of Ulster Unionism clear rewards from economic enterprises (for more details, see Coulter 1994, 1997). Even so, there is little evidence that this section of Unionism expresses considerable support for the desirability of a unitary Irish state.

The bulk of the Unionist community fears that economic unification will prove to be a project that offers few instrumental rewards but threatens to undermine the political status of Northern Ireland within the Union (Anderson and Goodman 1995, 1997). While there has been growing recognition during the contemporary period of the wider 'Irish dimension', not least in the North-South bodies formalised in the Good Friday Agreement, any Unionist support for such developments has been strictly limited. For most Unionists any symmetry between Ireland as geographical entity and Ireland as political unity must be resisted and the Irish Nationalist position of 'geographical statehood' exposed as a falsehood.

Some Conclusions

Unionism as an ideology and as a political force is in no small state of upheaval and internal flux. This may perhaps result in a modification of its form. It may result in a more progressive Unionism. It is, however, just as likely to conclude in a strong restatement of Unionism's core values. There are clearly those who wish to reinforce the traditional Unionist agenda. The DUP remains foremost in its continued criticism of those Unionists engaged in the contemporary search for a settlement. Any attempt to do so is seen as undermining the Union. Furthermore, the discourses the DUP and its supporters construct are capable of rallying significant sections of Unionism against any settlement.

Elsewhere, the views being expressed by the political leadership of the PUP, and by at least some sections of the Protestant working class, offer a clear attempt to reassess traditional Unionist discourses. Central to this has been the challenge offered to the authority of the established Unionist political leadership. Whilst sectarian politics remain fundamental to the realities of 'Protestant' communities, their expression of 'Britishness' as conscious political identity can no longer be thought of as either stable or homogeneous (McAuley 1994, 1996, 1998).

What remains consistent is the set of ideas to which these people have returned – in this case, culturally a British identity and politically Unionist, or at least anti-united Ireland. It has, however, become increasingly transparent that the Union and Unionism mean different things to different people. For the time being most forms of political identity within the Protestant community remain subordinate to the all-embracing representation of 'Britishness'. The different perceptions and locations of Protestant cultural identity outlined above have political consequences. Unionist identity is complex, encompassing much social experience that is influenced directly by a distinct understanding of history and pattern of socialisation. It is partly this that synthesises the differing strands of Unionism, binding it together by a common set of symbols, myths and shared beliefs that promotes a sense of togetherness among those from that tradition (Bryan et al. 1995; Cecil 1997; Jarman 1997, 1998; Jarman and Bryan 1996).

Unionists, however, are also separated by other social and political views, for example, those surrounding economic development, resource redistribution and the provision of welfare services. In the face of rapidly changing social conditions, economic decline and fragmenting political relations, traditional Unionism has found it increasingly difficult to dominate the discourse of identity. Unionist hegemony is increasingly being challenged from within – by those with alternative notions of the nature of Unionism, articulating a class and sometimes a gendered perspective, and who seek the right to include their respective politics within a redefinition of Unionist identity and political Unionism (Democratic Dialogue 1996; Rooney 1992; Sales 1997, 1998). Unionist identity is, however, also capable of closing around its most fundamental understandings of the world, particularly if it believes those fundamentals to be under direct external threat.

References

Althusser, L. 1971. 'Ideology and Ideological State Apparatuses', in *Lenin and Philosophy and Other Essays*, ed. L. Althusser. London.

Anderson, J. and Goodman, J. 1995. 'Regions, States and the European Union. Modernist Reaction or Postmodernist Adaptation?', in *Review of International Political Economy* vol. 2, no. 4 (1995).

————1997. 'Problems of North–South Economic Integration in Ireland', in *Irish Journal of Sociology* 7 (1997).

Aughey, A. 1995. 'The End of History, The End of the Union', in *Selling Unionism Home and Away*, ed. A. Aughey, D. Burnside, E. Harris, G. Adams and J. Donaldson. Belfast.

Bach, J. 1995. 'The Idea of the Union. Statements and Critiques in Support of the Union of Great Britain and Northern Ireland', ed. J. W. Foster. Canada.

———1996. 'The Union – Best for All', in *A Vision for the Union*, ed. R. Holmes. Belfast.

Ballymacarrett Think Tank. 1999a. *Puppets No More*. Newtownabbey.

———1999b. *Beyond King Billy?* Newtownabbey.

Bardon, J. 1992. *A History of Ulster*. Belfast.

Boyd, N. 2001. 'Agreement Has Weakened Union', letter to *Belfast News Letter*, 10th July 2001.

Bryan, D., Fraser, T. G. and Dunn, S. 1995. *Political Rituals: Loyalist Parades in Portadown*. Coleraine.

Cecil, R. 1997. 'The Marching Season in Northern Ireland. An Expression of Politico-Religious Identity', in *Inside European Identities*, ed. S. MacDonald. Oxford.

Cochrane, F. 1997. *Unionist Politics and the Politics of Unionism since the Anglo-Irish Agreement*. Cork.

Coulter, C. 1994. 'Class, Ethnicity and Political Identity in Northern Ireland', in *Irish Journal of Sociology* 4 (1994), pp. 1–26.

———1997. 'The Culture of Contentment. The Political Beliefs and Practice of the Unionist Middle Classes', in *Unionism, Protestantism and Loyalism in Northern Ireland*, ed. P. Shirlow and M. McGovern. London, pp. 114–39.

Democratic Dialogue. 1996. 'Power, Politics, Positionings. Women in Northern Ireland', *Report* No. 4. Belfast.

Dunn, S. and Morgan, B. 1994. *Protestant Alienation in Northern Ireland*. Coleraine.

———1997. 'Who Are "The People"?', in *Unionism, Protestantism and Loyalism in Northern Ireland*, ed. P. Shirlow and M. McGovern. London.

DUP. 1996. 'Election Special'. Belfast.

———1996a. 'Election Special'. Belfast.

———1996b. 'Our Covenant With the Ulster People', in *Manifesto for the Forum Election*. Belfast.

———1996c. 'The Framework of Shame and Sham. Yes the Framework Document is a One Way Road to Dublin'. Belfast.

———1996d. 'The Unionist Team You Can Trust', in *Election Communication*. Belfast.

———1999. 'The Tragedy of a False Peace', http://www.dup.org (21 January 1999).

Foster, R. F. 1998. Modern Ireland 1600–1972. Harmondsworth.

Gamson, W. A. 1992. 'The Social Psychology of Collective Action', in Frontiers in *Social Movement Theory*, ed. A. D. Morris and C. McClung Mueller. New Haven.

Gamson, W. A. et al. 1992. 'Media Images of the Social Construction of Reality', in *Annual Review of Sociology* vol. 18 (1992), pp. 373–93.

Hall, M. 1994. *Ulster's Protestant Working Class: A Community Exploration*. Belfast.

———1995. *Beyond the Fife and Drum*. Belfast.

———2000. *Seeds of Hope: Ex-prisoners Project*. Newtownabbey.

Hanna, R., ed. 2001. *The Union: Essays on Ireland and the British Connection*. Newtownards.

Hennessey, T. 1997. *A History of Northern Ireland 1920–1996*. Dublin.

Hutchinson, B. 1995. 'Loyalist Leader Addresses Dublin Socialist Gathering', *Socialist Voice* vol. 5, no. 7 (1995), p. 3.

Jarman, N. 1997. Material Conflicts: Parades and Visual Displays in Northern Ireland. Oxford.

———1998. 'Material of Culture, Fabric of Identity', in Material Cultures: Why Some Things Matter, ed. D. Miller. London.

———1996. Parades and Protest: A Discussion of Parading Disputes in Northern Ireland. Coleraine.

Laclau, E. 1994. The Making of Political Identities. London.

Laclau, E. and Mouffe, C. 1985. Hegemony and Socialist Strategy. London.

McAuley, J. W. 1994. The Politics of Identity: a Loyalist Community in Belfast. Aldershot.

———1996. '(Re)Constructing Ulster Loyalism. Political Responses to the 'Peace Process', in Irish Journal of Sociology 6 (1996), pp. 127–153.

———1997a. 'Divided Loyalists, Divided Loyalties: Conflict and Continuities in Contemporary Unionist Ideologies', in Peace or War? Understanding the Peace Process in Northern Ireland, ed. J. Tonge and C. Gilligan. Aldershot, pp. 37–53.

———1997b. 'Flying the One-Winged Bird: Ulster Unionism and the Peace Process', in Unionism, Protestantism and Loyalism in Northern Ireland, ed. P. Shirlow and M. McGovern. London.

———1998. 'A Process of Surrender? Loyalist Perceptions of a Settlement', in Dis/Agreeing Ireland Contexts, Obstacle, Hopes, ed. J. Anderson and J. Goodman. London.

McAuley, J. W. and Tonge, J. 2001. The Role of 'Extra-Constitutional' Parties in the Northern Ireland Assembly. Final Report to the ESRC.

McCartney, R. 1999. 'Northern Ireland – A Warning for Britain', http://web.ukonline.co.uk/stuart.n2/nbrit/mccartney.html (21. 9. 1999).

McCartney, R. 2001. Reflections on Liberty, Democracy and the Union. Dublin.

McMichael, G. 1999. An Ulster Voice: In Search of Common Ground in Northern Ireland. Colorado.

Miller, D. W. 1978. Queen's Rebels: Ulster Loyalism in Historical Perspective. Dublin.

Paisley, I. 1997. 'DUP Rebuff Trimble Remarks', DUP Press Statement, 24 March 1997.

———1998. 'The Fruits of Appeasement', DUP Press Statement, 3 September 1998.

PUP. 1996a. 'Manifesto for the Forum Election'. Belfast.

———1996b. 'Support the Progressive Unionists', in Election Communication. Belfast.

Robinson, P. 1999a. 'Speech to DUP Annual Conference 1998', http://www.dup.org (21 September 1999).

———1999. 'Understanding Northern Ireland – A Part of the United Kingdom', http://www.dup.org (21 September 1999).

Rooney, E. 1992. 'Women, Community and Politics in Northern Ireland – Isms in Action', in Journal of Gender Studies vol. 1, no. 4 (1992), pp. 475–91.

Rosenbaum, S. 1912. Against Home Rule. The Case for the Union. London.

Sales, R. 1997. 'Gender and Protestantism in Northern Ireland', in Unionism, Protestantism and Loyalism in Northern Ireland, ed. P. Shirlow and M. McGovern. London.

———1998. 'Women, the Peace Makers?', in Dis/Agreeing Ireland Contexts, Obstacle, Hopes, ed. J. Anderson and J. Goodman. London.

Shankill Think Tank. 1995. A New Beginning. Newtownabbey.

———1998. At the Crossroads? Newtownabbey.

Todd, J. 1987. 'Two Traditions in Unionist Political Culture', in Irish Political Studies 2 (1987), pp. 1–26.

————1994. 'History and Structure in Loyalist Ideology. The Possibilities of Ideological Change', in *Irish Journal of Sociology* 4 (1994), pp. 67–79.

UDP. 1996a. 'Look to the Future', in *Election Communication*. Belfast.

————1996b. 'Look to the Future', in *Manifesto for the Forum Election*. Belfast.

CHAPTER SIX

Drumcree: Marching towards Peace in Northern Ireland?

Dominic Bryan

Introduction

From the mid-1990s until 2001, politics in Northern Ireland appeared to develop differently within two apparently separate public arenas. The 'peace process' was a stage which local political leaders have shared with members of the British, Irish and American governments. In contrast, the parade disputes, the best-known of which has become the Drumcree parade in Portadown, County Armagh, led to violent confrontations that served to question the emergence of a lasting peace. During these confrontations Protestant organisations – the Orange Order, the Apprentice Boys of Derry and the Royal Black Preceptories – generically termed the loyal orders, insisted that they have a right to hold 'traditional' parades in areas which have a predominantly Catholic population. There has been organised opposition to parades since the mid-1980s, but in recent years resident groups have conducted a concerted campaign against what they perceive as sectarian 'triumphalist' events. The defining images of both the parades and the disputes are of communal politics of the past (Bryan 1998). The fortifications erected in the fields around Drumcree Church from 1998 to 2000 by the Royal Ulster Constabulary (RUC) and the British Army to stop the Battle of the Boyne commemoration parade from returning via the Garvaghy Road created a scene worthy of equal regard to the original battle in 1690.

In this chapter, I will examine the apparent contrast between these two arenas and suggest that they are closely related, that the development of a peace process and increased conflict over public space are not at odds with each other. In particular, I will explore the political changes that are taking place within the Protestant community and argue that any simplistic view of ethnic politics in Northern Ireland will fail to comprehend the dynamics of the current situation.

Through revealing divisions of class and denomination, by examining the consequent development of political and paramilitary groups and by contrasting politics and power in rural and urban settings, we can better understand the part played by parades in local politics. The ritual parades, exhibiting a continuity in symbolic forms, appear as a manifestation of 'traditional' unchanging politico-ethnic relations but are better understood as complex political resources reflecting contemporary power relations:

> To the casual observer this continuity in symbolic forms seems to be a manifestation of conservatism and reaction, but careful analysis shows the old symbols are rearranged to serve new purposes under new political conditions. In ethnicity, old symbols and ideologies become strategies for the articulation of new interest groups that struggle for employment, housing, funds and other benefits. In Northern Ireland old religious symbols are used in a violent struggle over economic and political issues within the contemporary situation. (Cohen 1974: 39)

Parades and Power

As in many Western European countries, marches and demonstrations have played an important role in political life in Ireland. A calendar of events has developed in the north of Ireland, particularly through the second half of the nineteenth century, reflecting developing ethnic identifications of Irish/Catholic and British/Protestant (Bryan 1994; Jarman 1997). The anniversary of the Battle of the Boyne, commemorated on the 'Twelfth' of July, and the Siege of Derry (around 12 August) became central to a range of Protestant parading dates referred to as the marching season. Similar parading dates have varied in importance within the Catholic community, particularly, St Patrick's Day (17 March) and Lady's Day (15 August), and more recently the Easter Rising, Bloody Sunday (around 30 January), Hunger Strikes (early May) and Internment (second Sunday of August) (Jarman and Bryan 1998). In addition there are large numbers of commemorative events taking place within communities in Northern Ireland throughout the year.[1] In 1999, there were a total of 3,390 parades in Northern Ireland, of which the RUC defined 2,661 as 'Loyalist', 204 as 'Nationalist', and 525 as 'Other' (Chief Constable's Report 1999/2000). Ignoring the issue of how exactly an event is defined, there is an obvious difference in the numbers organised within communities. A brief exploration of the development of the parading 'tradition', combined with an explanation of how the ritual events function, provides a better understanding of the recent disputes.

Every parade, every ritual, is the focus for a range of social and political relations. They reflect the broader and general ethnic identifications

1 For an overview see Fraser (2000).

playing a role in sustaining the 'imagined' or 'socially constructed' community (Anderson 1983; Cohen 1985). Most are legitimised as 'traditional', carrying historical resonance reflecting a 'social memory' (Connerton 1989; Jarman 1997). However, although the continuity suggested by the reenactment of 'tradition' is highlighted by participants and media coverage, it masks the unique reworking and reinterpretation of each (Tonkin and Bryan 1997). Events have always reflected contemporary politics and are used as a political resource by politicians. Different sections of communities, political groups and economic interests work upon the event. Crucially, the relationship of communities with the policing and legal institutions of the state provides the environment in which the events take place.

The largest organisation holding annual parades is the Orange Institution, commonly termed the Orange Order. Formed in County Armagh in 1795, the Orange Order, whilst maintaining its basic structure, has adapted to changing social and economic conditions. Presently, nearly 1,400 local 'private' lodges are grouped together into 126 District Lodges, then divided into twelve County Grand Lodges and the Grand Orange Lodge of Ireland. Precise membership figures are not available but can be estimated at between 40,000 and 50,000 men. Although the Grand Lodge is the highest authority for Orangeism in Ireland, there has always been an egalitarian ethos and a strong sense of local identity to the organisation. From its inception, the central event that annually brought Orangemen together was the commemoration of the Battle of the Boyne in 1690 when King William III, Prince of Orange, defeated the Catholic King James. The Orange Order could be characterised as a 'defensive' localised friendly society for Protestants – even if the actions of members rarely appeared as defensive.

From 1795 until well into the second half of the nineteenth century, the Orange Order struggled for respectability (Bryan 2000; Smyth 1995). Its early members were predominantly lower-class small landowners and rural workers; however, some larger landowners, both in northern counties and in Dublin, soon saw its utility as a political power-base. Popular Orangeism organised around small, localised parades, which in some areas frequently clashed with Catholic Ribbonmen. The carrying of weapons at parades was common, as was the consumption of alcohol. Whilst predominantly Protestant magistrates were often supportive of Orangemen brought before them for the frequent breaches of the peace at Orange parades, the government only found the Orange Order of use in times of crisis, such as the uprising of the United Irishmen in 1798. At other times, Orange parades increased local civil disorder. Senior members of the Orange Order, seeking to have political influence in Dublin and London, were often embarrassed by popular Orangeism. From 1832 to 1845 and from 1850 to 1872, Processions Acts banned parades in Ire-land.

By the end of the nineteenth century the role of parades in the north of Ireland had changed dramatically. A widening of the franchise required that politics needed to be conducted in new ways. The Orange Order had become a central organising institution in Unionist politics just as in the north of Ireland the Ancient Order of Hibernians was important within Irish Nationalism. Orange lodges found a new role in facilitating Protestant patronage and labour exclusivity in the industries of Belfast (Gibbon 1975: 96). The Twelfth of July parades were bigger, facilitated by public transport, and Unionist politicians used them for popular appeal. A more conservative strain of Presbyterianism also embraced Orangeism. The parades and symbols of Orangeism became a focus for the developing Ulster Protestant identity. Orange parades were still regularly the focus of violent civil unrest, particularly in Belfast, Lur-gan and Portadown, and played an important role in developing territo-rial sectarianism, but they now played a much broader role in community life. An industrial bourgeoisie, as well as the rural aristocracy, invested in the Orange Order. Orange halls became social centres as well as political meeting places. Parades showed increasing signs of respectability, with better organised bands replacing the rough drumming parties and a dra-matic development in the imagery appearing on banners held by each lodge. Often the local landowner or factory owner appeared on the reverse side of the banner from King William at the Battle of the Boyne. In short, the Orange Order and its associated parades provided an organ-isational and political resource with which a pan-Protestant, Unionist identity could be forged in spite of different class, denominational and political interests. Aristocratic landowner, factory owner, tenant farmer, labourer, Presbyterian, Episcopalian, Methodist, abstainer and drunk, Liberal and Conservative Unionist, and even trade unionist could march under an Orange banner.

Within the quasi-state of Northern Ireland the Orange Order was in an unprecedented position of power. Between 1921 and 1969 all but three cabinet ministers were in the Orange Order, although three others resigned or were expelled from the institution after achieving their post (Harbinson 1973). Many police officers and civil servants were also in the Orange Order (Weitzer 1995). The Twelfth of July parades effec-tively became rituals of state.

A review of the speeches by senior politicians, leading Orangemen and local Protestant ministers on such occasions clearly indicates the internal divisions that existed within the Protestant community and within the Unionist block. There were constant references to maintaining Unionist unity in the face not only of Nationalism and Republicanism but also of socialism and the electoral successes of the Northern Ireland Labour

Party. While Orange parades were the hegemonic expression of Protestant identity, they nevertheless remained a very loose coalition of interests represented by Loyalist symbols and an opposition to Nationalism, but also under varying degrees of threat from within the Protestant community. Threats to that hegemony came from more fundamentalist Protestantism, eventually manifested in Ian Paisley, which continually argued that senior Orangemen and government ministers were too liberal; from socialism and trade unionism, which always had a base in Belfast and Derry; and, in the late 1950s and 1960s, from tentative modernisers in Unionism itself. This hegemonic struggle, which existed right through the existence of the quasi-state, was to crystallise in the 1960s.

Public space, which had been contested in the previous century, was dominated by Orangeism. Emergency powers under the Civil Authorities (Special Powers) Act of 1922 and the nature of policing ensured that in the 1920s and 1930s Republican commemorations were largely suppressed. St Patrick's Day and Lady's Day parades organised by the Ancient Order of Hibernians only took place in small, predominantly Nationalist villages. Although the Hibernians' political strength was by then well on the wane (Foy 1976), their parades were still viewed as threatening and were sometimes attacked (Jarman and Bryan 1998: 41–50). Confrontations over Orange and Green parades became particularly intense after 1931, with de Valera being elected in the Free State in 1932 and the organisation of a large Catholic Eucharistic congress in Dublin increasing the level of public representations of Catholicism in the North. The Apprentice Boys of Derry also started to organise parades on Easter Monday, apparently to 'recover' Easter from 'Republicans' (Apprentice Boys of Derry 1989). Special powers were used to stop certain demonstrations organised by the labour movement in the 1930s (Farrell 1980).

After the Second World War, under pressure from the British government, the situation eased slightly and, by the late 1950s, limited Republican events were taking place. There were also occasions when the RUC and government ministers stopped Orange parades on the assumption that they were likely to cause disorder or threaten local community relations (Jarman and Bryan 1998: 51–68). Nevertheless, particularly in the late 1940s and 1950s, the RUC regularly took action against any demonstration or public meeting at which Irish tricolours were displayed, while the Stormont administration introduced the Public Order Act (NI) in 1951 and the Flags and Emblems (Display) Act (NI) in 1954. The first of these acts was particularly important since it demanded that forty-eight hours notice be given for a procession unless it was 'customarily held along a particular route'. In other words, the practice of having 'traditional' Orange parades, which had developed in large part due to political dominance, was now enshrined in law. That is not to say that the holding of Orange parades was simply about political domination – they have far broader communal, social and cultural significance. Nor were most Orange parades particularly threatening, nor did most go through predominantly Catholic areas. Nevertheless, their prevalence and development was in large part a function of Unionist political power and Orange hegemony within the Protestant community.

War and Peace

I have tried briefly to place parades within a dynamic historical context and argue that they are complex rituals mixing communal paternalism, patronage and sectarianism, and drawing on 'tradition' and symbolic resonance which is used as a resource by changing political interests. Their place in the identity politics of Catholic and particularly Protestant communities was gained over time but was never unchallenged and depended to a great extent on the reaction of the police, magistrates and government. Orangeism became central to Unionism and hegemonic within the Protestant identity. However, this was only sustainable given a convergence of class interests and the particular power structures securing the quasi-state of Northern Ireland. From the 1960s onwards these structures were no longer sustainable and in the 1990s, during the peace process, Orange hegemony has been partially dissipated.

Within the communal, legal and political environment of Northern Ireland in the 1960s it can be no surprise that the Civil Rights movement, taking to the streets, caused the reaction it did. Apart from issues of housing, electoral fairness and employment that were being highlighted, Civil Rights demonstrators were demanding the right to march. Confrontations with the RUC became inevitable when Ian Paisley organised opposition protests in the centre of Northern Irish towns and cities. Even before the development of the Civil Rights movement, Orangeism was struggling with divisions within Unionism, as those taking a more moderate stance over relations with the Irish Republic were opposed by Paisley and others. The speeches on the Twelfth of July became a public site for these confrontations as Orangemen argued with each other. Many senior Unionist politicians started to stay away from the parades. The Civil Rights movement further exposed those divisions, and as civil disorder grew, the British government could no longer ignore what was taking place.

In the following years, a whole range of factors undermined the position of the Orange Order, particularly the role of the Unionist-Orange elite controlling the Unionist Party and the Grand Lodge. As civil disorder grew, government ministers felt bound to take action to reduce public confrontations. Much to the annoyance of hardliners, there were some bans and restrictions placed on some loyal order parades. But in 1969 and 1970 communal violence grew, territorial boundaries became more defined and Orange parades became increasingly contested. Senior members of the Orange Order, in order to maintain respectability, changed key parade routes in areas like West Belfast. But strategies within increasingly embattled and politicised working-class Nationalist communities shifted from marching at civic centres to demand political rights to keeping the state out of their communities in the form of 'No Go' areas. Local cultures of resistance were developing with the focus less on Civil Rights but on the paramilitarism of the IRA. At the same time, the British government disbanded the so-called B-Specials, an exclusively Protestant auxiliary police force, adding to Protestant insecurity. For many working-class Protestants, the Orange Order looked increasingly impotent, and soon the Ulster Defence Association (UDA) joined the Ulster Volunteer Force (UVF) in paramilitary sectarian attacks on the Catholic community.

Orange parades had growing numbers of rough 'blood and thunder' bands taking part and stressing the development of communal defence in Protestant working-class areas. The parades appeared more assertive and confrontational. Yet just as for many hardliners the Orange Order had not done enough, for some in the middle class or in moderate Unionism it began to represent sectarian communal confrontation. In addition, the collapse of local industry and its eventual takeover by international corporations significantly reduced the role of the Orange Order in offering economic patronage. The political environment within which the Orange Order worked became all the more difficult when Stormont was prorogued in 1972 and direct rule from Westminster introduced. Its main avenue of political influence was now gone. For all these reasons, the Orange Order appeared no longer to hold the banner Protestants rallied to in the face of organised Nationalist opposition – rather, the Order lost membership.

Parades and Protest

The policing context within which parades took place started to change. To begin with, the introduction of the British Army made a difference. Whilst it was soon at war with Republicans, at the same time it was not hugely sympathetic or understanding of loyal order parades, and confrontations in Protestant areas of west Belfast were not uncommon. Although in the late 1970s, in a significant policy change, the RUC resumed as the dominant partner in policing, it was under pressure to be seen to police even-handedly.

Although most loyal order parades were, and have remained, unproblematic in terms of policing, a small but significant number impinge on or go through areas perceived as Catholic. By the 1980s many of those parades had bands carrying flags and wearing uniforms representing paramilitary groups. There is some evidence that the number of parades was increasing even if the number of people participating was decreasing (Jarman and Bryan 1996).

Whilst Nationalist opposition to parades was not highly organised, tension in some areas was ever-present. In the early 1980s, there was a series of disputes over loyal order and band parades in Castlewellan, Downpatrick and Ballynahinch in County Down. In 1984, the RUC issued new 'force orders' directing police policy that discussed 'an upsurge in the number of bands whose members are predisposed to overt and unruly displays of sectarian bitterness' (Belfast Telegraph, 4 July 1986). John Hermon (1997: 171f.), the then Chief Constable, has since reflected on the changing attitudes of the police:

> By mid-May 1985, the Force the RUC was fully prepared to address the smoldering problem of Loyalist parades. Over almost a century, these had been given a special position in Northern Ireland and appeared to have acquired a sort of temporal sanctity. Participants believed they could march wherever and whenever they chose. Their marches epitomised the right to civil and religious liberty, as long as the religion in question was Protestantism.... I was not alone in believing that the superior attitude of the Loyalists, in respect to their marches, had to be changed.

In the summer of 1985 there were serious confrontations over loyal order parades in Portadown after protesting Unionist councillors blocked a small Nationalist parade on St. Patrick's Day. The signing of the Anglo-Irish Agreement further heightened tensions over Orange parades, particularly in the Tunnel and Garvaghy Road areas of the town (Bryan et al. 1995; Bryan 1997). Changes in the policing of the parades were depicted by many Unionists as Dublin interference and an attack on Protestant traditions. During serious disturbances on Easter Monday, 1 April 1986, at a banned Apprentice Boys parade in the town, Keith White was hit by a plastic bullet and later died from his injuries. Over the summer, Loyalists intimidated many families of police officers out of their homes. The loyal orders have not been allowed to march their 'traditional' route through the Tunnel since 1986. In 1987 the British government introduced the Public Order (Northern Ireland) Act which, although similar to English and Welsh legislation introduced in the wake of the miners' strike and a series of urban riots in the 1980s, significantly did not recognise 'traditional' parades. Under the new legislation parade organisers had to give seven days' notice of their event. Quite obviously, relations between the state and loyal order parades had undergone a massive change since the 1950s and 1960s.

A further significant change must be noted. Nationalist and Republican events, although still a small fraction of the total number of parades, have been allowed into areas where previously they would always have

been stopped. Most significantly, in 1993, the main Internment commemoration parade was allowed into the centre of Belfast with a meeting being held in front of the City Council building. In places like
Armagh, Derry, Lurgan and Castlederg, fewer restrictions were placed on
Republican events. Also, Nationalist groups such as the Ancient Order
of Hibernians have held parades in Derry for the first time. On 26 July
1996 the Bogside Residents Group, campaigning against aspects of loyal
order parades in the city, retraced the route of the October 1968 Civil
Rights march from the Waterside to Waterloo Place; however, this time
there was no intervention by the police (Jarman and Bryan 1998: 69–84).
I am not suggesting that the position of the Nationalist community, in
terms of the use of public space, in any way approaches parity with the
Protestant community. Nor would I suggest that relations between the
police and the Protestant community are the same as between the police
and the Nationalist community. However, it is undeniable that significant changes in relations of power have taken place.

It is in this context that one can begin to understand the series of
parade disputes that have coincided with the peace process. The development of the peace process is in part due to the changing nature of
Republican politics (Bean 1994). The development of a political strategy
has meant greater stress being placed upon many of the Civil Rights
issues – particularly what has come to be termed the equality agenda.
Closer relations with the SDLP and Dublin governments have also been
evident. Greater emphasis has been placed upon community development through events such as the West Belfast Festival (De Rosa 1998).
And the cessation of violence called by the IRA from August 1994 to
February 1996 and then since July 1997 has been vital. At the same time,
better organised opposition to certain parades in predominantly Nationalist areas developed: on the lower Ormeau Road from 1992, on the Garvaghy Road and in other areas from 1995 (Jarman and Bryan 1996:
42–84 and 1998: 80–84). Unionists, based on some recorded remarks
made by Gerry Adams, argue that the rise of residents groups was all part
of an overall Republican strategy.[2] This underestimates local community
dynamics that have long been in existence in places such as the Garvaghy
Road and the political space which the peace process had created for
public opposition to parades (Garvaghy Residents 1999). Ironically, the
fact that in a number of cases, particularly on the Ormeau Road, the
RUC were no longer prepared to defend a status quo of Orange parades
taking place without question, made it obvious that concerted campaigns
by residents could be effective. The changing relations of power in
Northern Ireland produced new dispensations both in the political arena
and in the utilisation of public space. The development of community

2   See Dudley Edwards (1999) for a recent restatement of this position.

opposition to parades owes more to a process of political change and discovery than conspiracy.

This being said, however, I would suggest that the dynamics of the parade disputes has as much to do with what has taken place within Unionism as within the politics of Irish Nationalism. I have suggested that the political and economic circumstances played a part in the impotency of the Orange Order and the apparent loss of membership since the 1960s. What is more important, direct opposition to Orange parades since 1995 has only mobilised the Orange Order for relatively short periods of time and with disastrous consequences. The fundamental problem for the Orange Order has been that the divisions and differing interests, which at other times held it together, have not been reconcilable. In addition, the disparate nature of authority within the organisation and parades has made it incapable of developing any strategy likely to be politically effective.

On 9 July 1995, with Garvaghy Road residents holding a protest on the road, the RUC decided to block the Drumcree church parade. The local District Master of Portadown No.1 District, Harold Gracey, reacted by saying that they would stay at the fields around the church until they were allowed down. So began the first Drumcree stand-off, or 'Siege of Drumcree' as Orangemen later termed it. There were sporadic attacks on police lines as it went through the night and into the next day. Various Unionist politicians became involved although Grand Master and Ulster Unionist MP for South Belfast, Martin Smyth, remained absent. On the Monday night a political meeting was held at the field. By far the biggest reception was given to Ian Paisley – indeed, some accused him of encouraging the crowd to attack the police, although I could see that those attacks were already taking place whilst he spoke. Overnight, after rain had cooled tempers, a process of negotiation led to an apparent resolution whereby the parade and a protest took place, although subsequently there have been different interpretations about what was agreed. Crucially, much to the annoyance of the resident groups and others involved in the negotiations, Paisley and local UUP MP David Trimble, clasping hands in victory, joined the parade as it came through Portadown.

As so often in the past, Unionists looked to this Orange parade as providing a sign of Unionist unity. However, an alternative interpretation can be made which provides clues to the dynamic situation that was to develop in the years that followed. It rests on a number of peculiarities of the 'Siege of Drumcree': most obviously, the presence of Ian Paisley, who has not been a member of the Orange Order since 1958; the sense in which the two major Unionist parties were competing with each other; and, for whatever reason, the nonappearance of Martin Smyth. Paisley emerged from the event as the 'Orange' hero, and criticisms of the Grand Master grew in the months that followed. A ginger group developed within the Orange Order, called the 'Spirit of Drumcree', which agitated on a range of issues, including making the Orange Order more democratic, the resignation of Martin Smyth and a hard line on the parades issue. Trimble, for a time, was a hero and by September was leader of the UUP.

This party-political fissure within Orangeism was one of a number of divisions that became more acute between 1996 and 1998 as the peace process gathered momentum and parades disputes increased in hostility. On 7 July 1996 the RUC again blocked the return section of the Drumcree parade. The Orange Order had rejected any attempts to engage with the Garvaghy Road Residents Coalition, which they envisioned as organised by Republicans. The tactic employed by the Orange Order was to organise parades all over Northern Ireland, stretching the security forces to the limit. The days that followed saw widespread disorder in many areas, particularly in Belfast. Trimble, along with many other senior Orangemen, was prominent at the protest but the massive nature of the confrontation with the police and Army raised questions amongst many in the Protestant community, caused alarm in UUP ranks, was widely criticised by leaders of the main Protestant churches and business leaders, and seemed to shock many within the Orange Order who were totally unable to control what was taking place. A Catholic taxi driver was shot dead outside Lurgan, probably by the mid-Ulster UVF. On 11 July, the Chief Constable, Hugh Annesley, reversed the decision, the parade proceeded down the Garvaghy Road and the Orange Order claimed victory. There followed nights of rioting in Nationalist areas.

The price of Drumcree 1996 was very high: one man was dead, hundreds of people injured, hundreds intimidated out of homes and great financial damage caused, largely by Protestant rioters in Protestant areas to Protestan-owned businesses. There was significant tension in all sections of Nationalism at the reversed decision but also in the rest of Ireland, Britain and overseas. Politically it was a disaster for the Orange Order. The Secretary of State, Patrick Mayhew, initiated an independent enquiry into parades, which recommended the setting up of the Parades Commission to make 'determinations' over disputed parades (Northet al. 1997). The new commission was formed in the spring of 1997 but only had legislative powers after the Public Processions Act became law in April 1998 (Jarman 1999). A shift in power that had started in the 1960s was taking legal hold in the 1990s.

Parades and Peace

All of this took place in a new political environment, with the IRA rein-stating its cessation of violence in July 1997 after the new Labour gov-ernment promised Sinn Féin's early entry into talks. This initiated a walkout by the DUP and UKUP, whilst the PUP (politically aligned to the UVF) and the UDP (politically aligned to the UDA) continued their involvement. Crucially, it split the UUP, with many of their MPs failing to back David Trimble's decision to stay in. The parade disputes were now an arena in which Unionism fought out its fundamental differences. Whereas Trimble had begun a slow engagement with Sinn Fein, the dis-pute at Drumcree symbolised for many Unionists their opposition to Republicanism. Many Unionists, once again, viewed the Orange Order as the institution through which opposition to the peace process and, subsequently, to the Good Friday Agreement could be mounted. Yet if the Grand Lodge had taken this stance it would have been in opposition to UUP policy and a significant minority of Orangemen themselves. Consequently the Grand Lodge came under constant attack form hard-liners in the 'Spirit of Drumcree' group for not being tough enough, yet effectively alienated members committed at least to Unionist participa-tion in the peace process.

If one examines the parades and the dispute in Portadown more closely, the situation becomes even more complex. An important con-stituent of all parades is the marching bands (Bell 1990; Bryan 2000; Jar-man 2000). The bands are, in the main, independent of the Orange Order and as well as being involved in loyal order parades have many parades of their own. Quite a number of the bands, however, are con-nected to Loyalist paramilitary groups and show their allegiance by car-rying flags and emblems. It has not been uncommon for disputes between the UVF and UDA in particular areas to be played out in phys-ical confrontations between bands. Days after the signing of the Good Friday Agreement, at the 1998 Easter Monday Apprentice Boys parade in Ballymena, there was a significant physical confrontation involving a UVF band, apparently after jibes from anti-Agreement supporters. Another important issue is the stance over prisoners, since the Loyalist paramilitary groups were keen for prisoner releases under the Agree-ment, a position opposed by the DUP.

The politics of the paramilitary groups therefore affects the parades. During the peace process, a significant split took place between the Belfast-based UVF, who through the PUP were committed to the peace process, as well as to a broadly left-wing working-class agenda, and the Mid-Ulster UVF, underpinned by a more fundamentalist Protestant, broadly Pais-leyite, ideology. This urban–rural split is one that has always been signifi-cant within Unionism (as it has in Republicanism). The Mid-Ulster UVF was a significant player at Drumcree. After his expulsion, a former leader of the Mid-Ulster UVF, Billy Wright, formed the Loyalist Volunteer Force (LVF), which drew significant support in rural areas of Northern Ireland. Support for the stance of the LVF was high in Portadown and on at least one occasion District Master Harold Gracey appeared on a platform with Wright. When the Parades Commission banned the return of the Drumcree parade in 1998, Loyalist politicians and paramilitaries in Belfast worked hard to avoid a repeat of the street violence seen in 1996. Yet, in Portadown the dynamic was quite different and there were serious confrontations with the police, during which shots were fired at police lines. There is no doubt that sympathy for the Drumcree stand-off was high in Loyalist areas of Belfast, but there were also apprehensions concerning involvment. It would have been unsafe for PUP politicians to be present and there were no large appearances of UVF bands at Drumcree.

The stand-off at Drumcree in 1998 threw the divisions into relief. The banning was widely predicted. That the Orange Order would not talk to the Parades Commission, let alone resident group leaders, did not help. Between Good Friday, when the Agreement was signed, and the Drumcree parade, the referendum on the agreement and the election to the new Northern Ireland Assembly were held. There were precisely enough pro-Agreement Unionists in the Assembly to give David Trimble a majority of Unionist members in the Assembly. In the days leading up to Drumcree, Trimble was elected First Minister Designate. Estimates vary, but at least a sizeable minority of the UUP were anti-Agreement, including most of the Westminster MPs, and many more were not exactly positive about the negotiations. Many members of the Grand Orange Lodge of Ireland were opposed to the Agreement, although they stopped short of statements completely rejecting it. However, the newspaper produced by the Grand Lodge was clear in its rejection (Orange Standard, June 1998). Drumcree became a focus for anti-agreement Unionist forces. Consequently, in an amazing turnaround, David Trimble did not appear at Drumcree.

In 1997 the RUC and the British Army had conducted a massive operation and violently removed protesters in the middle of the night to allow the parade to take place the next day. For the 1998 Drumcree parade on Sunday, 5 July, they constructed major fortifications, using miles of barbed wire and a huge barrier, to enforce the Parades Commission's decision. Given that the Orange Order was unwilling to conduct the type of Northern Ireland campaign it used in 1996, Portadown was again the focus. Although there were relatively few incidents on the first few nights, it again became obvious that the Orange Order was in no position to control the developments. By Tuesday, groups of Loyalists were conducting attacks on the barriers and in the nights that followed the attacks became more serious, including the use of blast bombs and a gun attack. Each morning, Orangemen from the local District Lodge and the Grand Lodge tried to distance themselves from what was taking place but they were either unwilling or unable to control the situation. Actually the dynamics of the situation were familiar to anyone watching confrontations between the Orange Order and the police in previous years. Members of the Orange Order organise the protest, but apparently cannot control it, and eventually finding themselves having to explain injuries to RUC officers, with the consequence of diminishing support for the protest within the Protestant community. At Drumcree all this happened live on television. Towards the end of the week, the numbers gathering at the field in solidarity with their Portadown brethren had already started to fall. On Saturday 11 July, during a Drumcree protest in Ballymoney, County Antrim, a petrol bomb was thrown into a house of a Catholic family and three young boys were burnt to death. Immediately the Reverend William Bingham, an Orangeman who had been prominent in supporting the Portadown Orangemen, called for the protest to end. Others in the Protestant community joined the call. The numbers at the protest dropped dramatically. At the Twelfth of July parades, confrontations within the Orange Order were made public as 'Spirit of Drumcree' leader Joel Patten heckled the Reverend Bingham as he spoke.

The Drumcree protest had revealed itself to be just a brief moment at which a weak coalition of interests, representing a significant section of the Protestant community, came together. But as soon as it confronted the forces of the state in any substantial way, as certain sections of the protest were keen to do, the coalition was shattered. In the months that followed, condemnation of the Orange Order was particularly noticeable from senior ministers in the Church of Ireland, Presbyterian and Methodist Churches. The Church of Ireland initiated a report that, amongst other things, looked at the use of churches by the Orange Order. Whilst the Orange Order is well represented in all three churches, there is increasing discontent in the churches over the role played by an institution set up to defend Protestantism. Equally, membership of the loyal orders has been seen as increasingly incompatible with membership of the police. The Report of the Independent Commission on Policing in Northern Ireland has recommended that all officers should register their interests and associations with the Police Ombudsman (Independent Commission on Policing for Northern Ireland 1999). The annual stand-off at Drumcree has been repeated in 2001. A bomb killed one police officer in associated violence. At intervals, talks have taken place, some hosted by Prime Minister Tony Blair, but the Orange Order has yet to agree to meet residents' representatives face to face, or talk to the Parades Commission.

At the parade in July 1999, the RUC and the Army constructed an even bigger set of fortifications. Local Orangemen walked up to police lines but then turned away and dispersed. There have been consistent rumours that a number of religious ministers who were in the Orange Order would leave if confrontations with the police developed again. On the other hand, the spokesperson of the 'Spirit of Drumcree' Group, Joel Patten, has been suspended from the Orange Order and has made clear his disenchantment with the institution.

In terms of numbers, the protest at Drumcree has slowly declined in support. Perhaps the most striking moment of the protests in 2000 and 2001 came in July 2000 when the leader of the UDA in the Shankill Road, Johnny 'Mad Dog' Adair, made a set-piece appearance to lend his support. He was then pictured attending an LVF show of strength with guns being fired. In the days after that Drumcree parade the UDA was also involved in protests in Belfast, blocking a number of roads and confronting the police. This all served to give the perception that paramilitaries, not the Orange Order, were determining the nature of the protest. It was also in marked contrast to the scenes of 1995 and 1996 when prominent Unionist politicians had been involved. As such, the Drumcree protest has become slowly less respectable. The parade disputes and the peace process have underlined the present impotency of the Institution derived from fundamental political, social and economic changes in Northern Ireland.

Some Conclusions

Parades have played an important role in the development of ethnic identification in the north of Ireland. The predominant understanding of Orange parades is that they are 'traditional', and therefore unchanging, and are frequently used to represent the Protestant community. However, if the events are approached as ritual occasions being manipulated and interpreted in contemporary circumstances, then one can better understand how they work as a political resource. The dominant hegemonic position of Orange parades in public space, and the dominant position of Orangeism as a representation of the Protestant community, developed in particular economic and political circumstances. But the position of Orangeism has never gone unopposed even within the Protestant community. To understand its development one needs to explore relations of power within the Protestant community, the relations between that community and the Irish/Catholic community, and with the rest of Britain. Of most importance since the 1960s is the way the parades have moved from being rituals of state to, in some circumstances, rituals of resistance. The parade disputes are therefore part of the same dynamic process of altering political relations that have brought about the peace process. They not only indicate the developing political power of Nationalist politics but, perhaps more crucially, the change in the position of the Orange Order within the Protestant community and the relationship of the British state, through the police, Army and legislation, to Orangeism. As Frank Wright has pointed out, the Unionist periphery in Ireland frequently finds itself at odds with the metropolitan centre of the United Kingdom (Wright 1987: 1–27).

The referendum vote on the Agreement in 1998 revealed deep divisions within the Protestant community over political development in Northern Ireland. The total of 71 percent vote in favour of the Agreement in Northern Ireland suggests that only little more than 50 percent of Protestants were pro-Agreement. This highlighted the difficulties for Unionist politicians and for the peace process generally. But it was a most significant problem for, historically, the two major political bodies in the Protestant community: the UUP and the Orange Order. For the Orange Order, the problems were compounded by the ongoing parades disputes. They had been predominant in public space and they had spent years with vital access to political and economic power. As the peace process and parades disputes progressed, senior Orangemen had to cope with their apparent political impotence; a Protestant community, which they sought to represent, divided on their way forward; and increasing antagonism with institutions, such as the major Protestant churches and the RUC, with which historically they had been so closely associated. As for so many other political groups and parties, the conditions provided by the peace process and the Good Friday Agreement have put questions to the Orange Order on its role in communities which, as yet, it has not been able to answer. The position of Orangeism as central to Protestant ethnic identification is under threat.

References

Anderson, B. 1983. *Imagined Communities. Reflections on the Origin and Spread of Nationalism*. London.

Apprentice Boys of Derry. 1989. *Official Brochure of the Tercentenary Celebrations of the Apprentice Boys of Derry Association*. Derry/Londonderry.

Bean, K. 1994. *The New Departure. Recent Developments in the Irish Republican Ideology and Strategy*. Liverpool.

Bell, D. 1990. *Acts of Union*. London.

Bryan, D. 1994. 'Interpreting the Twelfth', in *History Ireland* vol. 2, no. 2 (1994), pp. 37–41.

———1997. 'The Right to March. Parading a Loyal Protestant Identity in Northern Ireland', in *International Journal on Minority and Group Rights* 4 (1997), pp. 373–89.

———1998. '"Ireland's Very Own Jurassic Park". The Mass Media and the Discourse of 'Tradition' on Orange Parades', in *Symbols in Northern Ireland*, ed. T. Buckley. Belfast, pp. 23–42.

———2000. *Orange Parades: The Politics of Ritual, Tradition and Control*. London.

Bryan, D., Fraser, T. and Dunn, S. 1995. *Political Rituals. Loyalist Parades in Portadown*. Coleraine.

Chief Constable's Report on the Royal Ulster Constabulary 1997/98. Belfast.

Chief Constable's Report on the Royal Ulster Constabulary 1999/2000. Belfast.

Cohen, A. 1974. *Two-Dimensional Man: An Essay on the Anthropology and Symbolism in Complex Society*. London.

———1985. *The Symbolic Construction of Community*. London.

Connerton, P. 1989. *How Societies Remember*. Cambridge.

De Rosa, C. 1998. 'Playing Nationalism', in *Symbols in Northern Ireland*, ed. Anthony Buckley. Belfast, pp. 99–116.

Dudley Edwards, R. 1999. *The Faithful Tribe: An Intimate Portrait of the Loyal Institutions*. London.

Farrell, M. 1980. *Northern Ireland. The Orange State*. London.

Foy, M. T. 1976. 'The AOH: An Irish Politico-Religious Pressure Group 1884–1975.' Belfast (unpublished MA thesis).

Fraser, T., ed. 2000. *The Irish Parading Tradition: We'll Follow the Drum*. Basingstoke.

Garvaghy Residents. 1999. *Garvaghy: A Community Under Siege*. Belfast.

Gibbon, P. 1975. *The Origins of Ulster Unionism*. Manchester.

Harbinson, J. 1973. *The Ulster Unionist Party, 1882–1973: Its Development and Organisation*. Belfast.

Hermon, J. 1997. *Holding the Line: An Autobiography*. Dublin.

Independent Commission on Policing for Northern Ireland. 1999. *A New Beginning: Policing in Northern Ireland*. Norwich.

Jarman, N. 2000. 'For God and Ulster: Blood and Thunder Bands and Loyalist Political Culture', in *The Irish Parading Tradition: Following The Drum*, ed. T. Fraser. Basingstoke, pp. 158–172.

Jarman, N. and Bryan, D. 1996. *Parades and Protest. A Discussion of Parading Disputes in Northern Ireland*. Coleraine.

———1998. *From Riots to Rights. Nationalist Parades in the North of Ireland*. Coleraine.

Jarman, N. 1997. *Material Conflicts. Parades and Visual Displays in Northern Ireland*. Oxford.

———1999. 'Regulating Rights and Managing Public Order. Parade Disputes and the Peace Process, 1995–1998', in *Fordham International Law Journal* vol. 22, no. 4 (1999), pp. 1415–39.

North, P., Dunlop, J. and Crilly, O. 1997. *The Independent Review of Parades and Marches in Northern Ireland*. Belfast.

Smyth, J. 1995. 'The Men of No Popery. The Origins of the Orange Order', in *History Ireland* vol. 3, no. 3 (1995), pp. 48–53.

Tonkin, E. and Bryan, D. 1997. 'Political Ritual. Temporality and Tradition', in *Political Ritual*, ed. Asa Boholm. Gothenburg, pp. 14–36.

Weitzer, R. 1995. *Policing Under Fire: Ethnic Conflict and Police-Community Relations in Northern Ireland*. Albany.

Wright, F. 1987. *Northern Ireland: A Comparative Analysis*. Dublin.

CHAPTER SEVEN

Images of Peace: The News Media, Politics and the Good Friday Agreement

Thomas Taafe

> Spin is… the burnishing of an irrelevancy until it appears to be genuine, the redirection of a truth until it appears to be 'the' truth… the creation of pseudo attitudes, the momentary feelings that are produced in response to artificially assembled information and images.
>
> Randall Rothenberg, Journalist

Introduction

The news media heralded the Good Friday Agreement throughout the world as a 'new dawn' in Northern Ireland. Indeed, the cover image on the published version of the Agreement was one of the 'nuclear unit' (Mum, Dad, two children) silhouetted against a sun rising on the coast. The image was, in fact, a sunset. The photo was taken in South Africa, against a western sky (Northern Ireland has no western coastline). Its slogan proclaimed 'It's your choice.'

On the evening of the referendum vote, I sat in a bar with several magazine photographers. Most were from outside Ireland and had come during the final week of the referendum campaign to capture 'the image' that would summarise the mood of this 'historic' occasion. The absence of images frustrated the photographers. What they found were the predictable 'photo opportunities' of politicians at the polling booth or at press conferences, or similar opportunities created by the 'Yes Campaign'. Rather than meeting a jubilant Northern Ireland, they met a quiet electorate, and occasionally a bomb or killing by paramilitaries opposed to the Agreement.

For a variety of reasons, the mood of the electorate might more aptly be described as either 'cautiously optimistic' or 'cynically pessimistic'. Why then was there such a discrepancy between the banner headlines and the heady proclamations, and a citizenry marked at best by a quiet and cautious deliberation, and at worst by acts of violence or declarations of betrayal?

A remarkable convergence of contradictory political forces occurred within and outside Northern Ireland to make the Good Friday Agreement possible. Yet the Agreement did not resolve the national argument of the conflict. Rather, it sought to create a framework to move that struggle from a low-level civil war to a constitutional struggle. The news media have played an important role throughout 'the Troubles', as all sides sought to advance their cause through the news media or (in the British and Irish governments' case) contain and manage its discourse (Miller 1994: 70–2, Wilson 1997: 31–5). The Good Friday Agreement marked a new phase of this 'propaganda war', as it radically expanded the political domain and created new structures for political struggle. Yet the effort to change the plane of political struggle meant a shift of power in Northern Ireland, not only from paramilitaries and security forces, but from the working-classes of either community to political and professional elites, including the media.

This chapter will look at the interactions between the political realm and the production of news in the moments before the Good Friday Agreement up until its ratification by the people of Northern Ireland.[1] The goal of this effort is to understand how hegemonies are produced out of these interactions. By examining these interactions in the effort to establish a 'peace discourse', we can see both the tactics of a media-based political effort to constitute hegemonies and the limitations of such strategies. In doing so, it will be necessary to examine 'spin', soundbites, leaks, rumours and other discursive strategies, which are a part of what we understand as news. It will also be necessary to consider the social processes of producing 'the news' and the conditions under which journalists do their work. By looking at the social processes of news production and the interactions between political actors and news professionals, I hope to illuminate some ways in which hegemonies are produced, within the news industry and in the political realms they report on.

Hegemony and the News

As Mouffe and Laclau and others have argued, meaning is never fixed; rather there is always an overflow of meaning attached to any object or idea (discursive formation) (Laclau and Mouffe 1985). The process of

---

1   This chapter is based on four years of archival and ethnographic research, which consisted of travelling with the press pack, attending press conferences, peace talks, marches and riots as well as dozens of interviews with local, national and international reporters, politicians, press officers and other news subjects. It also included the extensive review of newspapers, radio and television accounts of that period.

articulation is a process of negotiation, of constructing a link or connection between a word and an object, a speaker and listener. While speech relies on a framework of 'agreed upon' meanings and rules, close examination of any discourse will expose a variety of disjunctions, nonagreements, differing interpretations etc. These ensure that any statement received will be interpreted differently to one degree or another. Thus, the goal of speech, or of political discourse, is to achieve relative agreement, sufficient to proceed on to the next moment. This is a part of the constitutive process of hegemonic formation.

Raymond Williams offered a generally acceptable meaning of hegemony as 'political rule or domination' (1977: 108). In the writings of Antonio Gramsci, however, the term came to hold a complex set of meanings for understanding social processes and relations of power. Gramsci made a distinction between direct physical coercion or domination, which he understood to mean rule without hegemony, and leadership, which entailed an ideological production process that legitimated the right to rule, by 'consent' from the masses. This entailed a conversation of power or a hegemonic political process. Central to the hegemonic production process is the role of the intellectual. As Gramsci observed:

> Every social group, coming into existence on the original terrain of an essential function in the world of economic production, creates with itself, organically, one or more strata of intellectuals which give it homogeneity and an awareness of its own function not only in the economic but also in the social and political fields. (1971: 5)

But Gramsci's concept of hegemony goes beyond economics and ideology; its effects are naturalised into the fabric of the social. As Williams notes:

> What is decisive is not only the conscious system of ideas and beliefs, but the whol-lived social process as practically lived by specific and dominant meanings and values. (1977: 108–9)

Thus hegemonic formations are grounded in – and are productions of – the experiences, beliefs and ideas of those who live and express them. These formations are imbued with, and driven by, the social, economic and historical forces that come to bear on any given moment (Grossman 1996: 42). They are also conditioned by the relations of power at play in that given moment (Foucault 1980: 122), expressed in values and meanings, and reinforced through the lived experiences of those in that relationship. While hegemonic formations may be institutionalised in some form or codified in law, those laws or institutions are continually tested and open to interpretation. Likewise, the social processes within hegemonic formations are ongoing and in flux. They are manifested in the creation and recreation of articulatory linkages between objects, ideas, meanings, and the need to sustain, transform, modify or disrupt those linkages. Hegemonic formations occur in sentence construction and in the communication of that sentence to another. They develop in the production and reproduction of ideas (knowledge), which are conditioned by the discursive limitations established, maintained or opposed by regimes of power (Foucault 1980: 112). These formations blossom into – or are experienced as – 'paradigms' and 'identities'. They are themselves made up of countless micro-hegemonic constructions, which do not necessarily resolve into each other. Large hegemonic formations are constantly negotiated and challenged, revised and rejected, from within and outside. Political discourse is the whole complex of those contestations; conditioned and situated within the relations of power and within the socioeconomic and historical forces of any given moment. Hegemonic formations can, and do, produce counter-hegemonic formations, which are in direct conflict with, or antagonistic towards, each other.

Within the news media, the formation of a story is the assemblage of words the meanings of which convey concepts, beliefs and images. Imbedded in any story are countless meanings – some intended, some unrecognised by the speaker, some approximations by the speaker. The process of communication is itself a negotiation: between the speaker and the listeners, between those in authority over the speaker, and those referenced by the speaker. It is conditioned and constrained within the limits of speech permitted by law, within the limits of time and space, within the conditions and technologies used by the speaker, and so on. As Stuart Hall (1990: 90–103) has noted, that assemblage is interpreted variously by its listeners or readers. Consequently, a statement that 'resonates' as intended to one group of people, can resonate entirely differently to another.

This discourse is rampant in Northern Ireland. In a divided society such as that, a message received in one way by one group may be interpreted with a dichotomous set of meanings by another.

Legislating the Limits of Discourse

The media have provided (and denied) a central stage in the conflict that all participants attempt to access or control (Curtis 1998). This 'propaganda war' increasingly led the states directly involved (the UK and the Republic of Ireland) to legislate access to the news media. For thirty years, the British and Irish governments have resorted to a variety of tactics, including outright censorship, to contain primarily Irish Republican voices, although the tactics used have also affected some Loyalists (Curtis 1998; Miller 1994; Rolston and Miller 1996). Overall, the British government has enacted more than eighty-four different laws that restrict or shape the terms of news gathering and dissemination. The Republic of Ireland went even further than the British government and prohibited the images, words and voices of Sinn Fein and IRA members from 1976 to 1994 (and intermittently before then). This was done even though Sinn Fein was never a proscribed group in the Republic and had dozens of elected representatives in the Republic and even more in the North (McGonagle 1996: 16, 28–9, 249–54). The consequence of this long effort is that such laws and the silencing of critical voices have significantly conditioned the media's discourse on Northern Ireland.

The legal system has also affected the news media through the limitations imposed by libel laws. While a full discussion of libel law is not possible here, it is important to note its impact on the limits of permissible discourse. Statements made in Parliament, or made by security forces (and those who quote them) are protected by the law (Welsh and Greenwood 1997: 160, 166, 170). Libel suits are very expensive and are considered 'a rich man's sport' (McGonagle 1996: 62f.). Since libel is based on the value set by 'right thinking people', who 'have no reputation to lose', those convicted of serious crimes, people who have engaged in 'sedition' or are deemed by security forces to belong to proscribed organisations are unprotected; and if they are from lower-class backgrounds, they do not have the resources to defend themselves (Welsh and Greenwood 1997: 134f., 190f.). Thus, security forces, the rich and the elected are protected, while the poor, Irish Republicans and Loyalist paramilitaries are exposed. In the context of a thirty-year war, these laws intersect with rumour and black propaganda to 'normalise' negative and defamatory statements about certain people and communities. This has compounded and reinforced economic and ethnonational inequalities and, in general, privileged the Unionist/British establishment at the expense of Irish Republican voices, persons and communities (Taaffe 1998: 2f.).

But such strategies must struggle against ideals of journalistic freedom, perceived audience interests, expectations, demands and knowledge, and the complexities of news production in competitive (yet interactive) markets crowded by bureaucratic, profit-orientated, and party organ modes of production.[2] The multiplicity of socioeconomic interests constantly subverts the strategies of policing the hegemonic positions of the dominant perspective, not the least of which is the potential recourse to violence.

Propaganda and the Good Friday Agreement

Although seventy-one percent of the electorate ratified the Good Friday Agreement, what had been 'agreed to' and who agreed to it remains sur-

2   'Bureaucratic' news organisations are those which are funded in some means by the state. 'Profit-orientated' organisations are those supported by capitalist means. 'Party organ' publications are those published by specific organisations, and generally advance the organisation's point of view.

prisingly open. As the months and years since April 1998 have shown, the question of whether it will produce 'peace' equally remains open. In the vague language of the Agreement, both sides could find (or seem to find) that which they wanted to see. In the campaign to secure support for this Agreement, both sides trumpeted their gains. Both sides made contradictory claims about the same document (e.g. 'the Union is safe" versus 'a stepping stone to a united Ireland'). With the world's media catching every word uttered by Northern Ireland's politicians, new problems emerged when disparate and sometimes antagonistic groups received a politician's statement in very different and contradictory ways.

The propaganda war now entered a new phase. Three governments – the UK, Ireland and the US – committed their political and economic resources to convincing the electorate of the merits of the Agreement. 'Photo opportunities' abounded as politicians and celebrities weighed in with their support. Pundits trumpeted the bounty that awaited Northern Ireland if peace were secured, often referring to the Irish Republic's growing economy. Britain, the EU and the US made promises of money to ease the transition.

The events surrounding the Agreement brought a circus-like atmosphere to the political realm. The conduit for this circus was the news media, and the news media arrived in droves. But the news industry is not a passive conduit of information; it is made up of active political agents, with their own political views and with responsibilities to please their employers. Cook has pointed out:

> Newsmaking and its place in the political system is best conceived not as a linear, unidirectional process but as interactive and interdependent. ... Political actors and journalists (and only occasionally citizens) interact in a constant but implicit series of negotiations over who controls the agenda, what can be asked, where and how, and what a suitable answer will be. (1998: 12)

Thus, the news producers are manifestly a part of the political sphere. Those in the state apparatus have the potential to shape, advance or stymie journalists' careers. But journalists also have a similar potential from a different position. While the political struggle in Northern Ireland shifts fitfully from a street war to a constitutional struggle, the media take on an even more nuanced role as the gatekeeper through which all parties seek to advance their agendas.

In most cases, news organisations enthusiastically supported the Agreement and the efforts of the British government to ratify it.[3] As we will see, the role of British media management was central to that effort.

---

3 Exceptions were the sceptical *Sunday Business Post*, an Irish weekly, and the outright anti-Agreement Orange Order's *Orange Standard*.

The News Producers and Northern Ireland

Allan Baird (1996: 174) has noted that 'throughout ... "the Troubles", the people of Northern Ireland were particularly news-conscious. This is scarcely surprising given that they were living in a part of the world whose problems generated so much world-wide media attention'. Baird argued that this interest was driven, in part, by the desire to participate in, or observe, political debates on issues that affected their lives. He also commented that:

> ... people also turned to the media to hear about ways in which their day-to-day routine might be adversely affected by 'the Troubles'... they would listen to radio news reports for information about bomb scares and traffic disruption or about what was happening in another part of their city or town or even at the other end of their street. (1996: 174)

Given this interest and Northern Ireland's deep political divisions, it is not surprising that a wide variety of options are available to the consumer. These options reflect both provincial and national (i.e., Northern Irish, Irish and British) news companies. There are three regional dailies, four major British broadsheets (plus the daily Financial Times), four British and two Scottish tabloids, most of which produce Irish or Northern Irish editions. Two Irish broadsheets are available. Most of these papers also provide a Sunday edition, and there are also four weekly Irish or Northern Irish papers that come out on Sunday, as well as at least forty local weekly newspapers. There are also papers that serve specific organisations such as the Orange Standard (Orange Order) and An Phoblacht/Republican News (Sinn Féin). A variety of local magazines are also available which cover the whole political spectrum. All local newspapers consciously direct their news towards one ethnonational community or the other, though some, such as the Belfast Telegraph, 'claim' the middle ground between communities.

On broadcast television (apart from cable), there are two BBC channels, as well as two commercial organisations (UTV/ITN and Channel 4). More than a third of all Northern Irish homes also receive RTE (two channels, plus another Irish language channel), the Irish public television company. For those who have cable, there is also CNN, BBC News 24 and Sky News. On the radio, the BBC offers two regional stations as well as its national radio services. RTE also broadcasts in much of Northern Ireland. There are many commercial radio stations that provide news coverage. Though none of the radio or noncable television stations offer a 24-hour news service, BBC, UTV, ITN and RTE provide a menu-driven Teletext service, which offers short three- or four-paragraph updates on the top six to twelve major stories. Several news wire services also operate in Northern Ireland, all of which provide text, audio and video to news organisations around the world. These are the British Press Association (PA), Reuters and Associated Press (AP).

The ownership of news corporations in Northern Ireland is primarily in Unionist or British hands. Tom Collins (1998), former editor of the Nationalist Irish News has pointed out that 'of the five big media organisations ... only one has grown out of the Nationalist tradition'. Since the smallest of the five is the only voice of Irish Nationalism, the media's discursive plane is structurally tipped towards British or Unionist interests, values and perspectives. Though television and radio 'claim' a transcommunity position, this effort contains the space of news production around a discourse that integrates the critiques and complaints of both communities. These complaints are arranged along a hierarchy of social, political and economic positions, within a centralising logic of the status quo.

Some news organisations (mostly Irish or British) keep staff in Northern Ireland. Most British and foreign journalists are stationed in London. Of the American news organisations, only AP and the Boston Herald keep a journalist on the ground in Northern Ireland. The New York Times and the Boston Globe have a reporter in Dublin, and a few international organisations base their staffs on the European continent. The international journalists stationed in London often have a very wide turf to cover. A single nonEuropean journalist may be responsible for all of Europe. Consequently, their preparation for Irish politics is often limited to a review of old press clippings, the odd book, discussions with other journalists and information gleaned in their daily work.

The BBC, as the largest news organisation, and the PA, the national wire service, form the gravitational centre of news production because of their mass and scope. The discursive limits within these organisations affect the reportage of other organisations that rely on their accounts. Since most outside reporters cover Northern Ireland from London, how PA and the BBC report a story shapes how many others will as well. Most news stories written by those outside Northern Ireland come from PA and BBC reports. Thus the recycling of news stories begins from the preparation stage (reviewing old press clippings) and continues with the daily work of filing new stories. While some have a fairly good grasp of the events and actors involved in Northern Ireland, others have little knowledge of the history and politics of the region. The tendency is to repeat the British government's interpretation of events. This is exceptionally true of the American press. Journalist/academic Jack Holland has pointed out:

> ... the British government's official 'line' on Northern Ireland, like that of the major newspapers and magazines in the U.S. held the problem to be a sectarian conflict between recalcitrant religious groups kept apart only by the intervention of Britain acting as a kind of 'bobby.' The view of Britain was that of a detached, patient and objective arbiter doing its best to convince two irrational, hate-filled communities to

live together in harmony. Constantly undermining these noble efforts was the IRA, portrayed as a gang of mindless criminals and psychopaths bent on destruction. In later years, this portrait was touched up somewhat by the rising concern over 'international terrorism'. (1997: 197)

Without paying attention to the roots of 'the Troubles' in the complex history of conflict between Northern Irish communities and Britain's active role in that conflict, the British and international press have adopted the analysis of 'terrorism as cause' rather than 'discrimination as cause'. This perspective has become the hegemonic definition of 'the Troubles' in the minds of many influential British politicians and in the minds of the British and international media (Wilson 1997: 21).

British perspectives in international and particularly American news coverage is facilitated by the lack of time allocated to independent journalism, distance from events and the lack of in-depth knowledge. This knowledge is further constrained by the cost of moving a reporter from London to Belfast (estimated by some reporters to be as high as US$10,000 a week). Inadequate space or time further constrains the ability to explain a complex sociopolitical situation. International journalists usually have to begin every story as if the reader had never heard of Northern Ireland or 'the Troubles'. Such stories usually run between 250 and 500 words or less than two minutes.

The Circulation of News

In Belfast, stories travel from one news organisation to another, as each takes its turn in the forefront of the daily news cycle. The speed with which information travels combines with the pressures to publish quickly and reduces the opportunity for independent investigation, which increases the tendency to rewrite (with additions or edits) what was already presented in another medium. Thus, stories develop incrementally throughout the day, with each organisation adding another bit of information to the story. That most such stories are based on secondhand accounts and taken from BBC and PA reports, exacerbates this process on the national and international level. The process of story consolidation also goes on within the 'press pack' as journalists share bits of information and meet to discuss a given moment and consolidate information into a news story (Taaffe 1998: 2).

These discussions form a part of the production of hegemonic interpretations in the news media. Journalism, which primarily reports on relations of power, tends to privilege political groups in direct relationship to their ability to express power (Fawcett 1996: 22f.). Larger parties are privileged at the expense of smaller parties or groups. Since journalists are dependent on relations with politicians for access to news stories, the tendency is to refrain from speaking in ways that might damage those relationships. Following the referendum vote, women and the small working-class Loyalist parties virtually disappeared from the media's stage, while Republicans were usually only quoted in response to Unionist charges. Over and over, I was told that the central story was the disagreement within Unionism. In an atmosphere charged with accusations of 'betrayal', the political discourse of Unionism shifted to the right, driven also by the polarising hostilities of the marching season. This reinforced the hegemony of Unionist positions, either pro- or anti-Agreement, leaving Nationalists and other pro-Agreement parties answering issues raised within the discourse of Unionism – a discourse that has structurally negated, marginalised and vilified Irish Nationalism since its emergence. These forces also increasingly marginalised women and progressive, working-class Loyalists, except when they reinforced the dominant order. This inequality of access to news media's 'soundstage' shapes the political landscape. It can also lead to violent attempts to access that stage (Taaffe 1998: 4).

The accelerated speed of events from the Talks to the 1998 stand-off at Drumcree[4] placed increasing pressures on both politics and news production. Twelve to sixteen hour work days were often the norm. Events increased the 'call and response' between politicians and news professionals, the technology of news production and the speed at which journalists were pressured to report them. The compression of space to explain events, the speed demanded by their agencies and the circumstances under which reporters worked, encouraged a superficial grasp of events by outside reporters and an over-reliance on second-hand reporting. This compression led, in turn, to greater use of heightened dramatic language, soundbites and a simplification of situations. These reductions heighten tensions and magnify conflict, while reducing complexity. This atmosphere tends to elevate personalities over the issues. It requires that reporters often rely on their instincts, and even preconceived notions, rather than on research.

Shifting the Plane of Political Discourse

Perhaps more than any previous British Prime Minister, Tony Blair understands the power of image in a postmodern Western liberal democracy. He drew on the media strategies of the American political system, and particularly those of Bill Clinton, to secure his success in the 1997 elections. Using some of the same 'spin doctors' and advisers that had propelled Clinton into office, the 'new' Labour Party packaged Blair, and

4   See Dominic Bryan's chapter in this volume on the significance of the Drumcree march.

sold him to the British electorate. Fresh from his success at the polls, Blair turned his postmodern image machine on Northern Ireland.

However, Northern Ireland is not a Western liberal democracy. Such a political structure is based on the premise of a 'consented' state (i.e., acceptance of a geopolitical entity by all significant political ideologies in that geo-political entity). But no such state has ever existed in Northern Ireland. The very existence of an Irish Republican ideology undermines that consensus. Conversely, Loyalism also reveals ambivalent tendencies towards the state as it is slowly separated from its institutional power. Consequently, explicit military force sustains the existence of Northern Ireland. For the most part, London-appointed committees, civil servants and the security apparatus handle the affairs of the state. Whatever trappings may exist of an elective political system, elected political positions have little administrative power. Elected politicians have few duties other to than to 'speak for' their constituencies, or to advance their careers. In the Assembly elections, only 8.5 percent of the first-preference votes were for cross-community parties, and their strength is primarily among urban, professional-class voters (Belfast Telegraph, 27 June 1998). Political struggle is still very much a street-level affair (through political protest, civil disobedience, the contentious marching season, paramilitary and sectarian violence). The political discourse remains centred on the national question and the violence surrounding it.

The framework of the Good Friday Agreement created new political dynamics to overlie the older, more violent, plane of struggle. While the terms of participation (the Mitchell Principles) and the Agreement restricted the discursive space for paramilitary violence,[5] this violence became increasingly subdued, but none the less remains present. The inclusive process of the peace talks elevated previously delegitimated political actors and groups into the political spotlight. Assembly elections further expanded the realm of 'legitimate' political actors and discourse. The hegemonic power of the 'peace discourse', driven by three governments and supported by most parties and the media, as well as increased attention from the news media, opened new terrains for political discourse. But while it shifted the terms of discourse, it also highlighted the nonagreements that exist in the social dimension. In the bright glare of the international media spotlight, this emergent discourse produced both surprising continuities and familiar discontinuities within a radically changing political context. However, this context increasingly restricted the space for discourse that supported or legitimated violence.

---

5   The Mitchell Principles were the terms laid out by George Mitchell for participation in the talks and have been integrated into the Assembly's Oath of Office and the foundation for participation in the devolved government. See Stefan Wolff's introductory chapter.

Bits and Pieces: Soundbites, Spin and the Emerging Political

While the peace talks were primarily a conversation between the parties involved, they were also a conversation between those parties and the news media. It was through the media that politicians, parties and governments reassured constituencies, applied pressure on other parties, and sought the spotlight of international attention. The terms of the Good Friday Agreement were largely negotiated between the British and Irish Prime Ministers, supported by their civil servants. The political parties then negotiated and revised that document. Although the Talks were inclusive, the two governments primarily handled the negotiation process in a bilateral or trilateral manner.[6] That meant that the majority of the participants had time on their hands. They were often left wondering what was happening in meetings in which they were not involved. Each day in the final week, the press gathered in increasing numbers outside the gates of the Castle Buildings, Stormont, where the negotiations were held.

Since no party leaked the final draft document, the press was left to assemble its understanding of the talks based on what was already known and what information could be gathered from politicians and others.

The flowering and maturity of both the postmodern news media and the public relations industry created the conditions, context and resources necessary for the transformation of the political realm ever further into a project of image creation. In a political world where every statement or comment, action or image of action is instantaneously transmitted, reacted and counter-reacted to through the news media, the role of public relations in positioning those images, statements and actions becomes critical.

Within that context, 'spin' is a constructed discursive formation, created to engage with, or reinforce the dominant hegemonic formation of a given moment. It is an explicitly conscious construction. It is the discursive part of an organised campaign to achieve a political objective. It is manifested in a statement or series of statements, and is supported by calculated images and specifically constructed information, which reinforce the political position being advanced. The increasing speed with which the news industry disseminates information combines with the collapse of time and space available to express, analyse or contest political ideas, and leads to a focus on the 'surface' and/or 'image' of events or debates at the expense of depth. Since public political discourse is manifested through the media, spin is a strategy for establishing, reinforcing or altering the hegemonic formations of institutionalised politics and its reflection in the news media. In its most institutional form, it is an effort to become or remain the dominant hegemonic formation. A 'soundbite'

---

6   See Stephen Farry's analysis of the negotiation process in Chapter 2 of this volume.

is a short, catchy statement, crafted to achieve repeated airings in a variety of media venues. It is a discursive 'bullet' intended to smite other political agendas. Spin and soundbites do not exist in a vacuum. They are modified discursive strategies adapted to be effective on the stage provided by the news media.

In a highly active political arena, politicians are able to set the stage in accordance with their degree of power. Those expressing state power are in the best position to set the daily agenda, but power is not always derived from the state. A wide variety of political entities and constituencies, including those outside institutional politics, affect the political agenda of the state. Certainly paramilitaries are their own power centres, and can affect the political discourse through the media as well as through violence. The political terrain is not even, but it is always in contest. Power is circulated, as Foucault has pointed out, and the process of expressing power is also the process of negotiating power (1980: 99–100). In a postmodern context the news media are often the primary transmitter of political discourse and social events. Thus, they play a critical role in the dissemination, censoring, contextualising and editing of political discourse, daily events and expressions of power. The interactive nature of political discourse and news production manifested itself at the Talks. Both journalists and politicians fed each other information in a mutual effort to understand what was going on, affect the terms of the Agreement, and galvanise sectors of the electorate or world opinion to their position.

In a moment like the Stormont Talks – where no journalist is likely to hear all statements – the community of journalists assemble the bits and pieces of the puzzle through regular consultation. Journalists quite readily traded information with each other, despite the competitive nature of their business. While there were hierarchies and rivalries among them, the cooperation was surprising. The process of putting together all the pieces continued as they rang back to their offices, called across to the Castle Buildings and caught news reports coming in from other places. The circulatory processes of news production are not situated in one place, but remain in constant motion. Stories move from one medium to another, one production company to another, as each adds or edits for a complex set of reasons, including new information, audience interests, space or time needs and political agenda.

Politicians used the media for personal and collective advantage, negotiating through the media with other parties in the talks, reassuring their support base, or talking across community lines. Given the time on their hands and the extraordinary opportunity of the world's media at their door, the politicians took full advantage of the situation. Often many of them would be out at the same time, especially as the evening news hour beckoned. The British press secretary also conducted off-the-record briefings (where cameras or tape recorders were forbidden) to establish a 'master narrative' on the proceedings. A journalist listening to political discourse listens with an 'editor's ear' for the statement or phrase that crystallises the point of view being presented. These key phrases, which may be intentionally or unintentionally given, become part of the story that will shortly be written. While the print journalist has the opportunity to probe and paraphrase the position given, the radio or television journalist ideally needs that 'key phrase' captured on tape. The need of the media for short, concise statements, and the need of political actors to gain effective access to the media 'sound stage' shows how the production of soundbites is again interactive.

Secrets, Myths and the Profitable Troubles

News stories emerge in Northern Ireland like a thin crust of ice on a rich sea of rumour. In a world of 'open secrets', it is the land of 'everybody knows'. Although the news media are the most powerful forms of information dissemination, 'word of mouth' can have enormous power. Rumours pass quickly throughout the region, and are used by political groups, state representatives and security forces to spread 'black propaganda'. Sometimes a community may be more likely to accept a rumour than a published report. Secret societies proliferate in Northern Ireland, including the Loyal Orders, paramilitaries, the British military and its intelligence branches. Power, rumour and secrecy intersect to encourage a mystification of events.

But journalists are themselves storytellers, and their employers capitalists. The daily need for new stories meets the constant flow of rumours (Gans 1979: 293f.). Reporters hear these rumours and assess their worth. Rumours can have many lives, true or not, as entertainment, in newspapers or in books written about Northern Ireland. There are always speculative stories being run about secret organisations or persons identified by the security forces as belonging to them. Rumours and black propaganda intersect with libel laws to permit statements about Irish Republicans as well as Loyalist paramilitaries and their allies – often by unnamed security sources – that are not permissible about 'legitimate' and usually Unionist politicians. For a variety of reasons, 'the Troubles' have become a cottage industry, providing a steady stream of stories to its readers. Journalists and academics are the producers in this industry and Northern Ireland is always ready, story in hand, to oblige.

Stories, Objectivity and Drama

In my discussions with news professionals, 'objectivity' usually trans-lated as 'accuracy' or 'balance'. Balance was usually defined as 'showing both sides'. But balance can often become a mechanical process of matching two or more quotes that undermine, expose or contradict another, establish an argument, or frame the terms and parameters of debate. This juxtaposition or montage of statements – the editing of countless comments, bits and pieces of information and rumours into a 'story' – is necessarily a manipulation of information and political dis-course. Whether the intention is to be 'accurate', 'impartial', to con-sciously affect the political terrain, or simply to fit the material into a limited time and space, a story is an assemblage of images, statements and data made linear by narrative. The process of juxtaposition or mon-tage continues with story placement. Given the crowded, competitive environment of news production, the importance of drama cannot be underestimated. When used effectively, it heightens emotions on the part of the audience. Given the symbiotic relationships between politi-cians, the news media and the audiences or electorate, drama is often an important element in story production for both news producers and political actors. Given the emotional investment in the peace process, events like the Stormont Talks can produce high drama. While this sells newspapers, it also shapes the political discourse.

The politicians, in their statements and actions at Stormont, did not disappoint the news industry's need for stories. Their political need for space in the newspapers – to advance their political agendas, to address and reassure their constituencies, challenge or disarm their adversaries, affect the negotiations and perpetuate or build their political careers – intersects with the news industry's need for a great story. A story must justify the enormous expense of moving large amounts of equipment and staff to Northern Ireland. The Good Friday Agreement was a good story, one that could make anyone feel good. It was also well constructed. It had dramatic highs, depressing lows, walkouts, tantrums, warnings and the emphasised possibility of nonagreement. Most importantly, it was a story with a happy ending. As the Talks came to a close, I listened as an American reporter asked a long-time Northern Ireland correspondent what he would do, now that 'the Troubles' were over.

But if the talks could be defined as a suspenseful cliff-hanger, the cam-paign for the referendum was a blockbuster movie. Though not all went according to plan, all felt the overpowering effect of the British spin pro-ject. The combined force of pro-Agreement parties and three govern-ments (including the USA), as well as all the individuals and organisations they could draw on for support, had a dominating effect that was radiated out by the media.

One BBC, Many NIO?

At a press briefing just after the Talks concluded, a BBC business reporter quipped, 'just as there is not one BBC, there is not one NIO (Northern Ireland Office)'. Even the best laid plans do go awry. The two largest Unionist parties have enormous support among the civil servants in the NIO (79 percent of senior staff are Protestant, 75 percent of all staff). As George Mitchell pointed out in a recent BBC interview: 'What was unique about many of the leaks from the Northern Ireland Office is that they were designed to undermine the policy of the British government of which they were part' (quoted in Cracknell 1999). This strategy of releasing information facilitates 'journalistic work and pushes stories in directions ... they would otherwise not go' (Negrine 1996: 38). Documents were regularly leaked to both the anti-Agreement DUP and the nominally pro-Agreement UUP. The problem of leaks became so dramatic that the then Secretary of State, Mo Mowlam, was forced to withdraw her confidences from all NIO staff and keep counsel only with those who had come with her from London. But the strategy of 'leaking' information was not limited to disgruntled civil servants; as George Mitchell noted: 'I was surprised when I went there at the extent to which both governments and all the political parties actively leaked to the press in an effort to influence news coverage and therefore public opinion' (quoted in Cracknell 1999).

Shortly after the talks were concluded, the DUP leaked a confidential NIO document to the press. This document, drafted on 4 March 1998 (over a month before the Agreement and before a deadline for the talks was announced), detailed the NIO's plans to ensure a positive outcome to the Talks and the referendum:

> During the next ten weeks we need to convince the Northern Ireland public both of the importance of what is at stake, and... that not only is agreement possible, but they have a vital role to play in endorsing it... the government's message needs to be clear simple and direct. It needs to prioritise its key messages, and keep repeating them at every opportunity... It should be a message that is not afraid to recognise and build on the public's desire for peace, and uses that... to build a momentum as we approach the referendum and subsequently the election to a new administration... that will require a sustained, committed and coherent effort right across government. The message needs to be reinforced on every conceivable opportunity and the benefits of an agreement underlined in every possible way. The Northern Ireland public needs to be in no doubt about how a deal will improve every aspect of their quality of life... That means a concerted effort by all ministers and departments in every speech, interview and meeting. The momentum towards an agreement and the people's decision in a referendum must become a central part of every message government sends ... It can be the central part of every piece of communication we do. (*Irish News*, 28 March 1998)

The document recommended a steady stream of respected community and church leaders to endorse the Agreement. It suggested that 'a carefully coordinated timetable of statements from these people will be helpful in giving our message credibility with those they represent. It has the added benefit of providing a fresh face for that message, and ensuring that it is not only government which is seen to be selling the process.'

The media were a primary target for this strategy, not only as conduit for endorsements, but as advocate as well. The leaked strategy document further proposed that the NIO 'encourage some degree of public opinion polling by ... newspapers and current affairs programmes, where we believe the results are likely to be supportive ... this can be encouraged during meetings and briefings of senior media people.' To that end, it suggested that

> [w]e will wish to put more emphasis on briefing of media people... to ensure that they are fully informed and to encourage them to develop their own ideas for programmes on the talks process and later the referendum. We will be particularly anxious to use this means of exerting some influence on the content and quality of media coverage. The many weekly newspapers around Northern Ireland offer considerable scope for us to present our message and the editors of these papers should feature in the efforts of Ministers to cultivate the media... meeting and briefing media representatives should be spread around all of the Ministerial team and there is no reason why on occasions officials shouldn't carry some of this burden.

The second largest public relations firm in the world, McCann-Erickson, bolstered these efforts. The NIO commissioned them to provide both quantitative and qualitative research, as well as to handle advertising. However, the document cautioned that 'any overt manipulation could be counterproductive'. It also underscored that those responsible should ensure that the project was 'carried out without it being seen to be government inspired'. To that end it noted:

> Advertising on its own will not convince the public to vote in favour of the referendum. But as part of an integrated campaign it could play a crucial role in alerting the public to see precisely what is at stake... serious consideration needs to be given to the timing and content of any messages because it could be seen as 'big government' imposing its view, which would be entirely counterproductive... the focus should be on selling the concept of an agreed future, rather than its precise details. The central message will be 'It's your choice'. Initially that choice will be posed as being between the failure of the past and the future towards which we are making progress. Once an agreement is in place, the message will change to encouraging people to vote for their future.

While the embarrassment of revelation resulting from the 'release' of the document, in turn, caused some consternation in the NIO and angered those public figures (like Bishop Eames) mentioned in the leaked document, it did not stop the plan from being implemented. On the contrary, the British government pulled out all the stops in a choreographed way to affect public opinion and ensure a positive outcome of the vote. The Chancellor of the Exchequer cobbled together a package of tax breaks, job training and subsidies for businesses, along with money for road improvements and other programmes. Money was made available for the 'victims of the Troubles'. Blair made several trips to Northern Ireland, and provided a steady stream of photo opportunities, media events and soundbites. Former Prime Minister John Major made an appearance with Blair to show his support and the then Liberal Democrat leader Paddy Ashdown also stopped by to add his backing. President Clinton, Pope John Paul, Nelson Mandela and many other international figures weighed in with their support. South Africa sent several ANC leaders over to help Sinn Féin encourage its membership to swallow the many compromises that were a part of the Agreement. Entertainers like U2 and Kenneth Branagh cheered on the 'Yes' vote. Local academics, particularly Unionist ones, were put into service to argue for an affirmative vote.

But despite this formidable public relations project, the question of whether it actually changed many minds is debatable. Some political commentators have noted that the people of Northern Ireland are notoriously immune to spin doctoring. Most people vote along party or community lines. While the Nationalist communities have long been involved in discussions around ending the conflict, those discussions did not happen to the same degree in the Unionist community. Thus, Nationalists voted overwhelmingly for the Agreement, while in Unionist circles the landscape was quite different. The two major anti-Agreement parties (DUP and UKUP) accounted for 47 percent of first-preference votes in the Assembly. Anti-Agreement parties are two votes short of a majority of Unionist votes in the Assembly. The Orange Order – which claims around 50,000 Protestant members – was openly anti-Agreement. The UUP was split at the top of its leadership over the Agreement, though its party congress supported the Agreement by a plurality of 70 percent. Significantly, the British spent much of their energy assuaging Unionist fears of shared government with Sinn Féin. In the end, exit polls showed that only slightly more than 50 percent of the Unionist electorate voted for the Agreement.

Conclusions

The Blair government sought to use the refined discursive strategies (spin, soundbites, strategic leaks etc.) that were successful in Britain in an attempt to bring *closure* to 'the Troubles'. The overwhelming use of media management to achieve a 'yes' vote established a patina of democratic structure on a still divided society. Thus the 'image of peace' was far more evident in the news media than on the ground in Northern Ireland. It was reflected in the banner headlines and the hegemonic belief within the international media that the Agreement meant the return of 'normality' to Northern Ireland, in the form of a 'Western liberal democracy'.

But in Northern Ireland (in the absence of a consented state), the media have had, at best, a situated impact on the interpretations of events. Information can move by word of mouth, as well as through the media, and people interpret information, critically based on experiences, knowledge and beliefs. While the media can influence and legitimate events and political discourse, they serve more as a conduit, or gate-keeper, between political actors and their constituencies, rather than as the primary definer of events and their meanings.

The contradictory ambitions of all parties, combined with the perceived desire by a majority of people for an end to violent conflict, created the convergence known as the Good Friday Agreement. This hegemonic formation, with great power and seemingly wide appeal, was created out of the parties' (and Anglo-Irish) agreement and international support, and the British media campaign and the willingness of the media to facilitate that campaign. But as the NIO's document shows, even this image of peace was, to some degree, 'produced'. Because of ideological contradictions among the 'pro-Agreement' parties, this hegemonic formation was extremely unstable. While the peace discourse forced political actors to adapt familiar agendas to a 'peace' discourse, it did not necessarily alter their national aspirations or intentions.

When the state sets out with a specific agenda and has the infrastructure and discourse to back it up, it can have enormous power to affect the news. But the interests of news producers do not operate in step with state interests, even when they facilitate those interests (Miller 1994: 277). As the leaking of NIO documents and the whispers from unnamed security sources show, the state does not speak with one voice, even when it has a plan and wide political support.

Competition in the news media for audience and sales increases the need for stories that have dramatic action, and contestations in the political arena provide the action for that drama. This links with the need of opposition groups to access the media's sound stage. Thus, even the best-laid plans of the state can be undermined by events or counter-hegemonic forces.

The flow of information from one organisation to another means that news is not the domain of any single news company or political entity. Nor is news simply produced in a dichotomous relationship between representatives of the state and the news media. Rather it is an interactive and competitive relationship, situated in the relations of power, conditioned by prior discursive formations and the laws of the land, as well as the agendas of those who produce the news. Politicians, news producers and audiences or constituencies are in a symbiotic relationship that produces political discourse. Making a decision on what is news and how it is reported is a negotiation within this symbiotic relationship. This negotiation is situated within the news media, based on the hierarchies of value placed on different audiences, communities and political groups involved. The media's discourse has, over many years, privileged British and Unionist interests, while marginalising Irish and Irish Republican interests (Feeney 1997; Greenslade 1998). It has also marginalized women[7] and, in more complex ways, Loyalists (Fawcett 1996: 18–23; Parkinson: 1998).

While the media have had a limited effect in Northern Ireland, outside that region they became the primary definer of events. The fact that many stories about the peace process emanated from London – combined with the lack of experienced international or British reporters in Northern Ireland and the limitations of space – allowed a hegemonic interpretation of events in the international and British press that was discordant with the experienced realities of those living in Northern Ireland. The reduction of 'the Troubles', over a thirty-year period, to a master narrative – effected in no small part by successive British governments – has allowed a superficial understanding of the history, causes, activities and events of 'the Troubles' to be perpetuated in the media and in international opinion (Curtis 1998; Miller 1994; Rolston 1991). This, in turn, encouraged a simplistic international understanding of the peace process and the role of the Good Friday Agreement.

Just as the news media provided a central stage for the struggle of the past thirty years, their role in an emergent 'peace' discourse is even more crucial. The transformation of 'the Troubles' from a street struggle to a legislative one will not be possible if the media do not reflect the broad range of political positions evident in society, including anti-Agreement positions on all sides. If inclusion made agreement possible, only inclusion will sustain peace. In any case, national and international understanding and decisions will be based in no small measure on information provided by the news (Riffe 1986).

Whether the sun is rising or setting on Northern Ireland, resolution will not be aided by recycling British interpretations, but by independent reportage, from a wide variety of positions, based on first-hand, in-depth knowledge, not second-hand reports.

---

7   See Valerie Morgan's contribution to this volume.

References

'How Ulster Voted', *Belfast Telegraph*, 27 June 1998.

Baird, A. 1996. 'The Media', in *Northern Ireland Politics*, ed. A. Aughey and D. Morrow. Essex.

Collins, T. 1998. 'Broadcasting has played its role in the battle of Drumcree', *Irish News*, 14 July 1998.

Cook, T. 1998. *Governing with the News: The News Media as a Political Institution*. Chicago.

Cracknell, D. 1999. 'Government Lashed Over Ulster Leaks', *Electronic Telegraph*, 29 August 1999.

Curtis, L. 1998. *Ireland and the Propaganda War*. London.

'DUP Leaks NIO Peace Strategy', *Irish News*, 28 March 1998.

Fawcett, L. 1996. *Confining to Stereotypes in Power, Politics and Positionings: Women in Northern Ireland*. Belfast.

Feeney, B. 1997. 'The Peace Process. Who Defines the News – The Media or Government Press Offices?', in *Media in Ireland: The Search for Diversity*, ed. Damien Kiberd,. Dublin, pp. 41–58.

Foucault, M. 1980. *Power/Knowledge. Selected Interviews and Other Writings, 1972–1977*. New York.

Gans, H. 1979. *Making What's News: A Study of CBS Evening News, NBC Nightly News, Newsweek and Time*. New York.

Gramsci, A. 1971. *Prison Notebooks*. New York.

Greenslade, R. 1998. 'The Damien Walsh Memorial Lecture 1998'. Belfast.

Grossman, L. 1996. 'On Postmodernism and Cultural Studies. An Interview with Stuart Hall', in *Stuart Hall. Critical Dialogues in Cultural Studies*, ed. David Morley and Kuan-Hsing Chen. New York.

Hall, S. 1993. 'Encoding, Decoding', in *The Cultural Studies Reader*, ed. Simon During. New York, pp. 90–103.

Holland, J. 1999. *The American Connection: U.S. Guns, Money, and Influence in Northern Ireland*. Boulder, CO.

Laclau, E. and Mouffe, C. 1985. *Hegemony and Socialist Thought: Towards a Radical Democratic Politics*. New York.

McGonagle, M. 1996. *A Textbook on Media Law*. Dublin.

Miller, D. 1994. *Don't Mention the War: Northern Ireland, Propaganda and the Media*. London.

Negrine, R. 1996. *Politics and the Mass Media in Britain*. New York.

Parkinson, A. F. 1998. *Ulster Loyalism and the British Media*. Dublin.

Riffe, D. 1986. 'Gatekeeping and the Network News Mix', in *Journalism Quarterly* vol. 63, no. 2 (1986), pp. 315–21.

Rolston, B., ed. 1991. *The Media and Northern Ireland: Covering the Troubles*. Basingstoke.

Rolston, B. and Miller, D. 1996. *War and Words. The Northern Ireland Media Reader*. Belfast.

Taaffe, T. 1998. 'Negotiating Legal Fences. Libel and the Limits of Media Discourse in Northern Ireland' (paper presented at the American Anthropological Association). Philadelphia.

Welsh, T. and Greenwood, W. 1997. *McNae's Essential Law for Journalists*. Fourteenth edition. London.

Williams, R. 1977. *Marxism and Literature*. Oxford.

Wilson, R. 1997. *Media and Intra-State Conflict in Northern Ireland*. Amsterdam.

CHAPTER EIGHT

The Perception of Economic Aid in Northern Ireland and its Role in the Peace Process*

Cynthia Irvin and Sean Byrne

Introduction

In the new world order, external economic aid is used as an integral part of the post-conflict peace-building process in protracted ethnopolitical conflicts (cf. Agnew and Corbridge 1994; Esman 1997, 1998). Yet, policymakers and academics continue to debate over whether an organic sustainable social-economic development model is a more appropriate intervention than a free-market interdependent economic model (Byrne and Ayulo 1998; Lederach 1997). Within the context of the Northern Ireland conflict, external economic aid from the International Fund for Ireland (IFI) and the European Union (EU) Special Support Programme for Peace and Reconciliation in Ireland, coupled with fragile negotiations for the establishment of a power-sharing executive in Belfast, has set the context of the peace agenda, and holds out the promise of a new civic culture (Byrne and Irvin 2001; Tomlinson 1995a).

In the past, the British economic subvention was used by populist politicians to sustain a politics of sectarianism in Northern Ireland that discriminated against Catholics in housing, public sector employment and economic development (Bew, et al. 1995; Cunningham 1991; Farrell 1980; Munck 1985; O'Dowd et al. 1980; Probert 1978). From 1969 to 1994, the war economy has cost the British exchequer £18.205 billion, and civilians have made up 53 percent of the war deaths (Fay et al. 1998: 65; O'Leary and McGarry 1993: 8–54; Tomlinson 1994: 26). Northern Ireland's economy, on the periphery of the United Kingdom (UK), boasts one of the highest unemployment rates in the EU (Tomlinson 1995b: 13). The Nationalist and Unionist working-classes have begun to mobilise in support of fair employment and employment equality as well as for an

* This project was supported by a United States Institute of Peace research grant. The authors would like to thank Jessica Senehi for critically commenting on an earlier draft.

opportunity to create indigenous economic development projects (McVey 1995: 3; Miller 1995: 74; Price 1995: 65; Sheehan 1995: 79).

In response to the situation in Northern Ireland, the Clinton administration was most active as a third-party intermediary in the peacebuilding process. In his address to the White House Conference on Trade and Investment in May 1995, President Clinton remarked:

> As everyone knows, peace is more than cease-fires and formal agreements. It demands real hope and progress in the hearts of people. It demands common striving for the common good. It is time for those who have been most affected by the fighting to feel this kind of hope and this sense of progress...There must be a peace dividend in Northern Ireland and the border counties so that everyone of us is convinced that the future belongs to those who build, not those who destroy; so that the majority that supports peace is strengthened; so that there is no slipping back into the violence that frustration breed. This is why this conference is so important. It underscores that all sides have an interest in investing in the future of Northern Ireland, and that all sides will benefit from the peace.

It is important to point out that the Bush administration initially has not taken the same kind of interest in the Northern Ireland conflict. This in no small way contributed to the impasse reached in the summer of 2001. However, as Stefan Wolff has already pointed out in his introduction, the events of 11 September 2001 have fundamentally changed the international context of the Northern Ireland peace process and increased American pressure from the Bush administration and from within the Irish-American community has made a significant contribution to bringing about the beginning of IRA decommissioning.

This chapter focuses on the issues of public awareness of external aid in Northern Ireland, the perceived equity of its distribution, and its effectiveness in the reduction of violence. The findings are based on the results of a public opinion survey commissioned to assess public perceptions of the impact of funding from the United States (US) via the IFI and from the EU through the Special Support Programme for Peace and Reconciliation in Ireland.[1]

Public Awareness of Funding Source

The International Fund for Ireland was created in September 1986 by the British and Irish governments, based on objectives stated in Article 10(a) of the Anglo-Irish Agreement of 1985:

> The two Governments shall cooperate to promote the economic and social development of those areas of both parts of Ireland which have suffered most severely from

---

1   Please note that the August 1997 Ulster Marketing Survey results we are presenting below represent only a preliminary and cursory analysis of the descriptive data. The research findings are based on a representative sample of 610 Northern Irish citizens.

the consequences of the instability of recent years, and shall consider the possibility of securing international support for this work.

The language of the law authorising the US contribution makes clear the relationship the US administration and Congress perceived between peace and economic development:

The purpose of this Act is to provide for the United States contributions in support of the Anglo-Irish Agreement, such contributions to consist of economic support fund assistance for payment to the International Fund... as well as other assistance to serve as an incentive for economic development and reconciliation in Ireland and Northern Ireland... in which all may live in peace, free from discrimination, terrorism, and intolerance and with the opportunity for both communities to participate fully in the structures and processes of government.

Successive US Administrations and the US Congress have continued to view economic development as a key to fostering peace in Northern Ireland. As support for both Republican and Loyalist paramilitaries has traditionally been strongest in those communities which suffer the highest level of unemployment and economic deprivation, many advocates of the Fund view the creation of jobs and economic opportunity as an essential component in reaching a solution to the political conflict in Northern Ireland (Irvin 1999: 56). The following comments made by Senator Patrick Leahy regarding the Fund underscore this sentiment:

Lasting peace means urgently dealing with the terrible problem of unemployment in the North. People need to have confidence in their government, but they also need jobs; they need economic security as well as physical security... I am reminded of what Senator Mitchell, quoting Franklin Roosevelt said to an audience in Dublin: 'In the dark days of our Great Depression', President Roosevelt said, 'the only thing we have to fear is fear itself.' He also said, 'the best social programme is a job.' (Leahy 1995: 2917)

As Table 8.1 indicates, financial support for the Fund from the USA, while not on the same level as aid provisions to other conflict-torn areas, such as the Palestine Authority,[2] nevertheless has remained relatively constant since its initial seed funding.

Table 8.1: US Contributions to the IFI

Financial Year	US$ (millions)	Financial Year	US$ (millions)
1986	50	1993	19.7
1987	35	1994	19.6
1988	35	1995	19.6
1989	10	1996	19.6
1990	20	1997	19.6
1991	20	1998	19.6
1992	19.7		

2   US funds pledged as of November 1996 reached US$500 million. EU funds pledged (excluding those from the European Investment Bank) reached US$300 million. For additional information see Byrne (1996).

Other donors to the IFI include the European Union (EU), Canada, New Zealand and Australia. Since 1989, the EU has contributed approximately US$18.3 million per year. In response to the 1994 cease-fires, the EU has increased its annual contribution to approximately US$24.4 million per year, supplanting the USA as the largest donor to the fund.

Northern Ireland and the Republic of Ireland also receive substantial EU assistance through the EU structural funds for economically depressed regions and the Special Support Programme for Peace and Reconciliation in Ireland, (EU Peace Fund) (Byrne and Ayulo 1998: 421–4). During the period 1989–94, Northern Ireland received over one billion ECU from the European Structural Funds.

The EU Peace Fund was an initiative by the President of the European Commission, Jacques Delors, introduced in the weeks following the announcements of the Irish Republican Army (IRA) and Combined Loyalist Military Command (CLMC) cease-fire in the autumn of 1994, and promised 300 million ECU (US$393 million) for the period 1995–8 (Byrne and Irvin 2001). The Commission has since proposed over US$220 million additional funds. Together with the structural funds applied to the Republic of Ireland, the EU will have invested over 1.2 billion ECU by the year 2000 in the island of Ireland. As stated in its programme summary, the strategic aims of the Peace Fund are 'to reinforce progress towards a peaceful and stable society and to promote reconciliation by increasing economic development and employment, promoting urban and rural regeneration, developing cross-border cooperation and extending social inclusion', its strategic objectives being 'to promote the social inclusion of those at the margins of economic and social life' and to 'to exploit the opportunities and address the needs arising from the peace process in order to boost economic growth and stimulate social and economic regeneration' (Special Support Programme).

Given the considerable amount of funds available through the IFI and the EU to the people of Northern Ireland, we wished to assess the public recognition of these donor sources partly as a means of testing the depth and breadth of the perceived availability and accessibility of external funds. Table 8.2 indicates widespread recognition of the IFI across both communities. The reduced level of recognition for the EU Peace and Reconciliation Fund is understandable given that the first funds were not distributed until 1996. Also, the lower level of recognition within the Protestant community is consistent with other reviews.[3] Within these reviews, the most commonly accepted explanation for the lower level of funding within deprived Protestant areas is the relative lack of community infrastructure in comparison to similar Catholic communities.

---

3   See, for example, reviews of the EU fund by the Northern Ireland Voluntary Trust (1997: 1-
30) and by Harvey (1997) for the Joseph Rowntree Charitable Trust.

With regard to the distribution of IFI funds, it is also important to note that while the explicit aims of the Fund are to promote reconciliation through focusing on economic and social regeneration through investment in the most deprived areas, its origins in the 1985 Anglo-Irish Agreement led to an initial boycott by Protestant community groups on the grounds that it represented 'blood-money'. Although Fund reports show increasing support of projects within Protestant communities our findings indicate that fewer Protestants than Catholics perceived the distribution of IFI funds between communities to be very fair or quite fair (see Table 8.3).

Table 8.2: Awareness of the IFI and the EU Peace Fund

Group	IFI % aware	EU Peace Fund % aware
All	77	39
By Sex		
F	71	34
M	84	44
By Class		
ABC1	86	45
C2	74	40
DE	68	30
By Religion		
Catholic	83	44
Protestant	74	36

Source: UMS Survey August 1997, N= 610

Table 8.3: Perceived Fairness of Distribution of IFI Funds Between Communities

	Very fair %	Quite fair %	Neutral %	Not very fair %	Not fair %	Don't know %
All	3	21	6	10	10	49
By sex						
F	3	18	4	9	9	57
M	4	25	8	10	12	41
By class						
ABC1	5	26	5	9	8	46
C2	1	19	8	12	11	52
DE	3	16	5	10	14	51
By religion						
Catholics	7	27	5	4	12	51
Protestants	2	17	6	13	13	48
By political party						
UUP	1	16	5	17	16	45
DUP	3	15	10	17	12	42
Alliance	2	40	9	2	2	45
PUP	0	13	0	17	39	30
UDP	5	23	23	5	9	36
UKUP	0	13	0	25	13	50
SDLP	6	33	7	4	6	43
Sinn Féin	13	21	6	6	2	51
Women's Coalition	0	17	0	17	0	67

Source: UMS Survey August 1997, N=601

Table 8.4: Perceived Fairness of Distribution of EU Funds Between Communities

	Very fair %	Quite fair %	Neutral %	Not very fair %	Not fair %	Don't know %
All	3	21	7	6	7	56
By sex						
F	2	17	7	7	6	62
M	4	27	7	5	8	49
By class						
ABC1	3	26	8	6	8	49
C2	4	14	7	7	6	62
DE	1	19	7	6	6	61
By religion						
Catholics	6	27	7	3	4	54
Protestants	1	18	8	8	8	57
By political party						
UUP	1	21	9	10	11	49
DUP	0	17	7	8	7	61
Alliance	4	32	11	2	2	49
PUP	0	4	4	13	26	52
UDP	0	23	23	9	5	50
UKUP	0	25	13	0	13	50
SDLP	6	25	6	5	6	53
Sinn Féin	13	23	11	2	2	49
Women's Coalition	0	17	0	17	17	50

Source: UMS Survey: August 1997, N=610

Table 8.5: Awareness of IFI and EU Projects

	IFI %	EU %
All	19	7
By class		
ABC1	26	10
C2	19	5
DE	11	6
By religion		
Catholics	24	7
Protestants	16	7
By political party		
UUP	18	7
DUP	17	0
Alliance	21	13
PUP	22	0
UDP	5	14
UKUP	13	38
SDLP	29	8
Sinn Féin	23	6
Women's Coalition	33	17

Source: UMS Survey (August 1997), N=610

Table 8.6: Top 3 Types of Projects Identified as Funded by IFI

(Top three)	%
Having local buildings renovated/new shops	45
Local restaurants/hotels/pubs built/refurbished	15
New clubs and youth projects	7

Looking at the perception of the fairness of the IFI distribution of funds by party, the differences between Catholics and Protestants are even more stark. As an aggregate voters for the Unionist/Loyalist block are far more likely to view the distribution of monetary funds as unfair than those supporting the nonconfessional Alliance and Women's coalition bloc or the Nationalist SDLP and Sinn Féin bloc. The highest overall ranking on fairness of distribution is held by Sinn Féin voters, which appears to indicate that the IFI is succeeding in targeting the more eco-nomically deprived areas.

Table 8.4, which illustrates attitudes regarding the perceived fairness of the distribution of EU Peace Funds, reveals a similar pattern to that associated with IFI funds. However, there appears to be a slightly less overall negative perception, even among voters for the Unionist/Loyalist parties. Given that the designers of the EU Peace and Reconciliation Fund had the IFI's successes and failures to draw upon in its modelling, and quite extensive community-group consultation, our findings would suggest that community-level consultation and input has contributed to a more equitable distribution of funds.

In contrast to the awareness of the IFI and the EU as funding sources, Table 8.5 indicates that far fewer respondents are actually aware of either IFI- or EU- funded projects within their communities. Again, looking at Table 8.5 we note that the pattern for greater awareness of funds holds with regards to consciousness of actual projects. Given the longer period in which the IFI has been active, it is not, perhaps, surprising that there is greater awareness of IFI-funded projects. Also of interest is that awareness of both funding and funded projects is greatest among the professional and skilled socioeconomic categories. Even though both the IFI and EU are committed to targeting the areas of greatest social and economic needs, it could be that even within those areas the skills to access the allocation of monetary aid remain confined to certain segments of those communities.

An area for further work for both the EU and IFI would, therefore, appear to be facilitating access to funding for the most marginalized groups within the deprived communities. Both organizations could work together to streamline the application process and application forms in a nontechnical way that would even-out the flow of resources to marginalized areas. During our fieldwork, we both frequently encountered complaints regarding the IFI use of funds on 'refurbishing banks and hotels' and reviews by such groups as the West Belfast Economic Forum, the Irish Congress of Trade Unions, and the Northern Ireland Trust also contained numerous references to IFI funds being spent on infrastructure projects. Such references also frequently appear in the Congressional Record, the following being characteristic of a number of entries:

> Mr. Eliot Engel: A number of years ago many of us held hearings... and we were very critical of the way the International Fund for Ireland was dispensing monies; to a large degree American monies. We heard horror stories about funding flying schools, diving schools, Chinese restaurants, and silly things like that. (Engel 1995)

Given the preferences of the US Congress for the funding of private enterprises and the direction of the Fund by members of the Irish and British government, it is understandable that both political vetting by the British government and the economic preferences of US donors would result in a heavy emphasis on support for investment in tangible enterprises that had already given some indication of success early in the implementation of the Fund. Table 8.6 would appear to indicate, however, that some ten years after the initial disbursement of funds, it remains most closely associated with building projects.

Tables 8.7 and 8.8 show that, despite the perceived differences in the fairness of the distribution of funds from the IFI and EU between the communities and the primary association by respondents of IFI funding with building renovations, both communities view the projects funded by these organisations as very important to their community's economic development. Table 8.7, for example, illustrates that close to two-thirds of respondents perceived that IFI projects were either very important or important to one's own community's economic development. This image cut right across political party and class orientation.

Table 8.7: Importance of IFI Projects to Your Community's Economic Development

	Very important %	Quite important %	Neutral %	Not very important %	Not important %	Don't know %
All	34	34	6	3	3	23
By sex						
F	31	37	5	2	0	25
M	37	30	7	5	1	20
By class						
ABC1	32	39	7	2	0	23
C2	38	28	5	5	0	23
DE	33	30	6	3	0	27
By religion						
Catholics	48	26	5	3	0	17
Protestants	27	38	6	3	1	25
By political party						
UUP	23	41	7	5	0	24
DUP	25	39	7	5	2	22
Alliance	34	32	9	2	0	23
PUP	48	35	4	4	0	9
UDP	36	14	9	5	0	36
UKUP	25	38	13	0	0	25
SDLP	50	24	6	3	1	17
Sinn Féin	38	36	4	4	0	17
Women's Coalition	0	67	17	0	0	17

Source: UMS Survey August 1997, N=610

Table 8.8 indicates that about two-thirds of the respondents' highlighted the importance of EU-funded projects to one's own community's economic development. These findings were also consistent across class and political party affiliation.

Table 8.8: Importance of EU Funded Projects to Your Community's Economic Development

	Very important %	Quite important %	Neutral %	Not very important %	Not important %	Don't know %
All	35	35	5	2	0	23
By sex						
F	33	37	5	1	0	25
M	38	32	6	3	0	21
By class	5	4	3	2	1	0
ABC1	33	39	6	1	0	20
C2	37	27	6	3	0	26
DE	37	33	5	1	0	24
By religion						
Catholics	48	26	5	2	0	19
Protestants	29	40	5	1	0	25
By political party						
UUP	26	40	7	1	0	27
DUP	29	44	7	2	0	19
Alliance	34	38	4	2	0	21
PUP	48	39	4	4	0	4
UDP	32	23	5	5	0	36
UKUP	25	38	13	13	0	13
SDLP	52	21	6	1	0	20
Sinn Féin	38	36	4	4	0	17
Women's Coalition	17	67	0	0	0	17

Source: UMS Survey August 1997, N=610

Looking at the responses by religion, we note that almost twice as many Catholics as Protestants viewed these projects as very important to their community's development although the total combined 'important' percentages were closer. These findings can be interpreted as supporting the effectiveness of both the IFI and the EU in targeting the areas of greatest social need, particularly within the Catholic community.

In its conclusion to a paper on the Special Support Programme for Peace and Reconciliation, the EU Commission states:

> The new circumstances provide a challenge to all to promote social inclusion, to put behind them alienation and marginalisation caused by violence. In particular, those who have been victims, whether individuals or whole communities, and those who have not benefited from life in a normal society, expect the new developments to bring about clear change.

The IFI in its annual reports similarly suggests that community economic development nurtures an environment in which peace can take hold. Specifically, both programmes suggest through their statements regarding strategic aims and objectives, that by providing those in the most disadvantaged areas with the opportunity for economic development, they can weaken the appeal of the paramilitaries by providing alternative incentives to young people.

Milton Esman (1991: 487), in his work on the relationship between economic performance, foreign aid and ethnic conflict, has noted that

> It has become an article of conventional wisdom that economic growth mitigates ethnic conflict. Simply put, when there is more to go around, everybody benefits, thus relieving material grievances and reducing incentives for conflict. To a great many people this would seem to be grass-roots common sense.

Against this 'common sense', Esman (1991: 489) argues that a more likely finding would be that:

> Vigorous and equitably distributed economic growth might be instrumental in reinforcing or protecting the settlement of underlying political or cultural issues among contending parties ... External agencies that wish to support political accords among conflicting ethnic communities may find in economic assistance a practical vehicle for contributing to and implementing such agreements. The main point, however, is the primacy of politics in the management of ethnic conflict. Economic performance can facilitate and reinforce but never substitute for political measures.

Table 8.9, in general, provides strong support for Esman's position. Overall, a majority of the respondents view external economic support as not having played a role in the reduction of violence, a finding which transcends class and gender lines as well as Unionist/Loyalist and non-confessional party lines. Looking at the Nationalist party block, however, we see a much higher percentage of respondents who view economic investment as having helped in reducing violence. Perhaps most surprisingly, it is among Sinn Féin supporters that we see the greatest belief in the positive role that external support has had. The escalation in sectarian violence, and the fact that the Secretary of State for Northern Ireland, John Reid, declared the cease-fires of the UDA and the Loyalist Volunteer Force to be over (after a number of attacks had been linked to the two organisations) certainly bears this point out.

These results, at least at this preliminary stage of analysis, suggest that IFI and EU investment in the disadvantaged areas within the

Catholic communities has had the desired effect of both offering alternatives to participation in acts of political and nonpolitical violence and securing participation in those alternatives.

Table 8.9: Belief that External Support Has Helped Reduce Level of Violence

	Yes %	No %	Don't know %
All	21	56	23
By sex			
F	20	53	27
M	23	59	18
By class			
ABC1	27	55	19
C2	19	60	21
DE	16	55	29
By religion			
Catholics	38	40	22
Protestants	13	65	22
By political party			
UUP	14	64	23
DUP	8	76	15
Alliance	17	64	19
PUP 4	48	48	
UDP	9	82	9
UKUP	0	88	13
SDLP	39	43	18
Sinn Féin	45	28	28
Women's Coalition	33	50	17

Source: UMS Survey (August 1997), N=610

In Table 8.10 we have categorised the principal explanations given by respondents for their view on the role of external support. These findings further suggest that political questions, especially distribution of funds, underlie the success at once of the economic development programmes of the IFI and EU, and, more importantly, of the peace process itself.

Table 8.10: Reasons for Attitudes Regarding Effectiveness of External Economic Support in Reducing the Level of Violence

Reasons mentioned for why external economic support has not reduced levels of violence

Political explanations
1) Nothing has changed – still violence and unsettlement
2) It has nothing to do with the political situation
3) Money is not the problem in Northern Ireland – compromise is needed
4) Should be politicians on both sides leading the way, not people from other countries

Socioeconomic explanations
1) It has helped to make more funds for the IRA and other such organisations
2) It has made it worse if anything/they should mind their own business
3) Money only goes to certain places
4) Money not used properly for both communities
5) Not enough money has been put in
6) Only helps those who are employed and not the unemployed

Reasons mentioned for why external economic support has reduced levels of violence

Political explanations
1) Helps bring people together in talks
2) Has helped since President Clinton's visit
3) It's good in that it puts pressure on the IRA and Sinn Féin politically

Socioeconomic explanations
1) It has given people more job opportunities
2) People are gaining financially from it
3) Gets people's minds off violence if they make more money

Table 8.11, which lists the top 3 reasons stated by supporters of each of the Northern Ireland political parties for their positive or negative view of the role of external economic support, shows that for the Unionist community, which has traditionally been privileged economically (albeit characterised by enormous discrepancies of wealth within the community), economic development has not effected a positive change in the political situation, at least in terms of reducing the level of violence. Within the nonconfessional and Nationalist bloc, however, there is greater support for the role of economic development in providing people with greater opportunities and in diminishing the level of violence.

Table 8.11: Most Frequently Mentioned Attitudes Regarding the Effect of External Economic Support on the Reduction of Levels of Violence – By Party

UUP	PUP
Nothing has changed	Nothing has changed
Helped make more funds available to IRA	Money only goes to certain places
Made things worse –	More IRA money
mind their own business	

DUP	UDP
Nothing has changed	Nothing has changed
More IRA money	Has made things worse – mind own business
Money not the problem – compromise is	Money not the problem – compromise is

Alliance	Women's Coalition
Nothng has changed	Has given people more opportunities
Given more people opportunities	Nothing has changed/people are gaining financially
People are gaining financially	Should be politicians on both sides – not from outside

SDLP	Sinn Féin
Nothing has changed	Given people more opportunities
Given people more opportunities	Nothing has changed
Has helped (how not specified)	People are gaining financially from it

From Table 8.12, in general, we do see that both communities perceive that paramilitaries, Northern Ireland's politicians and the security forces are the groups benefiting from 'the Troubles'. Looking at the responses by political party, we note that all of the Unionist and Loyalist parties rank the IRA as the primary benefactor of political violence. Interestingly, supporters of both the Nationalist and Republican political parties were of the opinion that the Royal Ulster Constabulary (RUC) was the net beneficiary of continuing political violence. These findings can be interpreted as supporting traditional political attitudes within both communities, to the root cause of the Northern Ireland conflict (McGarry and O'Leary 1995: 13–61).

A number of prolific scholars of the Northern Ireland conflict have noted the role of class conflict and escalated competition between both communities for scarce economic resources, which has resulted in bicommunal sectarian polarisation (McGarry and O'Leary 1995: 265–258; Rowthorn and Wayne 1988: 23–36; Whyte 1990: 52–66). Table 8.13 indicates that most respondents are aware that big business is benefiting from the peace process. Also of significant interest is the awareness that both working-class and middle-class communities have most to gain and most to lose from the current peace initiative. Our findings would suggest, therefore, that people are aware that the peace-building process is providing space for economic development, and employment opportunities for the working class in both communities.

Table 8.12: Groups Identified as Benefiting from 'the Troubles'

Top five Groups Mentioned

IRA	44	RUC	42	IRA	49
NI politicians	33	NI Politicans	37	NI Politicians	30
Loyalist paramilitaries	32	IRA	36	Loyalist paramilitaries	29
RUC	25	Prison staff	34	RUC	16
Prison staff	19	British govt.	15	Irish govt.	12

By Party (top three groups mentioned)

UUP		PUP		SDLP	
IRA	55	IRA	65	RUC	43
Loyalist paramilitaries	32	Irish govt.	39	IRA	39
NI politicians	30	NI politicians	26	Loyalist paramilitaries	35

DUP		UDP		Sinn Féin	
IRA	49	IRA	32	RUC	53
NI Politicians	27	L. paramilitaries	27	Prison staff	43
Loyalist paramilitaries	25	NI politicians	23	Loyalist paramilitaries	40

Alliance		UKUP		Women's Coalition	
IRA	55	IRA	63	IRA	67
Loyalist paramilitaries	53	RUC	38	Loyalist paramilitaries	50
NI politicians	55	Loyalist paramilitaries	38	RUC/Prison staff	33

Source: UMS Survey (August 1997), N=610

Table 8.13: Groups Benefiting from Peace (the five groups most frequently mentioned)

Top 5 Groups	Catholic %	Protestant %	All %
NI businesses	77	73	74
Nationalist working class	78	58	66
Unionist working class	70	59	63
Nationalist middle class	60	46	51
Unionist middle class	54	46	49

Source: UMS Survey (August 1997), N=610

Table 8.14, which lists the top five groups most frequently mentioned as not benefiting from the peace process, shows that for the majority of respondents, the peace process has not benefited the paramilitaries and the security forces.

Table 8.14: Groups Not Benefiting from Peace

Top 5 Groups	Catholic %	Protestant %	All %
IRA	42	46	45
Loyalist paramilitaries	42	35	38
RUC	22	10	14
NI politicians	15	13	14
Prison staff	16	10	11

Source: UMS Survey (August 1997), N=610

Analysis and Discussion

This preliminary analysis suggests that external economic assistance can play a positive role in nurturing an environment more conducive to political rather than violent resolutions of conflict. Indeed, if skilfully administered, it appears that development assistance can contribute at least to the mitigation of violence in ethnic conflicts. Certainly, as Tables 8.12–14 indicate, the people of Northern Ireland clearly perceive the potential of peace to bring prosperity. As these tables also illustrate, however, the advent of peace will 'negatively' affect both the paramilitaries and those employed in security services, whose livelihoods have also waxed and waned with the political conflict. Clearly, an important issue to be addressed in any study of the impact of peace on the economy and society of Northern Ireland is the investment that will be necessary both in the provision of skills and training for paramilitaries to assist in their reintegration into their communities, and in the retraining of those long employed in the regulation of those paramilitaries.

The peace-building process must, therefore, help to end poverty and the war economy by targeting economic resources at impoverished and marginalised members of both communities. However, a political process has to be created to institutionalise a culture of cooperation among Northern Ireland's political elites. Thus, the bilateral 'external ethnoguarantors' – the British and Irish governments – continue a carrot-and-stick approach to enforce a 'coercive consociational' power-sharing model on the government and politics of Northern Ireland (Byrne 2000). For example, the 1985 Anglo-Irish Agreement ended the Unionist veto, attempted to curb Nationalist support for Sinn Féin, and created the space for moderates within both communities to work together to create a power-sharing government. The 1991 Brooke Initiative, the 1993 Joint Declaration, the 1995 Framework Proposals, and the 1998 Good Friday Agreement have also continued the political mould that has seen both governments continuing to work together to shape and impose a power-sharing executive at Stormont (Byrne 2001; Byrne and Keashly 2000). The cooperative partnership of both governments and the power mediation of former President Bill Clinton were successful to a point in facilitating intercommunal negotiations.

However, the sectarian assassination of Rosemary Nelson in Portadown by the Red Hand Defenders, the August 1998 bombing of Omagh, Co. Tyrone by the Real IRA, the impasse over the decommissioning of arms, escalated tensions along Orange Order marching routes, and the sectarian violence surrounding the Holy Cross Community School in North Belfast clearly indicate the shaky and fragile nature of the peace settlement. While the beginning of IRA decommissioning may have overcome one set of hurdles, politicians in Northern Ireland remain ill at ease with each other within and across party-political divisions over the very direction of the peace process. In other words, stalemate, intransigence, and an unwillingness to compromise among the political parties could create a power vacuum to be filled by extremist armed elements (Byrne 1999). The 1998 Good Friday Agreement is not a panacea for an immediate resolution of the intractable conflict. Instead, a multimodal, multilevel contingency conflict intervention approach is integral to any peace-building efforts.

Such a complementarity and multitrack approach at multiple levels of intervention could successfully coordinate a variety of peace-building activities and actors within Northern Ireland's conflict context (Bloomfield 1996; Byrne and Keashly 2000; Diamond 1995; Dixon 1997; Galtung 1996; Keashly and Fisher 1996). Consequently, moving the conflict to a tractable mode of conflict resolution involves building a peace system within Northern Ireland that includes a variety of structural and psychocultural conflict resolution intervention strategies, as well as individuals, organisations and groups working together simultaneously to transform the conflict (Hume 1996; Love 1995; Ruane and Todd 1996). Participatory democracy, therefore, must seek to psychologically, politically and socioeconomically empower individuals and both communities in the politics of social justice, hope and participation (Schwerin 1995: 55–93, 161–189). Transformational ethnic conflict resolution also involves moving the people of Northern Ireland from a crisis mode to a desired change by developing their capacity to think about social change in time nodes of decades (Byrne 1995).

Conclusions

Ethnopolitical conflicts can be 'waged constructively' and in a transforming world 'many of our old paradigms are no longer valid.' (Kriesberg 1998: 370) 'Intangible and tangible interests' must be addressed by a constructive conflict resolution process (Senehi 2000). The findings from our public opinion survey certainly indicate that the respondents support the work of both the IFI and the EU Peace and Reconciliation Programme in economically empowering both communities.

In closing, we must admit that when we began this study we tended to agree with the third of Esman's hypotheses regarding the effect of economic growth on ethnic conflict, (1 being that it mitigates, 2 being that it exacerbates) – namely, that it has no significant effect on conflict. After four months of fieldwork during the summer of 1997, and buttressed somewhat by the findings of our survey, we are pleased to be reconsidering our initial position and leaning more towards the view that economic assistance, if indeed properly targeted, can provide communities with resources, both human and material, which builds self-confidence, increases self-esteem and nourishes an environment in which politics rather than violence can dominate the arena of conflict and negotiation. However, economic aid alone cannot resolve a problem that is political in nature and which demands a political solution.

References

Agnew, J. and Corbridge, S. 1994. *Mastering Space. Hegemony, Territory and International Political Economy.* New York.

Aughey, A. 2000a. 'The 1998 Agreement: Unionist Responses', in *A Farewell to Arms? From 'Long War' to Long Peace in Northern Ireland,* ed. Mick Cox, Adrian Guelke and Fiona Stephen. Manchester, pp. 62–77.

———2000b. 'Learning form "the Leopard"', in *Aspects of the Belfast Agreement,* ed. Rick Wilford. Oxford, p. 191.

Bew, P., Gibbon, P. and Patterson, H. 1995. *Northern Ireland. 1921–94: Political Forces and Social Classes.* London.

Bloomfield, D. 1996. *Peacemaking Strategies in Northern Ireland: Building Complementarity in Conflict Management Theory.* Basingstoke.

Brynen, R. 1996. 'International Aid to the West Bank and Gaza. A Primer', in *Journal of Palestine Studies* vol. 25, no. 2 (1996), pp. 10–34.

Byrne, S. and Ayulo, M. 1998. 'External Economic Aid in Ethnopolitical Conflict. A View From Northern Ireland', in *Security Dialogue* vol. 29, no. 4 (1998), pp. 421–34.

Byrne, S. and Irvin, C. 2000. 'Economic Aid and Policy Making: Building the Peace Dividend in Northern Ireland', in *Policy and Politics* vol. 29, no.4 (2000), pp. 413–429.

Byrne, S. and Keashly, L. 2000. 'Working with Ethno-Political Conflict: A Multi-Modal Approach', in *International Peacekeeping* vol. 7, no. 1 (2000), pp. 97–120.

Byrne, S. 1995. 'Conflict Regulation or Conflict Resolution. Third Party Intervention in the Northern Ireland Conflict. Prospects for Peace', in *Terrorism and Political Violence* vol. 7, no. 2 (1995), pp.1–24.

———1999. 'Israel, Northern Ireland and South Africa at a Cross-Roads: Understanding Intergroup Conflict, Peacebuilding, and Conflict Resolution', in *International Journal of Group Tensions* vol. 28. nos. 3/4 (1999), pp. 231–53.

———2000. 'Power Politics as Usual in Cyprus and Northern Ireland : Divided Islands and the Roles of External Ethno-Guarantors', *Nationalism and Ethnic Politics* vol. 6, no. 1 (2000), pp. 1–24.

————2001. 'Consociational and Civic Society Approaches to Peacebuilding in Northern Ireland', in *Journal of Peace Research* vol. 37, no. 3 (2001), pp. 321–53.

Cunningham, M. J. 1991. *British Government Policy in Northern Ireland, 1969–89.* Manchester.

Diamond, L. 1995. *Beyond Win/Win: The Heroic Journey of Conflict Transformation.* Washington, DC.

Dixon, P. 1997. 'Paths to Peace in Northern Ireland. Civil Society and Consociational Approaches', in *Democratization* vol. 4, no. 2 (1997), pp. 1–27.

Engel, E. 1995. 'U.S. Economic Role in the Peace Process in Northern Ireland', *Hearing before the Committee on International Relations,* House of Representatives, 104th Congress, 15 March 1995, p. 40.

Esman, M. J. 1991. 'Economic Performance and Ethnic Conflict', in *Conflict and Peacemaking in Multiethnic Societies,* ed. Joseph Montville. New York.

————1997. Peaceworks. Can Foreign Aid Moderate Ethnic Conflict? Washington, DC.

————1998. Global Crisis in Foreign Aid. The Foreign Aid Regime in Flux. Crisis or Tradition? Syracuse, NY.

Farrell, M. 1980. *Northern Ireland: The Orange State.* London.

Fay, M. T., Morrissey, M. and Smyth, M. 1998. *The Cost of the Troubles Study: Mapping Troubles-Related Deaths in Northern Ireland, 1969–1994.* Derry/Londonderry.

Galtung, J. 1996. *Peace by Peaceful Means: Peace and Conflict Development and Civilization.* London.

Guelke, A. 2000. 'International Dimensions of the Belfast Agreement', in *Aspects of the Belfast Agreement,* ed. Rick Wilford. Oxford.

Harvey, B. 1997. *Report on Programme for Peace and Reconciliation.* York.

Hume, J. 1996. *A New Ireland: Politics, Peace and Reconciliation.* Boulder, CO.

Irvin, C. 1999. *Militant Nationalism: Between Movement and Party in Northern Ireland and the Basque Country.* Duluth, MN.

Keashly, L. and Fisher, R. 1996. 'A Contingency Perspective on Conflict Interventions. Theoretical and Practical Considerations', in *Resolving International Conflicts: The Theory and Practice of Mediation,* ed. J. Bercovitch. Boulder, CO, pp. 235–63.

Kriesberg, L. 1998. *Constructive Conflicts: From Escalation to Resolution.* Boulder, CO.

Leahy, P. 1995. *Congressional Record,* 22 February 1995, p. s2917

Lederach, J. P. 1997. *Building Peace: Sustainable Reconciliation in Divided Societies.* Washington, DC.

Love, M. 1995. *Peace-Building Through Reconciliation in Northern Ireland.* Aldershot.

McGarry, J. and O'Leary, B. 1995. *Explaining Northern Ireland: Broken Images.* Cambridge, MA.

McVey, J. 1995. 'Public Views and Experiences of Fair Employment and Employment Equality', in *Public Views and Experiences of Fair Employment and Equality Issues in Northern Ireland,* ed. John McVey and Nigel Hutson. Belfast.

Miller, R. 1995. 'Public Opinion on Fair Employment Issues. Evidence from the Northern Ireland Social Attitude Surveys', in *Public Views and Experiences of Fair Employment and Equality Issues in Northern Ireland,* ed. John McVey and Nigel Hutson. Belfast.

Munck, R. 1985. *Ireland: Nation, State and Class Struggle.* Boulder, CO.

Northern Ireland Voluntary Trust. 1997. *Taking Risks for Peace: A Mid-term Review by an Intermediary Funding Body of the EU Peace Process.* Belfast.

O'Dowd, L., Rolston, B. and Tomlinson, M. 1980. *Northern Ireland: Between Civil Rights and Civil War.* London.

O'Leary, B. 1999. 'Academic Viewpoint: The Nature of the Agreement', in *Fordham International Law Journal* vol. 22, no. 1, (1999), pp. 628–643.

O'Leary, B. and McGarry, J. 1993. *The Politics of Antagonism: Understanding Northern Ireland.* London.

Price, J. 1995. 'Political Change and the Protestant Working-class', in *Race and Class* 37 (1995).

Probert, B. 1978. *Beyond Orange and Green: The Political Economy of the Northern Ireland State.* London.

Rowthorn, B. and Wayne, N. 1988. *Northern Ireland: The Political Economy of Conflict.* Cambridge.

Ruane, J. and Todd, J. 1996. *The Dynamics of Conflict in Northern Ireland. Power, Conflict and Emancipation.* Cambridge.

Schwerin, E. 1995. *Mediation, Citizen Empowerment and Transformational Politics.* Westport, CT.

Senehi, J. 2000. 'Constructive Storytelling in Intercommunal Conflicts: Building Community, Building Peace', in *Reconcilable Differences: Turning Points in Ethnopolitical Conflict,* ed. Sean Byrne and Cynthia Irvin. Hartford, CT, pp. 96–115.

Special Support Programme for Peace and Reconciliations in Northern Ireland and the Border Counties of Ireland 1995–1999

Tomlinson, M. 1994. *25 Years On: The Costs of War and the Dividends of Peace.* Belfast.

———1995a. 'Can Britain Leave Ireland? The Political Economy of War and Peace', in *Race and Class* 37 (1995).

———1995b. 'The British Economic Subvention and the Irish Peace Process', in *International Policy Review* vol. 5, no. 2 (1995), pp. 69–74.

Whyte, J. 1990. *Interpreting Northern Ireland.* Oxford.

CHAPTER NINE

Women and a 'New' Northern Ireland

Valerie Morgan

Introduction

Given the range and complexity of problems which Ireland has faced for almost all of its recorded history, it is hardly surprising that the interaction between women and the changing political, social and economic structures of Irish society has been tortuous and even contradictory (Bitel 1995; Condren 1996). Women and their attitudes and achievements have at one and the same time been regarded as crucial symbols of various cultural and national identities and as of marginal practical importance – a dichotomy which has run across both major traditions (Edge 1998). In the nineteenth century women were frequently idealised in both the literary and the visual arts as representative of the spirit of Ireland. Variously portrayed as defenceless maidens, suffering mothers or indomitable defenders of tradition, they figured in cartoons of popular mass-circulation journals, in the propaganda of the pro- and anti-Home Rule campaigns and in the poems and plays of the leading figures of the Gaelic Revival (Foster 1993; Hutchinson 1987). Within the Catholic tradition this idealisation linked them to Our Lady, the Mother of God, providing a divine sanction for roles which simultaneously imposed unrealistic expectations and draconian restrictions (Kenny 1997). Beyond the rhetoric, however, the reality for the great majority of women in all parts of Ireland throughout the nineteenth century and well into the twentieth was hard work, limited rewards and exclusion from almost all political and economic power (Luddy 1997).

Although the specific context of the ongoing conflict over the relationship with Britain clearly influenced women in Ireland during the nineteenth century, many aspects of their experience and the social, political and economic disadvantages they faced were common across Western Europe (Rendall 1985). However, as women began to campaign for political rights at the end of the nineteenth century and into the early years of the twentieth century, those in Ireland had to face not only the familiar arguments about 'separate spheres' and questions about their intellectual and emotional capacity for political decision-making, but also problems of reconciling their national and gender identities. Would campaigning for women's rights before the 'national' question was settled represent betrayal? Could women only play an effective part in that struggle if they gained a formal political voice? Should gender rights and national rights be seen as linked facets of a wider struggle and hence be pursued in tandem? (Ward 1993)

The dramatic events of the first quarter of the twentieth century, culminating in the partition of Ireland and the creation of the independent 'Free State' (later the Republic of Ireland) and the Northern Ireland state, which remained a constituent part of the United Kingdom, did not remove such dilemmas for women, nor did they bring the anticipated advances in the economic, social or political status of women (MacCurtain 1985). Women's active roles in the events surrounding the Home Rule struggle, the Easter Rising and the Civil War were short-lived and quickly overtaken by the conservative reactions which established De Valera's 'Holy Catholic Ireland' and the Unionists' 'Protestant patriarchy' (Gardiner 1993). Although the period from the 1950s onwards saw an accelerating pace of social and economic change across Ireland, many of the images and issues which restricted and delayed women's active participation remained significant, particularly in Northern Ireland. Demands for constitutional change, and resistance to such demands, have continued to shape the political agenda, leaving most of the issues central to women's rights marginalised and women themselves facing dilemmas over their identity and priorities. Eavan Boland characterises the tensions in women's experiences: 'on the one hand was the idea of personal creativity and expression ... on the other there was the equally forceful idea of collective obligation with all its shadows of self denial, its requirement that the private will – the private feminine will, that is – be subsumed in the public good' (Boland 1995).

Women's Rights – National Rights

From the period in the late 1960s when the Civil Rights movement began to make its mark on the Northern Irish political scene, right through the abortive attempts at negotiated settlement in the 1970s and the subsequent long period of direct rule from Westminster, the constitutional issue has overshadowed all other aspects of politics. One result of this has been that those individuals and groups urging resolution of many pressing social and economic questions have not only been marginalised but frequently also treated with suspicion. Thus, those interested in feminism or women's rights and women campaigning directly for social, edu-cational and economic change have frequently been criticised from both sides of the community. Within much of Nationalist and Republican thinking there is a clear commitment to changing many of the structures and institutions of Northern Ireland. This often incorporates sympathy for a reassessment of the roles and rights of women, thereby challenging the status quo. But at the same time the centrality of the constitutional issue argues for its prioritisation. As a result of this tension, some Nationalists and Republicans feel that women's issues can only be dealt with effectively once a new set of government structures has been estab-lished and that until then women should concentrate their energies on work in support of the national question. This view has not been con-fined to male politicians in the parties identified with Nationalism and Republicanism, but has also been the source of extensive discussion, debate and sometimes dissension amongst women in these communities (Rooney 1992).

For women within the Unionist and Loyalist communities public iden-tification with feminist aspirations has posed even more difficulties. Cen-tral to much Unionist thinking is the belief that any change in social, political or cultural structures carries the seeds of danger. Preservation of the state of Northern Ireland is crucial and any demand for reform, even when it does not appear to have constitutional overtones, can be inter-preted as an implied criticism of the status quo and hence should be treated with suspicion. Against this background, feminism has been crit-icised as part of the process of destabilising Northern Ireland and as a 'tool' of Nationalism (Morgan 1996). In addition, elements of the theol-ogy of some evangelical and fundamentalist Protestant groups include clear statements that women should accept male leadership and author-ity.[1]

Thus, women on both sides of the community have been constrained by a background of political ideologies which potentially restrict their thinking and action and by a continuing use of symbolism which rein-forces the identification of women with their 'own' community (Aretxaga 1997). These may seem somewhat abstract considerations but they are important in a situation where women, and men, have deep commit-ments to their own cultural and national identity and are sensitive to anything which might undermine it. Discussion of the significance of commitment raises the question of women's attitudes to the Northern Ireland conflict. Some feminist writing and peace literature suggests that women are more peace-loving than men and more likely to be prepared to make compromises in conflict situations. Thus, in relation to North-

---

1   Cf. Rev. Ian Paisley's statement: 'I believe that the husband is the head of the wife and the home. I believe that the father should be prophet, priest and king in his home. As king, he should exercise rulership' (quoted from Fairweather 1984).

ern Ireland there have been claims that, if women had been in charge, the problem would have been solved 'long ago' (Morgan 1996; Vickers 1993). Such views are most certainly a serious oversimplification since the empirical data available indicate that women in Northern Ireland exhibit as wide a spectrum of political views as men and may even have marginally more negative stereotypes of the 'other' community (Morgan 1992). Whilst some women have been prominent in a number of peace initiatives and peace groups, others have also shown deep commitment to political parties across the whole spectrum, have supported the use of violence and have taken part in paramilitary operations. Even the large majority of women who have had no formal political role or voice and have not publicly expressed views or openly 'taken sides' may have contributed to the continuing divisions in the society by consciously or unconsciously passing on a culture which is divisive, and even sectarian, within the family. All this is not to suggest that there are no differences between the ways women and men have been involved in, and have reacted to, 'the Troubles' but rather to suggest that differences between the sexes in patterns of behaviour are more likely to be the product of social and cultural conventions than of fundamental contrasts in attitudes to the conflict (Morgan and Fraser 1995).

Women's Practical Contribution

Bearing in mind problems of interpretation and the serious dangers of generalisations which discuss 'women' as though they were a homogeneous group, it is still relevant to ask whether women have made a distinctive contribution to the evolution of Northern Ireland over the last thirty years. Even more important perhaps is the question of whether they have been making a significant contribution to the search for a way forward amid the complexities of the peace process and the intricacies of trying to establish and maintain some form of agreed, devolved government.

Monica McWilliams has argued that the form of women's involvement has changed considerably over the last thirty years. She suggests that six distinct stages of women's political involvement can be identified spanning the period from the mid-1960s to the late 1990s (McWilliams 1995). Generally, the growth of the women's rights movement over this period has introduced an element of pluralism into Northern Ireland's political life. By emphasising the existence of distinct concerns which cut across the conventional Nationalist/Unionist divide, women have drawn attention to the diversity within society and the inadequacy of working exclusively through the old dualism. This was illustrated in the early phases of the Civil Rights movement when women were extensively involved in housing protests, which focused on the absence of fair criteria in the allo-cation of public housing. Women from both communities joined in cam-paigns which defined issues in terms of personal oppression and individual disadvantage rather than clear political labels (McWilliams 1995; Rooney 1995).

As violence escalated rapidly during the 1970s, community divisions became increasingly entrenched. Cross-community action was, therefore, extremely difficult, but small groups of women did campaign along two distinct, though sometimes related, tracks. Some women were active in the peace groups which struggled to contain or end violence, such as Women Together, whilst others focused on women's rights issues. The Northern Ireland Women's Rights Movement, established in 1975, demanded the implementation of equality legislation in areas such as employment, welfare provision and education. Whilst there was no auto-matic cross-over between the two types of activity, a number of individ-uals did operate in both areas, and in the process they began to establish valuable contacts and alliances (Rooney 1995). In spite of the numerous attempts made to secure peace during the 1970s, including such high-profile mass movements as that spearheaded by the Peace People, vio-lence remained at a high level in the early 1980s (Morgan 1995; Sutton 1994). By this time, the British government and its 'direct rule' adminis-tration in Northern Ireland was shifting the focus of its policies. They were becoming convinced that a military solution probably could not be achieved and certainly would not be possible without increased Army activity. This Army intervention would antagonise public opinion not only in Northern Ireland but also in the rest of the United Kingdom, as well as heightening protests from the politically and economically sensi-tive European and North American arenas (Darby 1997; Dunn 1995). An alternative strategy gradually emerged, which has come to be referred to as the 'civil society' approach. This involved a range of policies which aimed at reducing intercommunity differentials in the areas of housing, employment, education and welfare provision, as well as supporting cross-community interaction and cooperation. This, it was hoped, would provide a basis for contact and ultimately the possibility of negotiation and political compromise between groups within Northern Ireland. Whilst the origins of such policies and their ultimate objectives have been a subject of controversy, in terms of women's involvement in pub-lic and political life they were of considerable significance (O'Leary et al. 1993).

With the shift away from the search for a single, all-embracing solu-tion to support for a series of activities which would address community relations and practical social and economic concerns on a local level, there was much greater interest in the sort of activities women were already involved in. Women had been becoming more active in local initiatives over issues such as child-care, provision for adolescents and employment opportunities, partially out of disillusionment over the failure of more ambitious but ultimately amorphous peace movements, such as the Peace People. In addition, the expansion of European Community financial support aided the expansion of community-based economic and social programmes. The combination of all these developments meant that during the 1980s women in Northern Ireland became increasingly active in what have been described as 'social arenas outside the state, private and market firms and the family where politically relevant discourse occurs and social trust is generated' (Scott 1999). Through such involvement, women were often contributing to the development of tolerance and understanding outside formal institutions and providing mechanisms for groups to act together and generate or articulate views which could ultimately affect policy-makers. Their activities spanned a wide range, from the development of local women's centres, through campaigns on specific issues (such as child care and domestic violence) to the creation of more formal organisations with a Northern Ireland-wide remit, such as the Women's Information Group, the Women's Support Network and the Women's Resource and Development Agency (McWilliams and McKernan 1993; Taillon 1992). In many of these initiatives women were working on areas of common interest and did not define their actions as linked to any 'peace' or 'community relations' agenda, but at the same time they were developing what Eilish Rooney has described as 'practical alliances' (Rooney 1995).

Whilst these 'alliances' have allowed women to work across the community divide on a wide range of issues, the difficulties should not be ignored. Throughout 'the Troubles' it has been difficult to maintain joint campaigns against a background of political division. For example in 1971, Margaret Thatcher, then Education Minister in a Conservative government, removed the general provision of a free daily allocation of milk for pupils in schools. This was opposed by women from both communities in Northern Ireland, who protested together about the impact in a region with high levels of child poverty and deprivation. However, Protestant women were pressured to withdraw from the protests by political leaders in their own community on the grounds that the campaign was linked to Nationalist demands and had a 'hidden agenda' of undermining the link with Britain. As a result of such early experiences, women have not been idealistic about their involvement in community action and rarely make exaggerated claims about its impact. Indeed, many women seek to distance themselves from being labelled as involved in 'community relations' activities and prefer to describe their work in more specific terms, focusing on its content, which avoid what could be controversial overtones.

The cautious reaction of many women is hardly surprising given the range and complexity of the difficulties women have encountered. As in so many other areas of Northern Irish life, even the apparently simple issues quickly acquire deeper significance. Thus, women have frequently encountered difficulties in resourcing their activities. Lack of funding has restricted the scope of many initiatives, but at the same time even where funding is offered, there can be difficulties about the acceptability of the source. For example, financial support from state or quasi-state bodies may generate controversy since some women may feel such funding would restrict their freedom of action or inaccurately identify them with government policy. Even support from charitable foundations can be problematic if the source is perceived as having 'links' to one side or the other, as some Irish-American groups have been. Money channelled through the European Community programmes to support peace and reconciliation has been one of the most productive sources for a wide range of voluntary groups including those in which women play leading roles.

Another set of practical difficulties arises from the segregated nature of housing and facilities in many parts of Northern Ireland. Organising meetings or finding a base for ongoing work when members of both communities are involved may be hard in areas where segregation levels are high. Participants may be anxious about travelling to some areas and many buildings may have associations which might make one of the groups uncomfortable. For example, most halls are linked to churches or organisations which have a close link with one section of the community, and even private facilities may be seen as belonging to one of the groups. All of this increases the practical problems for women, many of whom may have limited access to transport and find the time and cost of travelling to a mutually acceptable venue one more obstacle. Problems like this have been particularly strong deterrents for women in working-class areas who face high levels of poverty, as well as for women in rural areas where mobility is frequently a major difficulty. All these issues highlight the dangers in discussing women as a homogeneous group. Thus women's organisations with a largely middle-class, middle-aged membership who have time, resources and available private transport can easily work on a Northern Ireland-wide basis, whilst young mothers in rural areas face difficulties getting even to local events (Morgan and Fraser 1993).

Amid all these problems, women's achievements in community development have been remarkable. It has not always been possible to avoid sensitive and divisive political issues but there has been growing acceptance that this is inevitable and not wholly negative. Indeed one aspect of progress has been the increasing ability to recognise the importance and validity of differing perspectives and to make clear judgements about when they should be faced, how they can be handled sensitively and when it may be better to 'back off' for the moment. Obviously some issues have been more difficult than others. Abortion law reform and 'strip searching', for example, have generated serious dissension, though it is interesting that the two issues divided women along somewhat different lines. Abortion in Northern Ireland is still regulated by legal structures from the mid-nineteenth and early twentieth centuries which in effect render abortion, except on very narrowly defined medical grounds, illegal. A range of women's groups have campaigned for open debate of the issues surrounding the abortion question and reform of the law but other women have raised strong objections to any consideration of the question (Fuerdi 1995). Whilst the cross-currents of opinion are complex, it is clear that there is a coincidence of views opposing reform between women from traditional Catholic and fundamental, evangelical Protestant backgrounds (Rooney 1995). 'Strip searching', the intimate personal searching of women prisoners and sometimes of suspects or women visiting certain groups of prisoners, has been even more publicly contentious for Northern Ireland feminists (Loughran 1981). The women directly involved have almost all been from Republican backgrounds and the official argument has been that strip searching is necessary as part of 'counter-terrorism' to control major security risks, including attempts to smuggle weapons into prisons. As a result, the issues cover both feminist concerns over women's rights and divisive political questions. On the one hand, it has been argued that the central concern must be the personal violation of the women and as a result all women should be prepared to protest and campaign against 'strip searching'. The counter-view has been that, although the procedure is degrading and distasteful, security concerns must take precedence. There have even been suggestions that the women involved have 'brought the problem on themselves' because of their involvement with paramilitary groups. Not surprisingly the division here has been largely along traditional Nationalist/Unionist lines (McWilliams 1995).

Translating to the Larger Stage

The range and extent of women's involvement in community action and community development during the 1980s and early 1990s represents one of the major 'good news' stories from Northern Ireland. In the formal political arena, however, women made less impact. Throughout the period, Northern Ireland was represented in the Westminster and European parliaments exclusively by men. Even at local government level the district councils have been heavily male-dominated with few councils having more than 15 percent women members and some having no women councillors at all (Mahon and Morgan 1999). Overall, the political parties, across the spectrum, showed limited interest either in involving women in their organisational structures or in including issues of central concern to women in their policy formulation. This was particularly true on the Unionist side, where women remained 'token' figures, backroom workers and 'tea-makers' well into the 1990s (Miller et al. 1996; Wilford et al. 1993).

With the declaration of the first set of cease-fires in September and October 1994 and their subsequent reinstatement in late 1995 (after the temporary breakdown of the IRA cease-fire in early 1995), a major question for women activists was how they could make a significant contribution to transforming the political scene. The post cease-fire environment offered the first opportunity in over twenty years to restructure politics in Northern Ireland and reintroduce locally controlled democracy. Could the experience which women had gained at local level, and in the context of specific areas of social and economic development, be used to help to transform the Northern Ireland situation? Women in many areas were conscious from the outset both of the potential presented by the new context and the difficulties they were likely to face, and they tried to raise awareness through as many channels as possible. Even before the first cease-fires were announced, women had been voicing their concerns about the probability that secret negotiations were in progress to end violence, and that since women had no apparent voice in these, their interests might not be properly taken into account in the formulation of any new structures (Clar na mBan 1995). Whilst the Opsahl Commission was gathering information on a spectrum of political, legal, social, religious and cultural issues in Northern Ireland between May 1992 and June 1993, women made a wide range of individual and group contributions, emphasising their frustration with the existing political processes and their inability to influence them (Pollack 1993). In addition, in January 1995, the Northern Ireland Women's European Platform and the National Women's Council for Ireland presented a joint submission to the Forum for Peace and Reconciliation, which was held in Dublin and sponsored by the Irish government. In particular, they drew attention to the contrast between the contribution women had made to community relations and community development in Northern Ireland and their lack of recognition in formal bodies and structures (Forum for Peace and Reconciliation 1995).

After the publication of the Framework Documents in 1995, which set out the views of the British and Irish governments about possible future constitutional structures, women's groups found it difficult to get their views heard. The governments had called for general public debate and were particularly anxious to encourage 'grassroots' participation in the discussion. Many women's groups saw this as an opportunity to make a

positive contribution, but their limited financial resources made it difficult for them to organise meetings and disseminate material. As so often
in the past, potential sources of support had to be avoided because of
their political connotations; nevertheless two women's conferences to
discuss the Framework Documents were held in March and June 1995
(Hinds 1999).

What was becoming increasingly clear by early 1996 was that peace
negotiations were imminent. Therefore, groups of every type and shade
of political opinion were lobbying to ensure that their position was represented. A number of women's organisations, covering a wide regional
and socioeconomic spectrum, came together to try to strengthen the
impact of women's input. They included the Northern Ireland Women's
European Platform, the Derry Women's Centre and the Shankill
Women's Forum. The umbrella group they decided to establish became
the Northern Ireland Women's Coalition. Initially the consensus was
that the best way to make sure that women's concerns were addressed
was by putting pressure on existing political parties. When elections for
a body to facilitate negotiations, the Forum for Peace and Reconciliation,
were announced for May 1996, all the political parties were contacted
and asked to commit themselves to action on a range of issues which
directly affect women's lives, such as the provision of affordable child-
care. The result was disappointing, if hardly surprising. The only clear
and supportive response was from Sinn Féin, most parties did not even
reply. This created a dilemma: should women go on trying to work
through the existing parties or would they have a better chance of being
heard if they had their own candidates? During March and April 1996
there was heated debate and frantic activity, the outcome of which was
the formal registration of the Northern Ireland Women's Coalition as a
party putting forward seventy candidates in the election. Its stated aims
were 'to facilitate reconciliation through dialogue, accommodation and
inclusion, to include women on an equal footing with men and to achieve
an accommodation on which we can build a stable and peaceful future'.[2]
Initially, the Coalition seemed to have little chance of success, but complex electoral procedures were employed in the Forum elections specifically to facilitate the inclusion of smaller parties – especially those linked
to the Loyalist paramilitary groups. As a result, the Women's Coalition's
1.7 percent share of the vote, which placed them ninth in the ranking of
parties by overall support, gave them two seats.

The election of two representatives, Monica McWilliams and Pearl
Sager, attracted considerable media attention, but did it mark a real shift
either in women's political role or in the political structures of Northern

2   Northern Ireland Women's Coalition Website: http://www.pitt.edu/~novosel/northern.html
     (1999); also Hinds (1999).

Ireland? This is clearly a complex question. The inclusion of a wider range of parties, including the Women's Coalition, did introduce a further element of diversity and this continued to widen the cracks which had already begun to emerge in the long-established pattern of monolithic power blocks representing the Nationalist and Unionist communities respectively. On the other hand, the fact that women felt they had to move outside the recognised parties in order to make their voice heard can be read as a measure of the inflexibility of the political structures and an indication that women remain on the margins of political discourse. This uncertainty was mirrored in the debate within the women's movement. Whilst many individuals and groups were enthusiastic in their support for the decision to put forward candidates, others raised a number of concerns. Might the existence of a 'women's party' undermine women who were trying to establish a position within the existing political groupings? Was the Coalition so broad and amorphous that it would be unable to make a clear contribution whilst maintaining internal cohesion? Did the Coalition really represent the views and interests of the women who had been involved in grassroots community development during the 1980s and early 1990s, or was it a largely middle class grouping led by academics? Marie Mulholland, coordinator of the Women's Support Network, suggested that the Coalition was 'colluding with a system that was from the beginning weighted against radical organisations, and there's nothing in the talks process that's of any benefit to our constituencies' (McCafferty).

More significant in the long term, however, may be the question of whether the presence of Coalition representatives in the Forum and at the peace talks which led up to the Good Friday Agreement of April 1998 had any impact. Again judgement is complex and contested. Hard evidence is difficult to acquire given the semi-secret nature of much of the negotiation which preceded the Agreement and the selective leaking, claims and counter-claims which all parties have engaged in (Mitchell 1999). A positive, if subjective, view would be that the members of the Women's Coalition team were able to put forward views which other groups found it difficult to be identified with publicly and thus they could act as informal mediators. Certainly the profile of the Coalition was maintained during the Talks process, with frequent media attention to the representatives and their inputs, and they were able to make very clear their central belief that compromise should be regarded as a positive rather than a negative attribute. Their presence and visibility may also have begun to convince some of the other parties that they need to pay more attention to women's concerns and even to the better representation of women in party structures and policy-making bodies. Even the well-documented abuse which women received from male politicians, especially from members of the UUP and DUP, may have had a positive side. For example, when Monica McWilliams intervened in a debate on the flying of the Union Flag over the building where the Forum was meeting, Peter Robinson of the DUP ended an invective against the Women's Coalition with the comment 'Obviously, Ms McWilliams got out of the wrong side of the bed today. She would do well to cool her temper', whilst Ian Paisley, Jr., replying to a speech by Monica McWilliams on firearms control, commented that he was 'as ever, amazed at the mentality of the Women's Coalition' and in a later debate on contentious parades he interrupted her with shouts of 'moo, moo'. The fact that the women acted with dignity, absorbed abuse and invective and went on pursuing reasoned debate rather than indulging in trading insults helped to highlight the sexist nature of some of their male colleagues. Public distaste for the spectacle may in the long term make such behaviour unacceptable.

Conclusion

Drawing any conclusions about whether women will have a major political impact in a 'new' Northern Ireland remains difficult, especially when the stability and long-term viability of that entity is uncertain. The outcome of the elections in June 1998 for the new Assembly, designed to implement the Good Friday Agreement, did not suggest radical change. The gender balance amongst candidates put forward by the major parties remained predictable, with the Unionist parties still particularly male dominated:

Proportion of women candidates:
DUP   15 percent
Sinn Féin   32 percent
SDLP   27 percent
UUP   9 percent

Similarly, the pattern of those elected gave little indication of change. Of the 108 members of the Assembly 94 were men, with only 14 women (Alliance: 1, Northern Ireland Women's Coalition: 2, UUP: 2, DUP: 1, SDLP: 3, Sinn Féin: 5).[3] There were, however, one or two hopeful signs, the Women's Coalition retained representation in spite of a less favourable electoral system, and Sinn Féin continued to indicate a commitment to gender equality. In addition, in the process of setting up the Executive, two parties, the SDLP and Sinn Féin, nominated women for ministerial posts. Brid Rodgers (SDLP) became Minister of Agriculture and Bairbre de Brun (Sinn Féin) Minister of Health. Cynics have com-

3   See Northern Ireland Assembly Website: http:// www.ni-assembly.gov.uk (1999).

mented that women were given the 'poisoned chalices' of political responsibility, two areas where there are serious underlying problems and little hope of easy solutions. In reality both Ministers have proved decisive and effective, Brid Rodgers in tackling the threat of a major spread of foot and mouth disease from Britain and Bairbre de Brun in addressing the problems of restructuring the hospital service and closing or downgrading the numerous small hospitals in Northern Ireland.

Although the May 1999 elections for the European Parliament did not see a change in the province's all-male representation, the Westminster elections of June 2001 did suggest some movement, though perhaps less than the headline figure, of three women MPs from Northern Ireland, initially suggests. The gender breakdown of candidates, from the five major parties, indicates that although women were being nominated they remained in a minority, particularly in the Unionist parties:

	Male candidates	Female candidates
UUP	15	2
DUP	13	1
SDLP	12	6
Sinn Féin	15	3
Alliance	6	4

Turning to the three women who were elected (Michelle Giddernew – Sinn Féin, Sylvia Hermon – Ulster Unionist, and Iris Robinson – Democratic Unionist Party), it is interesting to note that the two Unionist women both had strong family links to the hierarchy of their respective parties and/or the social/political elite. Sylvia Hermon is the wife of the former Chief Constable of the RUC, Sir Jack Hermon, and Iris Robinson is the wife of Peter Robinson, deputy leader of the DUP.

Clearly there is no basis for complacency in relation to the political or economic progress women have made in Northern Ireland. Indeed it could be argued that the initial period since the establishment of a devolved government for Northern Ireland has been a difficult one. Amidst all the wrangling over decommissioning, police reform and prisoner releases, it has been difficult for women to ensure that their concerns are addressed and that the limited gains which have been made are not lost. Improvements in community relations may owe much to local initiatives in which women have taken the lead and the skills they have developed may be utilised by male community leaders. However, this does not mean that they will be accepted as equal partners. Instead, there may be a trend to mainstream community development and local activism in ways which could marginalise the women who pioneered such activities. The experiences of women in the newly independent Free State (later the Irish Republic) after partition illustrate the tendency of new regimes to revert to tradition in an attempt to establish stability.

Similarly, the treatment of women in many postcolonial contexts where governments have sought to restrict the role of women in the name of respecting cultural traditions and cultural diversity points to ominous possibilities. The difference in Northern Ireland, one hopes, will be that women are now sufficiently aware of the dangers to mount a clear and coherent defence of their rights and claims.

References

Aretxaga, B. 1997. *Shattering Silence: Women, Nationalism and Political Subjectivity in Northern Ireland*. Princeton, NJ.

Bitel, L. M. 1995. 'Do Not Marry the Fat Short One. Early Irish Wisdom on Women', in *Irish Women's Voices Past and Present*, ed. J. Hoff and M. Coulter. Bloomington (Journal of Women's History, Special Edition, vol. 6, no. 4 and vol.7, no. 1).

Boland, E. 1995. 'The Minds and Voices of Irish Women', in *Irish Women's Voices Past and Present*, ed. J. Hoff and M. Coulter, Bloomington (Journal of Women's History, Special Edition, vol. 6, no. 4 and vol.7, no. 1).

Clar na mBan. 1995. *Women's Agenda for Peace*. Belfast.

Condren, M. 1996. *The Serpent and the Goddess: Women, Religion and Power in Celtic Ireland*. San Francisco, CA.

Darby, J. 1997. *Scorpions in a Bottle: Conflicting Cultures in Northern Ireland*. London.

Dunn, S. 1995. *Facets of the Conflict in Northern Ireland*. London.

Edge, S. 1998. 'Representing Gender and National Identity', in *Rethinking Northern Ireland*, ed. D. Miller. London.

Fairweather, E. 1984. *Only the Rivers Run Free: Northern Ireland – the Women's War*. Dublin.

Forum for Peace and Reconciliation. 1995. *Presentations by Panel Drawn from Women's Representative Organisations*. Dublin.

Foster, R. F. 1993. *Paddy and Mr. Punch – Connections in Irish and English History*. London.

Fuerdi, A., ed. 1995. *The Abortion Law in Northern Ireland: Human Rights and Reproductive Choices*. Belfast.

Gardiner, F. 1993. 'Political Interest and Participation of Irish Women 1922 – 1992. The Unfinished Revolution', in *Irish Women's Studies Reader*, ed. A. Smyth. Dublin.

Governments of the United Kingdom and the Republic of Ireland. 1995. *A New Framework for Agreement*. Belfast/Dublin.

Hinds, B. 1999. 'Women Working for Peace in Northern Ireland', in *Contesting Politics: Women in Ireland North and South*, ed. Y. Galligan, E. Ward and R Wilford. Dublin.

Hutchinson, J. 1987. *The Dynamics of Cultural Nationalism: The Gaelic Revival and the Creation of the Irish Nation State*. London.

Kenny, M. 1997. *Goodbye to Catholic Ireland*. London.

Loughran, C. 1981. *Armagh and Feminist Strategy*. London.

Luddy, M. 1997. 'Women and Politics in Nineteenth-Century Ireland', in *Women and Irish History*, ed. M. G. Valiulis and M. O'Dowd. Dublin.

MacCurtain, M. 1985. 'The History Image', in *Irish Women: Image and Achievement*, ed. E. NiChilleanain. Dublin, pp. 37–50.

Mahon, E. and Morgan, V. 1999. 'State Feminism in Ireland', in *Contesting Politics: Women in Ireland North and South*, ed. Y. Galligan, E. Ward and R Wilford. Dublin.

McCafferty, N., 'A Women's Party Outwits the System in Northern Ireland', http://www.pitt.edu/~novosel/northern.html

McWilliams, M. 1995. 'Struggling for Peace and Justice. Reflections on Women's Activism in Northern Ireland', in *Irish Women's Voices Past and Present*, ed. J. Hoff and M. Coulter. Bloomington (Journal of Women's History, Special Edition, vol. 6, no. 4 and vol.7, no. 1).

McWilliams, M. and McKernan, J. 1993. *Bringing it Out to the Open: Domestic Violence in Northern Ireland*. Belfast.

Meek, C. E. and Simms, M. K., ed. 1996. *The Fragility of her Sex? Medieval Irish Women in their European Context*. Dublin.

Miller, R., Wilford, R. and Donaghue, F. 1996. *Women and Political Participation in Northern Ireland*. Aldershot.

Mitchell, G. 1999. *Making Peace*. London.

Morgan, V. 1992. 'Bridging the Divide: Women and Political and Community Issues', in *Social Attitudes in Northern Ireland. Second Report*, ed. P. Stringer and G. Robinson. Belfast.

———1995. 'Women and the Conflict in Northern Ireland', in *Terrorism's Laboratory. The Case of Northern Ireland*, ed. A. O'Day. Aldershot.

———1996. *Peacemakers? Peacekeepers? Women in Northern Ireland 1969–1995*. Derry/Londonderry.

Morgan, V. and Fraser, G. 1993. *The Company We Keep: Women, Community and Organisations in Northern Ireland*. Coleraine.

———1995. 'Women and the Northern Ireland Conflict. Experiences and Responses', in *Facets of the Conflict in Northern Ireland*, ed. S. Dunn. London.

O'Leary, B., Lyne, T., Marshall, J. and Rowthorn, B. 1993. *Northern Ireland – Sharing Authority*. London.

Pollack, A., ed. 1993. *A Citizen's Enquiry – the Opsahl Report on Northern Ireland*. Dublin.

Rendall, J. 1985. *The Origins of Modern Feminism: Women in Britain, France and the United States 1780–1860*. London.

Rooney, E. 1992. 'Women, Community and Politics in Northern Ireland – 'Isms' in Action', in *Journal of Gender Studies* 1: 4 (1992) pp. 475–491.

———1995. 'Political Division, Practical alliance, Problems for Women in Conflict', in *Irish Women's Voices Past and Present*, ed. J. Hoff and M. Coulter, Bloomington (Journal of Women's History, Special Edition, vol. 6, no. 4 and vol.7, no. 1).

Scott, S. L. 1999. *Between the People and Parliament. Local Context, Civil Society and the State in Northern Ireland*. Lexington, KY.

Sutton, M. 1994. *An Index of Deaths from the Conflict in Northern Ireland 1969–93*. Belfast.

Taillon, R. 1992. *Grant Aided – or Taken For Granted : Women's Voluntary Organisations in Northern Ireland*. Belfast.

Vickers, J. 1993. *Women and War*. London.

Ward, M. 1993. 'Suffrage First – Above all Else. An Account of the Irish Suffrage Movement', in *Irish Women's Studies Reader*, ed. A. Smyth. Dublin.

Wilford, R., Miller, R., Bell, Y. and Donaghue, F. 1993. 'In their Own Voices. Women Councillors in Northern Ireland', in *Public Administration* vol. 71, no. 3 (1993), pp. 341–55.

CHAPTER TEN

The Politics of Culture in Northern Ireland

Camille O'Reilly

> 'When I hear anyone talk of culture, I reach for my gun.'
>
> Attributed to Hermann Göhring

Introduction

The discourse of cultural identity is perhaps the most dominant political idiom today, displacing the politics of class. From identity-based social movements of the 1970s to the upheavals of 1989, from anticolonial struggles to ethnic conflict, the rise of the politics of culture has been a global phenomenon, as prevalent in the USA and Europe as in the post-colonial world. While the politics of culture has been a liberating force in some cases, it has also been used to mask or deny relations of power and ideology which underpin inequality and conflict in much of the world.

Culture is the common political currency, appearing in the form of ethnicity, nationality, social class, gender and sexuality, among others. Contemporary identities derive from an array of sources, as often conflicting as integrated or mutually supportive. Many have argued that we now have fragmented identities based on our different and multiple positions in the social world. Culture has come to be the primary idiom through which we express and discuss these identities. In the political sphere, a dominant theme is that all identities must be respected and understood in their own terms, often leading to extremes of cultural relativism which require acceptance and stifle opposition or dissent. In the politics of identity, culture is paramount and virtually untouchable, reified and incorporated into a hegemonic discourse of heritage and tradition.

Culture = Tradition = Legitimacy

This is the formula that dominates the politics of culture in Northern Ireland. Folk concepts of what constitutes 'culture' do include so-called 'high' culture, such as art and literature, but the primary focus of the politics of culture in the North is on certain creative and material manifestations of 'popular' culture, such as traditional music, dance, language, and public displays in the form of parading, mural painting and banners. Certain stereotypes lurk in the background, and occasionally appear on people's lips or in the press: 'Protestants do not have a culture', or, 'they do have a culture but one which is based on negation and hatred'. 'Catholics cling to a backward and old-fashioned culture which is centred on a dying language and a repressive religion', or, 'they have a rich culture and tradition deeply rooted in their Gaelic past'. The discourse of culture is tinged with power and ideology, whether explicit or implicit, and has increasingly become so during the last decade.

History, and the related concept of tradition, are key tools in the legitimisation and construction of culture – and in particular political and politicised culture – in the North. According to Bruce, 'tradition' enters into the politics of Northern Ireland with the Anglo-Irish Agreement, but culture has been a part of Northern Irish politics from the foundation of the state in 1921 (Bruce 1994). 'Protestant culture' – perceived as British and promoted through institutions like the Orange Order – was institutionalised as part of the Unionist state under Stormont, while 'Irish culture' was marginalised and seen as inimical to the state. With the end of the Stormont regime, some Protestants perceived their culture and way of life as being in retreat or under attack. At the same time, some Catholics began to see Protestants as being essentially without culture, at least in contrast with their own traditions.

Aspects of Irish culture became increasingly visible in the public sphere throughout the 1970s and 1980s, with the growth in popularity of traditional music and dancing, and then a revitalisation of the Irish language revival movement. During the 1980s, the politics of culture became institutionalised in a new way through the emerging concepts of 'common heritage' and 'two traditions' promoted by quasi-governmental bodies such as the Community Relations Council (CRC) and the Cultural Traditions Group (CTG). In part as a response to these developments, certain sections of the Protestant community began to promote Ullans as the native language of the eastern part of Ulster, adding still another dimension to the struggle over the politics of culture, and ultimately the legitimate right to govern Northern Ireland. These three developments will be investigated as case studies in Northern Ireland's politics of culture in the course of this chapter, which will conclude with an assessment of the overall relevance of the politics of culture to the future of the North.

Before addressing the specific case of Northern Ireland, it is helpful to look more closely at what is meant by the 'politics of culture'. For many English speakers, to 'be cultured' is to acquire tastes for the finer things in life – art, gourmet cuisine and classical music. Culture is used in this sense in Northern Ireland as well, but 'to have a culture' has somewhat different connotations. Anthropological definitions of culture can serve as a baseline for our discussion. Most introductory texts emphasise an ideational definition of culture – systems of shared ideas, concepts, meanings and beliefs – rather than using the term in a broader sense to include material culture.

A politics of culture, however, derives from an understanding of the concept that is both broader and narrower than this. It is broader in the sense that it includes many aspects of material culture which serve to identify and confirm the existence of a particular culture, and reaffirm the boundaries between one culture and another. It is narrower in the sense that it refers to those aspects of culture of which people tend to be consciously aware, rather than the systems of knowledge and beliefs through which we interpret our world and of which we are often not consciously aware. Handler (1988) discusses objectification as an inherent part of nationalist cultural production. It is the ability to see culture as a 'thing', to stand back and look at one's culture as an entity in itself. The implications of this are that culture is seen as being made up of particular traits, and is taken to be bounded and continuous in space and time. This leads to the idea that a culture 'bears' certain properties, and that individuals can 'have' a culture (rather than simply living it). In this chapter, I use the term 'politics of culture' to refer to a political idiom where action and belief are expressed, justified and explained in terms of culture, heritage and tradition, where culture is often understood in its popular sense as a quality that some people possess but others do not – a knowledge of the Irish language, for example, or a particular version of British history.

Along with the spread of nationalism as the dominant mode of political organisation in the world today, and the rise of ethnicity as a key means of constructing and expressing group identity, the politics of culture has become part of a hegemonic discourse of identity and political practice. Ethnic identity is as fundamental as gender identity and represents therefore an integral and 'primordial' aspect of our sense of individual self and group membership. For example, certain aspects of culture become reified through the process of nationalist cultural construction as an aspect of the politics of culture.

The last two terms – heritage and tradition – are complex, value-laden concepts that require some unpacking. In the general sense, 'heritage' and 'tradition' are part of a larger discourse which has come to dominate politics in much of the world. It is developing into a hegemonic discourse in the sense that it limits and shapes the options available for reply, and is difficult to dispute except within its own terms of debate. Cultural identity is as much about defining the 'Other' as about defining oneself. The use of heritage and tradition excludes those who do not or cannot share in it, and can thus be used as a tool of domination by one group over another. To cite just one example, Orange marches are now justified in terms of tradition, but are often used to intimidate and to assert ownership and dominance.[1]

Northern Ireland offers an interesting example of a politics of culture that has developed in recent decades within the context of violent conflict. Politics of culture is a long-standing phenomenon in Northern Ireland, predating the current phase of the conflict. Since the creation of the state, Catholic exclusion and Protestant dominance has been justified at least in part in cultural terms. Cultural stereotypes reinforced community division, and cultural practices such as Orange parades and mural painting were clearly used and interpreted as acts of dominance (Bryan 2000; Jarman 1997). The difference is primarily one of degree and of the contexts in which it is unfolding, both global and regional. Globally, the discourse of heritage and cultural tradition has become increasingly hegemonic. In Northern Ireland, the terms in which the conflict is carried out have shifted and changed. Culture is still used in the service of power, but increasingly it has been used to challenge and contest it as well. As a key aspect of the Good Friday Agreement and subsequent negotiations, the politics of culture continues to be an essential part of political life in Northern Ireland. To cite just one example, the ongoing struggle over the rerouting of Orange marches away from Catholic areas is perceived by many Protestants as symbolic of their loss of power and status over the last few years of political negotiation.[2]

Institutionalisation

Northern Ireland's political culture is deeply divided, and consequently so is the politics of culture. Irish folk traditions are considered by many to be Nationalist, as is the Irish language. Nationalists have a richer political symbolism on which to draw, particularly by dipping into the vocabulary of popular resistance from around the world. Because these cultural characteristics have come to be seen as Nationalist, they are considered to be off-limits and 'foreign' to Unionist political culture, which consequently has a much more limited scope of symbols on which to draw. This polarisation makes middle ground or neutral territory

1   See Dominic Bryan's chapter in this volume on marches and parades in Northern Ireland.
2   See Bryan's chapter.

extremely difficult to find or construct. When it is constructed, it can appear stilted and superficial as there is so little from which to make it that is not already taken up by one or another tradition.

Nevertheless, the search for consensus solutions has been a preferred mode of conflict management, particularly favoured by government. 'Righting wrongs' or tackling issues of sovereignty or political and economic inequality are not part of the strategy. In a pamphlet called 'Whither Cultural Diversity?' Maurice Hayes (1991), chairman of the CTG from 1990 to 1993, writes:

> Much of what presents itself as intergroup or ethnic conflict is, I believe, determined by the self-perception of the groups concerned, their perception of others, and their preconceptions of others' view of them. Underlying most of these conflicts is a failure of communication, a lack of empathy and understanding which results in stereotyping and scapegoating, and a basic lack of trust without which no social, political or other contract is conceivable. (Hayes 1991)

If this is how the problem is defined, solutions will tend to focus on integrationist programmes and projects that fall under the heading 'community relations'. The 'two traditions' and 'common heritage' approaches of the CRC and the CTG developed in a context where this was the dominant approach to the Northern Ireland conflict.

The word 'traditional' is heavily laden with meaning and connotation. It suggests deep roots, authenticity, goodness, realness, something that is 'ours', the correct way of doing things, that which is moral and right. By implication, that which is not traditional is shallow, recent, inauthentic, alienated, not good or even bad, foreign or imported, imposed or unwanted, immoral. To ask that traditional practices be changed or abandoned is tantamount to being the enemy of all that is moral and right. That which was made peripheral through processes of modernisation, perceived as 'backward' and perhaps undesirable, is now often seen as authentic and untouched by a soulless modernity (Chapman 1992; McDonald 1989; MacDonald 1997). 'Traditional' has become a desirable label in many contexts, and one which carries a great deal of political clout.

Particularly since the 1980s, the concept of heritage has been coopted into attempts to produce a shared version of Northern Ireland's history. Culture, especially in the form of heritage, is seen by many as a vehicle for political reconciliation. According to Bell (1998), the Northern Ireland Office (NIO) and its agencies promote this in discourse and action. Community relations politics, he argues, are an attempt to foster consensus within the structural status quo and avoid significant constitutional change. The heritage and cultural traditions industry also has economic goals, particularly linked to tourism, for example in the form of museums and interpretive centres. The politics and economics of heritage and tradition encourage a view of history as spectacle, fable and myth, presented to the viewer in static and reified form.

Constructing heritage and tradition is part of national and cultural imagining both inside and outside of Northern Ireland, and always has political implications. Its political use can and should be critiqued, however, and not simply accepted at face value. This is particularly true when discussing an organisation explicitly designed to deal with culture and tradition at an institutional level on behalf of powerful government bodies.

The CTG, founded in 1988 and coming under the umbrella of the CRC[3] in 1990, is an organisation with a remit 'to provide support and facilities for organisations, operating at local level, concerned with the development of community relations, awareness of cultural diversity and conflict resolution' (CTG 1995: 7). This is accomplished through the distribution of grants to community groups, language and history projects, and theatre productions; fellowships and the commissioning of relevant research; a media scheme which has produced a number of television programmes; and a publications scheme which produces teaching and learning materials for different organisations. A real challenge for the CTG has been to fund projects that will promote debate and challenge stereotypes, rather than simply reinforcing them.

The original agenda of the CTG was liberal in the classical sense – education and knowledge are liberating in and of themselves. This has proved to be a rather woolly concept on which to base decisions about which projects to fund. During 1999, the CRC underwent a process of restructuring in an attempt to be more proactive and to find ways of identifying and supporting projects with more of a critical 'edge'. From late 1999 the restructured CTG became known as the Cultural Diversity Programme. The aim of the programme will be to challenge overly simplistic ideas about the two main traditions in the North by promoting cultural diversity in a positive light in the public domain. A common criticism of the CTG has been that it tends to perpetuate an overly polarised view of two homogeneous, mutually exclusive communities, whether intentionally or not. The new Cultural Diversity Programme aims to rectify this by focusing on diversity both within the entire population of Northern Ireland, and within each community, taking greater account of the particular experiences of rural populations, women, the disabled, gays and lesbians, travellers, and ethnic minorities. It remains to be seen what impact these changes in the CRC will have, but it is clear that the fundamentally pluralist agenda remains.

Bell (1998) argues that the reconstruction of popular history through the heritage industry is part of the process of forging a political settlement in Northern Ireland around a distinctly pluralist agenda. This has

---

3   The CRC is a government-funded, grant-giving body with charitable status. It is funded by the Central Community Relations Unit, a part of the Department of Finance and Personnel.

led to attempts at mutual understanding through an awareness of what led to current divisions in society. The Tower Museum in Derry is one such example of the heritage industry attempting to confront modern divisions and promote pluralism through a display of both popular and academic accounts of history. Contemporary sectarian divisions can be dealt with openly in such a context, once they are rendered harmless by their presentation as 'cultural tradition' (Bell 1998: 239). The danger here, though, is that the 'two traditions' are being reified into two monoliths, unchanging and unchangeable. As Bruce (1994) points out, there is a risk that the cultural traditions project will simply produce more committed and better informed protagonists, and promote what Butler (1994) calls 'balanced sectarianism'.

Other heritage museums, however, strive to present a common heritage for all the people of Northern Ireland; an example is the Ulster Folk and Transport Museum, which studiously avoids direct references to culture or history that might be divisive. The implied message is that the two communities in the North have much in common in terms of both heritage and tradition. Again, although this is a laudable aim, it does little to address the root causes of conflict.

While the ultimate goal may be noble and sincere, a real problem with the presentation of the conflict as two opposing cultural traditions is that it tends to neutralise the power politics of a sectarian state. The politics of disenfranchisement and economic dominance become simply a matter of culture, and their solution an overly simplistic matter of increased understanding. The term 'tradition' is problematic in itself, because it implies something that is owed respect – simply another way of life, another interpretation among many equally valid interpretations. Sectarianism and bigotry, the legacy of generations of inequality and Unionist domination, are rendered nearly invisible.

This does have its advantages, and clearly helped to lay the groundwork for the political negotiations and progress since 1994. Nevertheless, bigotry is alive and well in spite of liberal wishful thinking. Events during the last years and the difficulties in setting up the Northern Ireland Executive in 1999 show that there are still some Unionists who refuse to share power with Catholics, no matter what the context or circumstances. This is not to say there is no bigotry emanating from the other side – there is – but the nature of current political structures means that Unionist sectarianism has the ability to make a far greater impact on political progress. Simple refusal to participate on the part of Unionists would be enough to collapse the process and possibly bring an end to the institutions established under the Good Friday Agreement.

Rolston (1998) offers a critique of the multiculturalist approach in Northern Ireland in an article on liberalism and the conflict. Four of his points are particularly relevant to a critique of the cultural traditions agenda. First, there is an over-reliance on sociopsychological explanations for the conflict. Sectarianism is seen as a structure of personal prejudice, with little attention paid to institutional aspects. Second, constructions of cultural tradition tend to either deny or depoliticise history. This is perhaps an inevitable outcome of attempts to find ground which will be acceptable to all, or at the very least offend none. Third, there is a tendency towards reductionism, with just about everything being boiled down to culture. Difficult structural issues such as colonialism, political institutions, triumphalism, institutionalised discrimination and state power are rarely taken into account. Fourth is the problematic concept of the 'two traditions'. The irony is that the discourse of two traditions has done a great deal to mask the complexities of diversity in the North, even as it attempts to promote diversity. From attempts to build a middle ground consensus to attempts to implement parity of esteem, the game has only two players.

Much of the work of the CTG has been very constructive, and it has no doubt contributed in its own way to helping create the conditions for political negotiations to take place. While there is clearly a place for an organisation which seeks to promote mutual understanding and cultural diversity, there are real problems with the pluralist approach and the promotion of a multicultural agenda if it takes the place of substantive efforts to change the root causes of conflict in Northern Ireland.

Politics of Culture, Politics of Resistance

Over the last decade, the Irish language has taken centre stage in the politics of culture in Northern Ireland. There is broad support for the language among Nationalists, and a rather generalised feeling that it is an important part of Irish identity. For many Nationalists, the status of the Irish language is seen as a sort of litmus test for 'parity of esteem' for Catholics in Northern Ireland.

Bell (1998) argues that the strategy of multiculturalism of the 1980s eventually took the form of calls for parity of esteem by the mid-1990s. In Bell's reading of the situation, the right to publicly celebrate Irishness in a cultural sense has been given in exchange for an acceptance from Nationalist political representatives of the principle of consent, which guarantees the constitutional *status quo* of Northern Ireland until a majority of the population of Northern Ireland votes otherwise. The public acceptance of expressions of Irishness gave some hope to Nationalists. Concrete evidence of this change came in the form of Nationalist marches being allowed into Belfast city centre for the first time in the early 1990s, and bit by bit through the provision of limited funding for Irish cultural projects, particularly those relating to the Irish language.

Since there was already a small but fairly healthy grassroots revival movement, Irish has become a key plank in this politico-cultural struggle
(O'Reilly 1996).

Despite an overall consensus of opinion among Nationalists on the
general value of the Irish language, the symbolic and practical meanings
of Irish and its revival are by no means agreed. Different groups seek to
advance their own interpretations of the importance and meaning of the
language, while representatives of the British government also compete
to neutralise the impact of this powerful symbol of identity. The contested nature of the language is reflected in different interpretations of
events and institutions associated with Irish, and is played out in the discourse used to talk about the language, its revival, and its social, cultural
and political role in Ireland today. The formation of the ULTACH Trust
and the controversy over the withdrawal of funding for the west Belfast
Irish language organisation 'Glór na nGael' were part of the trend
towards multiculturalism as a government policy and the struggle over
the political shape and significance of this new 'public' Irish identity
(O'Reilly 1997; 1999).

The politics of the Irish language do not begin here, however. Irish has
been a part of the politics of culture in Ireland since the turn of the last
century. As the language was coming to its final stages of decline as an
ordinary means of communication, it became the object of some intellectual interest. There was a surge of academic and antiquarian interest
in the Irish language in the 1830s and 1840s, but then there was a dip in
revival activities until the end of the century. The founding of the Gaelic
League in 1893 marked the beginning of a new phase of the revival, as
well as the beginning of the powerful association between the Irish language and Nationalism. As the Irish language revival became increasingly
associated with the struggle for Irish independence, it split the movement.[4] After the partition of the island in 1921, Irish became the official
language of the newly independent Irish Free State, even though the
vast majority of the population spoke English as their first language.

The fortunes of the language were quite different in the newly formed
state of Northern Ireland. For the fifty-year period from partition to
1972, the UUP (and its predecessor, the Unionist Party) ruled Northern
Ireland's parliament at Stormont. The dominant ideological forces of
Northern Irish society under this regime were inimical to the Irish language, and the state itself was self-consciously anti-Irish (Mac Póilin
1995). Official policy reflected the attitude that Irish was a foreign language, therefore negating its legitimacy in Northern Ireland. Throughout
the history of Northern Ireland, government policy has continued to

---

4   See Dunleavy and Dunleavy (1991) for the relationship between Nationalism and the Irish
    language revival movement at the turn of the century, and Hutchinson (1987).

oscillate between hostility and disregard, although more enlightened attitudes have been demonstrated on occasion since the fall of Stormont. For
example, in 1974 the Department of Education issued a report which
advocated second-language teaching in general, and which acknowledged
the particular attributes of Irish (Maguire 1991: 74). Unfortunately, this
was not reinforced in any concrete way through policy or planning initiatives.

In spite of official attitudes of indifference and antipathy, the Irish language has continued to find a niche in the North, and interest has been
growing at a steady rate for the last few decades. Over the past two
decades the Irish-medium schools have been the heart of the revival
movement. The first all-Irish primary school, Bunscoil Phobal Feirste,
was established in 1971 to cater for the children of the Shaws Road
Gaeltacht. Since then, eleven other primary schools and two secondary
schools have opened in Northern Ireland, all of them sponsored and supported by parents and the local community until government funding can
be obtained.

As the revival movement has grown it has become an increasingly
important part of the politics of culture that has come to prevail in the
North. As its influence has increased, the struggle to define the significance of the language and its revival has become more intense. The parameters of debate can be clearly seen through an examination of the
discourses of the revival movement – decolonising discourse, cultural
discourse and rights discourse.

At least since the split in the Gaelic League, which culminated in the
resignation of Douglas Hyde from his position as president in 1915, there
has been an ideological division between those who made a strong association between the Irish language and the political independence of Ireland,
and those who sought to keep politics outside of efforts to revive the language. The production, reproduction, contestation and transformation of
different ideologies in the struggle for hegemony in the Irish language
revival movement can be seen in writing and speech about the language.

Particularly in the first half of the 1980s, decolonising discourse was
associated with quite an extreme ideology. Irish was literally seen as a
weapon in the arsenal available to fight the British. A well-known statement demonstrates this position. A prominent member of Sinn Féin,
who is also an Irish-language activist, once said at a public meeting 'every
word of Irish spoken is like another bullet being fired in the struggle for
Irish freedom'. In the course of its development, decolonising discourse
seems to have been somewhat moderated. It would be relatively unusual,
for example, to hear someone make such a statement today, although
many continue to make a direct connection between freedom for Ireland
and the Irish language revival. For some people, the political struggle
goes hand in hand with the cultural struggle.

Certain key words, concepts and arguments indicate the use of the decolonising discourse: 'resistance' or 'cultural resistance', 'oppression', Irish as a 'weapon', cultural 'struggle', particularly as part of a wider anti-colonial struggle, and 'Republican', or a strong association made with Republican ideals or beliefs. Discourses of anti-imperialism, decolonisation or political struggle are frequently used in association with the Irish language. Connections are often explicitly made between a person's Nationalist political development and their interest in the Irish language. Speaking and learning Irish are seen as political acts. Irish is also seen as a particularly powerful expression of national, and not simply ethnic, identity.

Cultural discourse stands in ideological opposition to decolonising discourse. The clearest and most dominant feature of cultural discourse is the assertion that the Irish language and politics should be kept completely separate. The corollary is that the importance of the language lies in its beauty and cultural worth, not its political capital. What exactly is meant by 'politics', however, is not generally made explicit. When a person says the language should be kept apolitical, they are often making a veiled comment on the perceived relationship of the Irish language to Republicanism, usually casting it in an unfavourable light.

Like decolonising discourse, cultural discourse has a relatively long history. Probably the best-known advocate of an apolitical view of the Irish language was Douglas Hyde, president of the Gaelic League from its inception in 1893 until his resignation (over the issue of politics and the language) in 1915. According to Hutchinson (1987), Hyde was a cultural Nationalist embroiled in a classic confrontation with political Nationalists. He argues that the two forms of Nationalism articulate different conceptions of the nation and have diverging political strategies, as Hyde found to his detriment. It was during this period that the association between the ideology of Nationalism and the Irish language became so dominant that it was almost taken for granted as a 'natural' connection. The powerful association between Irish Nationalism and the Irish language remains to this day as a serious issue of debate.

In the ideology of cultural discourse, the Irish language must be kept strictly removed from party politics. The view of the relationship between politics and the language associated with cultural discourse is often strongly anti-Republican. The language ought to be kept wholly 'apolitical'. Instead of naturalising the relationship between Irish and Nationalism, this connection is challenged or denied, although some connection between romantic or cultural Nationalism is implicit.

There are certain key words, concepts and arguments that indicate the use of cultural discourse: 'apolitical', 'nonpolitical', 'depoliticise', 'beautiful language', 'heritage' and 'tradition', or 'cultural heritage' and 'cultural tradition' (as distinct from political heritage and traditions).

Accusations that the language is being politicised, or attacks on specific individuals or groups for politicising Irish, figure prominently. Anti-Republican discourse and the discourse of community relations are often associated with the language, and it appears frequently in the discourse of the CTG. A connection is frequently made between a person's interest in Irish and its inherent creativity, history, songs and literature. Speaking Irish is generally seen as a cultural activity, and it tends to be seen as an expression of ethnic or cultural identity (in contrast to the more dangerous and divisive political or Nationalist expressions of identity).

The first two discourses have congealed into a form that is heavily laden with meaning, creating a restrictive framework within which it is difficult to manoeuvre. Rights discourse is less straightforward than the decolonising and cultural discourses, in part because it is an attempt to sidestep the issues which lead into the political/apolitical deadlock, but also because it attempts to broaden and reframe the debate over politics and the Irish language. In recent years, this has been achieved primarily through the issue of rights for Irish speakers and a promotion of the idea of parity of esteem. Discourses of Civil Rights, human rights and minority rights have been adapted as a means of campaigning for the language and developing an ideology that challenges the confines of the dominant dichotomy.

The roots of rights discourse are not as historically deep as those of the other two discourses. Evidence of decolonising and cultural discourses can be found both at the turn of the century and in more recent debates over the relationship between politics and the Irish language. However, I have been unable to find evidence of a discourse similar to rights discourse preceding the current phase of the revival which roughly coincides with the start of 'the Troubles'. The lack of evidence of rights discourse from earlier periods suggests that it has more recent origins. Certainly there have always been people who did not engage in the debate over politics and the Irish language, but silence seems to have been the main alternative available to them.

Rights discourse is also signalled by particular key words, concepts and arguments: 'rights', 'Civil Rights' and 'human rights', 'you can't hijack a language', 'equality', 'parity of esteem', the responsibility of government to support minority cultures and uphold minority rights, and a denial that Irish can be wholly apolitical in the current sociopolitical context in Northern Ireland. Attempts are sometimes made to separate political allegiance from ethnic identity. And, importantly, the promotion of Irish is put above all other political and cultural considerations.

The following examples illustrate some of these characteristics. During a discussion of Sinn Féin's involvement with the Irish language, one man in his forties told me:

I have a problem with people who don't run around and promote the language. To people who say Sinn Féin has hijacked the language, I'd say go you and hijack the language. But I wouldn't even accept the charge that they have. I would urge people who do think so to go and try to beat them at their own game.

During a discussion about the rights of minority language speakers and the responsibilities of government, another person said:

C. O'R.: Do you see any conflict in trying to get the British government to do things in support of Irish, when you say you believe they don't belong here in the first place?

Answer: No, because we have to face the reality that we live under British rule whether we like it or not. If they left, then we'd have to face the same problems with an Irish administration. Whatever administration is there, it's there to provide us services. It owes us services because we pay for those services. The state claims that cultural diversity is a nice thing, but now they have to pay for it. They need to have a civil servant in every department that speaks Irish, and that costs money.

The essential difference between discourses is in the conceptualisation of the relationship between the Irish language, politics and culture. In decolonising discourse, Irish is nested firmly within party politics in general and Republicanism in particular. In cultural discourse, an attempt is made to remove Irish from party politics and to place it into the realm of culture, and occasionally into the politics of reconciliation. In rights discourse, politics in the general sense (as opposed to party politics) is nested within the struggle to revive Irish, which is seen as the primary objective and eclipses all other considerations in terms of importance.

Various campaigns to promote the Irish language – such as the campaign for bilingual Irish/English street signs in certain areas and efforts to get government funding for organisations that promote the language – have taken place over the last twenty years. These debates have occurred through the medium of these three discourses, contributing to their development at the same time as they work within their frameworks. Even as people struggle over particular issues, they are participating in a much wider debate about Irish identity and the position of Nationalists within a state that has historically been hostile to that identity.

Perhaps unsurprisingly, the CTG has played a key role in the politics of the Irish language. Irish has been an important part of the CTG's work from the beginning. 'From the outset', the booklet Giving Voices states, 'the new committee realized that it had to pass what was called the 'green litmus test' – finding a credible policy on the Irish language' (CTG 1995: 6).

The main object of the CTG is to promote discussion and debate about the validity of the various cultural traditions in Northern Ireland in a constructive and nonconfrontational atmosphere. One shorthand was to help Protestants to contemplate the Irish language without necessarily feeling offended by it, or for Catholics to look on Orange processions without feeling intimidated. Of course this rather begs the question that some Orange processions are indeed intended to assert a claim to territory, or to superiority, and sometimes to intimidate, and some manifestations of the Irish language are precisely employed in order to cause as much offence as possible to Unionists. (CTG 1995: 9)

In Hayes's view, the Irish language can be viewed as a kind of 'shorthand' for Catholic or Nationalist culture, and presented to Unionists as a nonthreatening manifestation of that culture. This is not entirely consistent with another view expressed by the CTG, where Irish is portrayed as belonging collectively to both Catholics and Protestants. The problem is indicative of two conflicting versions of the cultural traditions discourse. Hayes is drawing on the 'two traditions' version, while the latter view is from the 'common heritage' discourse (McCoy 1996).

Of course, the apolitical claims of organisations like the CTG are not taken at face value by everyone concerned. People and organisations which favour decolonising or rights discourses are not inclined to accept a situation which casts them in a less than favourable light. In a situation where the equation 'political equals bad' has come to predominate, three basic strategies can be taken to combat the status quo. First, it is often pointed out that the use and promotion of the cultural discourse is anything but apolitical in practice. This is reinforced easily enough with examples of the political use of this discourse, particularly with reference to the 'vilification' of Sinn Féin. Second, an attempt can be made to suggest that the connection between the Irish language and an Irish or Nationalist identity is a 'natural' one, usually by the use of historical references which connect the two, and occasionally by pointing out that Protestants/Unionists for the most part have no interest in the language. And third, the use of decolonising discourse and rights discourse continually challenges the representations created by cultural discourse.

The position of these three discourses in the political arena is continually in flux, as users adapt their approaches to suit changing circumstances. Since the implementation of the Good Friday Agreement began, decolonising discourse has become almost completely defunct, at least in public usage. Cultural discourse is still in use, but no longer holds the position of power it once had since it is no longer necessary to use it in order to gain access to funding or the ear of important government agencies and officials. Rights discourse, on the other hand, has very much come into its own. No longer the voice of the outsider but still oppositional in attitude, it is increasingly the discourse of the newly institutionalised sectors of the Irish language revival movement.

A Linguistic Counter-attack: Ulster-Scots

Ulster-Scots is closely related to Scots, which is spoken by many people in the lowland areas of Scotland. Scots grew out of the Northumbrian dialect of Old English, and has developed many characteristics that are distinct from modern English. Scots was the official language of the Scottish state during the fifteenth and sixteenth centuries, but was abandoned by James VI when he became James I of England. After 1707 when the Scottish parliament was dissolved, English became the dominant language of the upper classes and of literacy. However, Scots continued to be the language of ordinary people, and has its own literary tradition, best known through the works of the poet Robert Burns (1759-96). A literary Scots, which came to be known as Lallans, continued to develop and experienced a revival in the 1920s. The New Testament was translated into Lallans in the 1980s, and appears in such contemporary novels as Irvine Welsh's Trainspotting. Whether Scots is a dialect of English or a language in its own right is still a matter for debate among linguists and Scots alike.

Ulster-Scots, now sometimes referred to as Ullans, was brought to Ireland by Presbyterian Scots speakers during the plantations of the seventeenth century. Most settled in Counties Antrim, Down and Donegal, which are part of the historical province of Ulster. As local Catholics were exposed to Scots, a distinctive Ulster English developed which is now spoken by most of the residents of Ulster regardless of their religious or ethnic affiliation. The relationship of Ulster-English to Ulster-Scots is not entirely clear, and many would argue that they are much the same thing.

Ulster-Scots was never a language of education or officialdom, although it did develop something of a literary tradition, principally poetry. It is now spoken mostly by rural farming communities in Counties Antrim, Down and Donegal. Throughout the 1990s, Ulster-Scots has been drawn into the increasingly potent politics of culture in Northern Ireland. In 1992 the Ulster-Scots Language Society was formed with the following aims: to encourage an interest in Ulster-Scots literature; to support the use of Ulster-Scots in everyday speech and education; and to encourage the Ulster-Scots tradition in music, dance, song and storytelling. Throughout the 1990s, the CTG has supported projects related to Ulster-Scots, alongside its support for the Irish language. In 1993, Ulster-Scots was recognised as a variety of the Scots language by the European Bureau of Lesser-Used Languages, which makes its decisions based on the views of the language community concerned rather than solely linguistic criteria. The British government also recognised Ulster-Scots as a variety of the Scots language when it signed the European Charter for Lesser Used Languages in March 2000. In terms of the politics of culture in Northern Ireland, however, Ulster-Scots received its greatest boost through its inclusion in the Good Friday Agreement of 1998, which states:

> All participants recognise the importance of respect, understanding and tolerance in relation to linguistic diversity, including in Northern Ireland, the Irish language,

Ulster-Scots and the languages of the various ethnic communities, all of which are part of the cultural wealth of the island of Ireland.

As part of the new political structures that were established in the wake of the Agreement, a Linguistic Diversity Unit was formed within a branch of the Northern Ireland Office to deal with both Ulster-Scots and the Irish language (and in theory at least, other ethnic minority languages). Once cross-border institutions were established, the newly formed Language Implementation Body was given a remit to support both Ulster-Scots and Irish.

Within the framework of the politics of culture, there are certain essential traits or characteristics that must be present in order for a culture to be considered 'authentic'. The dominant popular model of an ethnically distinct group includes a fairly standardised set of cultural criteria, of which language is one of the most important elements. Some critics have argued that the promotion of Ulster-Scots as a language in its own right is an attempt by Unionists to compete with the level of authenticity enjoyed by Nationalist-dominated movements such as the Irish language revival. Rolston, for example, argues that the CTG supports Ulster-Scots as part of an artificial attempt to achieve symmetry with its support for the Irish language (Rolston 1998: 271). He sees efforts to categorise Ulster-Scots as a language as a kind of mimicry that substitutes for a genuine exploration of Unionist identity and culture.

McCoy argues that Unionists who wish to combat Nationalist cultural politics have four strategies.[5] They can denigrate Irish culture in general, and the Irish language in particular, as romantic nonsense. This is a common theme, and Irish is frequently referred to in some Unionist circles as a 'dead' language. Second, they can refuse to play the cultural 'game', opting instead to present Unionism as a rational political ideal with no need for nationalism of any kind. Nevertheless, some Unionists suffer from the suspicion that their political arguments are somehow weaker if they lack a cultural dimension. Third, a small minority of Unionists have attempted to appropriate aspects of Irish culture, attempting to disconnect Irish culture and Irish Nationalism. The suggestion is that it is possible to be culturally Irish, but politically Unionist and maintain a British identity, in much the same way as many Scots have a Scottish cultural identity but a British political identity. Fourth, they can engage in the politics of culture by promoting newly created or rediscovered traditions of their own. McCoy suggests that some Unionists who regard language as a valuable symbol of national identity want to promote their own language, Ulster-Scots, to compete directly with Nationalists who support the Irish language.

5   Gordon McCoy: personal communication.

The question of whether Ulster-Scots is a language, a dialect of English, a dialect of Scots, or simply 'English spoken with a Ballymena accent' (Ryder 1999) has been at the centre of debate concerning the legitimacy of the claims of its supporters as well as Unionist identity more generally. Opinions on this issue are strongly influenced by political agendas, with 'dialect' being perceived by some as a derogatory label, therefore utilising terms such as 'linguistic heritage', 'linguistic diversity', 'tradition' and 'tongue', which avoid taking a side in the language versus dialect debate. While some, like the Ulster-Scots Language Society, are willing to admit that Ulster-Scots is a dialect rather than a language, they tend to see it as a dialect of Scots rather than of English.

Without taking a strong stance on the language/dialect issue, Herbison (1989) points out that Ulster-Scots is part of a robust literary tradition not just through its association with Scots, but also through its own independent tradition as exemplified by the Rhyming Weavers, followers of the Burns poetic tradition, who wrote in their own vernacular. He argues that Ulster-Scots is an important part of the cultural identity of Ulster Presbyterians, and points out that it has been used with political impact as early as the late eighteenth and early nineteenth centuries (Herbison 1989: 6f.).

The constitution of the Ulster-Scots Language Society states that it is a nonsectarian and nonpolitical organisation. According to some sources, at least one member of Sinn Féin is also a member of the Society. Many are keen to point out that Catholics as well as Protestants speak Ulster-Scots. The key division is actually a rural/urban one rather than a sectarian one, with Ulster-Scots being spoken in some rural areas while urban areas are dominated by English. Nevertheless, for now at least, Ulster-Scots is firmly planted into the Unionist political and cultural arena. Parallel to Irish, most Ulster-Scots activities take place in Protestant areas. It is used symbolically on the notepaper of the Unionist-dominated Newtownards Borough Council, and many who are interested in it feel it expresses their Ulster Unionist identity.

Some Unionist politicians have turned the arguments used by Irish language activists to their benefit, arguing for parity of esteem for Ulster-Scots in relation to Irish, particularly with reference to funding. This stance tends to be associated with the more extreme wing of Unionism. For example, Ulster-Scots was used in the campaign literature of groups agitating for a 'no' vote to the Good Friday Agreement, and Ian Paisley's DUP used it on an election poster and in their manifesto. Language debates featured prominently in the early days of the new Northern Ireland Assembly, with some members addressing the Assembly in Irish, while others threatened to retaliate by speaking in Ulster-Scots. Meanwhile, many Nationalists see claims for status and funding for Ulster-Scots as spurious, nothing more than an attempt to undermine the status of Irish.

Since 1997, however, there has been increased cooperation between activists on both sides, in spite of their political differences. Funding bodies such as the CTG approve of cooperation methods, so these initiatives could be seen as a cynical attempt by both parties to secure more funding. On the other hand, cooperation could be interpreted as a kind of curiosity across the divide which should be welcomed and encouraged. According to McCoy, a primary reason for this increase in cooperation is that dialogue and diversity are now in political vogue because of the peace process.[6] Even Belfast City Council, site of considerable conflict over the Irish language in recent years, now has a Cultural Diversity Committee on which Irish and Ulster-Scots speakers work together to promote their respective languages.

In a personal communication to the author, McCoy relates the Ulster-Scots movement to challenges to Protestant identity in Northern Ireland. Relative economic decline, an increase in unemployment and the concomitant decline of working-class Protestant communities, along with political decisions such as the rerouting of some Orange parades, have contributed to a sense of retreat, alienation and grievance. McCoy and O'Reilly also relate the rise of the Ulster-Scots movement to the worldwide ethnic resurgence which has made minority status a desirable source of identity rather than a stigma or liability (McCoy and O'Reilly 2002). However, there are limits to the appeal of Ulster-Scots among the Protestant population of Northern Ireland. The emphasis on Presbyterianism and scriptural belief which characterises much of the Ulster-Scots movement alienates many Protestants of different denominations and those who identify with an increasingly secular dominant culture. In addition, many Unionists see themselves as part of a modern British state. Ulster-Scots and its accompanying rural-based traditions may appear too parochial to have widespread appeal.

Concluding Remarks

The discourse of cultural identity has come to dominate politics in Northern Ireland. The Northern Irish state has been characterised by a Unionist political culture and a British cultural identity. Although aspects of Irish culture became increasingly visible throughout the 1970s and 1980s, it was only in the 1990s that Irish culture, particularly in the form of the Irish language, became a force to be reckoned with. The development of a community relations and cultural traditions industry under the auspices of the state during the 1980s, along with increased Civil Rights and education for Catholics from the 1970s onwards,

6 Gordon McCoy. Personal communication.

encouraged the growth of a politics of culture in the Northern Irish context. As discourses of heritage and tradition became increasingly hegemonic on a global scale, the politics of culture took on an increasing salience and significance in Northern Ireland. The prominence given to linguistic and cultural issues in the Good Friday Agreement is evidence of the extent of its influence.

All parties, including the British government, the Northern Irish civil service, Unionists, Nationalists, and now an emerging devolved political infrastructure, have become fully engaged in the struggle for cultural capital and the political and economic rewards it promises. The stakes have become increasingly high, as new institutions are formed and struggles ensue over both their character and who will ultimately control them. The politics of culture is no longer simply a matter of obtaining a few hundred pounds for a community project – hundreds of thousands of pounds are now at stake, as is the future of a multitude of schools, and of cultural and political organisations. The debate over the political and cultural shape of a future Northern Ireland is now being played out in large part through the language of culture, heritage and tradition, squeezing out other alternative approaches – including attempts to increase the profile of class-based and feminist-influenced politics. The politics of culture is the new hegemony, and there is as yet no unified, effective discourse to oppose it.

References

Agreement Reached in the Multiparty Negotiations. 1998.

Bell, D. 1998. 'Modernising History. The Real Politik of Heritage and Cultural Tradition in Northern Ireland', in *Rethinking Northern Ireland*, ed. D. Miller. London, pp. 228-52.

Bruce, S. 1994. 'Cultural Traditions. A Double-Edged Sword?', in *Causeway*, Autumn (1994), pp. 21-4.

Bryan, D. 2000. *Orange Parades: The Politics of Ritual, Tradition and Control*, London.

Butler, D. 1994. 'The Study of Culture in Northern Ireland, or "What's So Bad About Peace, Love and Understanding?"', in *Causeway*, Summer (1994), pp. 50-5.

Chapman, M. 1992. *The Celts: The Construction of a Myth*. London.

CTG. 1995. *Giving Voices: The Work of the CTG 1990–1994*, Belfast.

Dunleavy, J. E. and Dunleavy, G. W. 1991. *Douglas Hyde, a Maker of Modern Ireland*. Oxford.

Handler, R. 1988. *Nationalism and the Politics of Culture in Quebec.* Madison and London.

Hayes, M. 1991. *Whither Cultural Diversity?* Belfast.

Herbison, I. 1989. *Language, Literature and Cultural Identity: An Ulster-Scots Perspective.* Dunclug.

Hutchinson, J. 1987. *The Dynamics of Cultural Nationalism: The Gaelic Revival and the Creation of the Irish Nation State.* London.

Jarman, N. 1997. *Material Conflicts: Parades and Visual Displays in Northern Ireland*. Oxford.

Mac Póilin, A. 1995. 'Aspects of the Irish Language Movement in Northern Ireland'. (Unpublished paper presented at the Language Policy and Planning in the European Union conference, Institute of Irish Studies, University of Liverpool).

Macdonald, S. 1997. *Reimagining Culture: Histories, Identities and the Gaelic Renaissance*. Oxford.

Maguire, G. 1991. *Our Own Language: An Irish Initiative*. Clevedon.

McCoy, G. 1996. 'Protestants and the Irish Language in Northern Ireland', Belfast (unpublished PhD thesis, Belfast).

McCoy, G. and O'Reilly, C. 2002. 'Essentialising Ulster? The Ulster-Scots Language Movement', in *Language and Tradition in Ireland*, ed. M. Tymoczko and C. Ireland. Dublin.

McDonald, M. 1989. *'We Are Not French!' Language, Culture, and Identity in Brittany*. London.

O'Reilly, C. 1996. 'The Irish Language – Litmus Test for Equality? Competing Discourses of Identity, Parity of Esteem and the Peace Process', in *Irish Journal of Sociology*, 6 (1996), pp. 154-78.

————1997. 'Nationalists and the Irish Language in Northern Ireland. Competing Perspectives', in *The Irish Language in Northern Ireland*, ed. A. Mac Póilin. Belfast, pp. 95-130.

————1999. *The Irish Language in Northern Ireland: The Politics of Culture and Identity*. London.

Rolston, B. 1998. 'What's Wrong With Multiculturalism? Liberalism and the Irish Conflict', in *Rethinking Northern Ireland*, ed. D. Miller. London, pp. 253-74.

Ryder, C. 1999. 'Ulster-Scots Will Trip Off Tongue Soon as Minority Language', *The Irish Times*, 13 May 1999.

CHAPTER ELEVEN

Sport and the Politics of Irish Nationalism: The Struggle for Ireland's Sporting Soul

Alan Bairner

Introduction: Sport, Politics, and Identity in Northern Ireland

Since the summer of 1999, much of the attention of commentators on the politics of Northern Ireland has focused on the difficulties faced by First Minister and leader of the UUP, David Trimble MP MLA, which came about as a consequence of his and his party's involvement in a power-sharing executive that included two Sinn Féin ministers, despite the fact that, until October 2001, there was no actual decommissioning of IRA weaponry. However, with the commencement of IRA decommissioning towards the end of 2001, there was a widespread feeling, not only amongst many Republicans, that a 'seismic shift' in Northern Irish politics had taken place.

Nationalist and Republican thinking clearly evolved during the period of 'the Troubles'. Moreover, it would be wrong to think that at any time during those years the Nationalist and Republican positions were identical or that either ideological position was itself monolithic. Rather, Nationalist and Republican worldviews have often contrasted starkly and within each camp there have been significant differences of opinion. One way of identifying these types of divisions is to use sport as a window through which to look at the cultural construction and reproduction of what is commonly described as the Nationalist community in the north of Ireland.

The relationship between sport and politics in Northern Ireland has been well documented in the past (e.g., Sugden and Bairner 1986, 1993; Sugden and Harvie 1995). Initially much of the discussion prompted an essentially descriptive discourse. More recently, however, attempts have been made to subject the raw data to more sophisticated theoretical analysis, drawing on such conceptual tools as spatiality, gender, post-modernity and postcolonialism (Bairner 1997, 1999; Bairner and Shirlow

1998). This chapter makes a further attempt to add analytical depth to the debate on the politico-cultural impact of sport in the north of Ireland, with specific reference to the relationship between sport and the changing politics of Nationalism and Republicanism. Specifically, it examines two separate episodes, one involving internal debates within the Gaelic Athletic Association (GAA), the other relating to divisions affecting the Irish Nationalist sporting culture more broadly. The issues which are considered are the GAA's Rule 21 (which prevented members of the British armed forces as well as the Royal Ulster Constabulary (RUC) from joining the GAA) and the discussions about whether Donegal Celtic football team situated in Nationalist West Belfast should play against the RUC. The former is discussed primarily with reference to rival theories of modernity, the latter in terms of postcolonial theory. The chapter's general purpose is to use sport as an entry point for an examination of contemporary representations of Irish national identity, particularly as expressed in the six counties of Northern Ireland.

Identities are the product of 'a multiplicity of often conflicting and variable criteria' (Graham 1997: 7). In this respect, Irish national identity is no different from countless other expressions of political and cultural identity. Indeed, according to Graham (1997: 7), 'there is little that is conceptually exceptional about the construction of Irish Nationalism'. Thus we can observe the politics of exclusion as well as crises of identity in any serious attempts to interpret Irish nationality. Kearney (1997: 102), for example, suggests that the globalisation of Irish culture demands 'a countervailing move to retrieve a sense of local belonging'. Indeed, he favours the linkage of local and cosmopolitan identity as a key element in the resolution of the British–Irish conflict in the north of Ireland. Certainly, at any given time, it is legitimate to speak in terms of a plurality of Irelands (Smyth 1997). For example, social class, gender and religion, amongst other factors, all impact upon the construction of national identity in Ireland as elsewhere.

Furthermore, in most societies, popular movements play a crucial role in the construction of at least one vision of the nation. Significant amongst these are sporting bodies because sports, as MacClancy (1996: 2) suggests, 'are vehicles of identity, providing people with a sense of difference and a way of classifying themselves and others, whether latitudinally or hierarchically'. It is gratifying, therefore, that more and more scholars are treating the relationship between sport and nationalism with increasing importance (Bairner 1996; Cronin 1999; Cronin and Mayall 1998; Mangan 1996). At the outset, it should be stated that the influence of sport on the construction of identity is often more strongly felt by men than by women (Messner 1992). Thus, national identities which are partially formed by way of involvement with sport are almost inevitably gendered identities as well. That said, of all the world's sporting organisations, the one most often cited as a vehicle for the promotion of national identity is arguably the GAA. The customary qualification as regards gender still needs to be made. As Healy (1998: 65) puts it, 'traditionally, women did not make the headlines in the GAA – they made the tea'. However, women have become increasingly active in a wide range of GAA activities in recent years; and for them, as well as for huge numbers of Irish men, the association plays a major role in the construction of identity. The fact remains, however, that Irish men (and women) also play and watch sports which do not operate under the aegis of the GAA. These activities have in the past been portrayed, especially by the devotees of the Gaelic games movement, as British, foreign and imperialist. If one takes the view that Ireland was unquestionably a British colony, then games such as cricket, rugby union and hockey would be regarded as inimical to a purist definition of Irish nationality. However, Ireland does not lend itself easily to traditional postcolonialist analysis. It was not only part of the British Empire as a subject colony, it was also imperialistic in its own right by virtue of its close ties to Britain. Thus, playing so-called 'foreign' games is intimately bound with being Irish at least in terms of a particular representation of what Irishness is.

Nevertheless, the GAA has certainly performed a central role in the reproduction of a particular form of Irish national identity since its formation in Thurles, Co. Tipperary, in 1884 to the present day, when images of hurlers promote a particular image of Ireland whilst simultaneously advertising beer. Today, according to Humphries, 'three-quarters of a million Irish people are members of the GAA, but that figure represents only a fraction of the Irish people who are touched by the games of football and hurling in their regular daily lives'. For Humphries (1996: 3), 'the GAA is more than a sports' organisation, it is a national trust, an entity which we feel we hold in common ownership'. In similarly lofty tones, Healy (1998: 151) claims that 'the Association has become a national movement, a driving force behind the people, a giant parental figure to the youth of the country'.

Gaelic Games and Irish Identities

Apart from its general role in Irish life, the GAA's contribution to the cause of Irish Nationalist politics has also been identified by certain commentators. For example, having reviewed the association's history up to 1924, Mandle (1987: 221) writes that 'it is arguable that no organisation had done more for Irish Nationalism than the GAA – not the IRB Irish Republican Brotherhood, so influential in its founding but now dissolved, not the Gaelic League, its linguistic counterpart which had failed in its mission to restore the national language, not the Irish Parliamentary party, which had been unable to adjust to the Nationalist revival, not even Sinn Féin, which had broken apart under the impact of the treaty'. Others, however, have questioned the importance of the association's political role and suggested there has been a widespread tendency, not least by GAA leaders themselves, to mythologise the organisation's con- tribution at key stages in the struggle to create an independent Irish state. Thus, Cronin (1996: 6) argues that 'the GAA was not, as it was projected in the post 1922 era, the mass spiritual home of physical force National- ism (which reached fruition following the events of 1916), but rather it was the home of populist national sentiment'. He is particularly dismis- sive of the GAA's role in the events leading up to and surrounding Bloody Sunday in 1920, when thirteen people were killed by British soldiers dur- ing a Gaelic football game at Croke Park in a retaliatory attack following the assassinations of a number of British secret service agents by the IRB. According to Cronin, 'the GAA itself did not plan, or were even party to the IRB's plans, but the vague connection between Nationalist violence and national sport allowed for martyrdom and legendary status' (Cronin 1996: 8). Cronin's attempt to deny the political importance of the GAA relies on an unfortunately narrow definition of the political. Even if few members of the association were directly involved in the key political events which determined the course of modern Ireland's development, there is no denying that the GAA clearly played a political role at the level of cultural resistance.

Moreover, the general influence of the GAA on Irish life remains undeniable. Today the association has a membership of around 800,000, with 2,700 clubs fielding approximately 20,000 teams. Although involve- ment is stronger in some parts of Ireland than others, its influence is felt throughout the thirty-two counties. For many players in particular, the identity which the GAA forges is essentially a sporting one relatively free from political connotations. Thus in the 1999 edition of the Irish Sports Almanac, writing about the challenges which currently face the GAA, the editor, Liam Horan, fails to comment on any of the issues dis- cussed in this chapter. Gaelic games have problems, according to this analysis, but they occur on the field of play and in technology rather than at the level of intellectual discourse on nationality (Horan 1998: 117). At least as significant, however, is the GAA's symbolic role in the construc- tion of the Irish landscape, both real and imagined. Gaelic pitches evoke a sense of Irishness even for those who do not see them regularly. Thus, they are very much part of Ireland's 'imagined community' (Anderson 1983). It should be added that Gaelic grounds are by no means unique in this respect. For example, in Ireland itself, certain soccer grounds are important symbolic spaces which contribute to the construction of Unionist and Loyalist identities (Bairner and Shirlow 1998).

Established in an effort to democratise access to leisure activities in Ireland and to resist the process whereby a British cultural hegemony was being consolidated in sport as in other spheres of activity, the GAA quickly laid down roots (particularly in the rural areas) of nineteenth century Ireland (de Búrca 1980; Mandle 1987). From the outset, it embraced representatives of all branches of Irish Nationalism, including the Catholic Church which has consistently played an important part in the reproduction of Irish national identity, even though this role has been greatly diminished in recent times. Despite the involvement of Protestant and even Unionist members in its formation, in a relatively short space of time, the association came to be regarded as providing sporting space for certain types of Irish people, mainly men and certainly Catholic and/or politically Nationalist. This development was assisted by a series of bans (1885, 1887 and 1905) which sought to prevent GAA members from playing or watching 'foreign' games, endeavoured to ensure that GAA facilities would not be used for such games and barred members of the British security forces from GAA membership. The foreign games rules were removed in 1971 but Rule 21 remained in force until the end of 2001 despite increasingly strenuous efforts over a number of years by leading figures within the association to have it rescinded. Responding to competition from other sporting activities, together with wrestling with the quasi-political question of how to react to the Crown forces, the GAA has been obliged increasingly to react to general changes in the way in which sport is organised globally in the direction of sponsorship and payment to players. In response to all of these issues, the association has revealed particular ways of representing Irishness whilst continuing to provoke hostile responses from those who believe that its representation of the nation is outmoded and inappropriate for the new, pluralist society which they deem to be emerging.

In regard to competition from rival sports, it is evident that even in the north of Ireland, where the original purpose of the GAA certainly would retain a greater degree of contemporary resonance than in the Irish Republic, numerous Nationalists and Republicans favour other sporting activities, most notably football. They do not regard this as in any sense indicating an abandonment of their Irishness. Indeed, as in Scotland, where 'Irish' identity has been maintained within the diaspora community by the very presence of a football team, Celtic FC, this 'foreign' game provides far greater opportunities for oppositional cultural resistance than is facilitated by separate, albeit distinctive, sporting traditions.

Debates about the current influence of the GAA in terms of representations of Irishness have tended to be conducted within a discourse centred around issues of tradition and modernity (or even postmodernity). Whilst this is an appropriate location for discussions concerning the growing commercialisation of Gaelic games and arguably the GAA's attitude towards 'foreign' games, the issue of Rule 21 needs to be approached from a different perspective, which takes account of rival conceptions of modernity as opposed to the dichotomy between the modern and the traditional. Moreover, for an accurate appreciation of the Donegal Celtic affair it is necessary to consider the relevance of postcolonial theory to the study of Irish Nationalism.

Before looking specifically at these debates, however, it is worth talking a little more about the overall political character of the GAA. In this regard, it is not enough to calculate how many or, indeed, how few Gaels have been directly involved in politics. Rather, one must be mindful of the extent to which by promoting a sense of Irishness, the association provided the broader Nationalist political movement with weapons of cultural resistance. In so doing, however, it also helped to establish in the minds of many Nationalists what it means to be Irish. Arguably, this GAA-inspired vision of the nation has remained influential to the present day. Above all, the image of Irish which the GAA has tended to promote has been exclusive in its implications (Bairner 1999). As Mullan (1995: 275) argues, 'the formation of the GAA in the 1880s represented something different in the development of Western sport; eschewing an integrationist approach, it organised its Gaelic revival around what would become a permanent state of conflict with established British bourgeois sport forms'.

The Ireland which the GAA represents is at least partly an imagined community. Far from actually reviving traditional native pastimes, the association is deeply implicated in a process through which Irish leisure was reinvented and placed in the service of the production of a specific elaboration of Irishness. Irish nationality, in GAA terms, has traditionally been presented in terms of Catholicism, ruralism and Celtic ethnicity. One does not have to be a Catholic, live in the countryside or be ethnically Irish to play Gaelic games, but the ideal Gael would be likely to combine at least two and frequently all three of these distinguishing features. According to de Búrca, for example, the influence of the founder of the GAA, Michael Cusack, on the development of the Irish nation state has been understated. For de Búrca (1999: 100), 'instead of being, as he [Cusack] is widely portrayed, merely an early advocate of Irish field games ... he had ... a much broader agenda which at a vital stage of his life and intermittently thereafter embraced the whole Celtic diaspora'. Not surprisingly, however, the close identification of Gaelic games with a purist, Celtic vision of what it means to be Irish has been viewed with suspicion by most Protestants, even those who would willingly describe themselves as Irish. Many town dwellers throughout Ireland (but particularly in Derry, Dublin and Belfast), who are themselves both ethnically Irish and Catholic, also view the manufactured identity with scepticism, favouring soccer as their chosen game. The GAA, as Mullan (1995: 275) suggests, 'consolidated its position within Ireland, especially in the rural

districts, through appeals to Catholic Nationalisms and the implementation of creative techniques of counterclosure, such as the athletic and
political bans on British games and those who played them'. It is against
this historical background that further doubts concerning the continuing
value of the GAA's contribution to the construction of Irishness have
been expressed in recent times. Specifically, these hesitations are in
response to certain controversial issues and in the context of the emergence of what some regard as a new, postmodern Ireland, which itself has
been accompanied, and arguably partially constructed, by a series of
influential revisionist readings of Ireland and the Irish.

It is claimed by de Búrca (1999: 111) that 'since the setting up of the
new state the GAA has become and remained a pillar of the new establishment and also championed, in the new era of professionalism and
sponsorship by commercial interests, all aspects of cultural Nationalism'.
According to Cronin (1996), on the other hand, there is no denying the
GAA's essentially outmoded and reactionary contribution to debates
about Irish nationality. Cronin's analysis is part of a more general
attempt to portray the GAA as being hopelessly out of touch with contemporary political representations of Irishness. In this respect, he is by
no means alone. The GAA has certainly not been without its critics for
the promotion of what has been perceived to be an essentially exclusive
vision of the nation. Cronin, Holmes and Free have argued in different
ways that soccer, as opposed to Gaelic games, is increasingly more in tune
not only with the people who live in a modern and pluralistic Ireland but
also with the identity of members of the Irish diaspora, particularly those
in England (Cronin 1994; Free 1998; Holmes 1994). However, to the
extent that soccer has contributed to the development of a more inclusive, although essentially 26-county Irishness, it has been assisted considerably by the fact that, in organisational terms, the game has followed
the lines established by partition (Sugden and Bairner 1993). The GAA's
influence vis-à-vis the construction of Irish national identity has clearly
been affected by the fact that Ireland itself is an example of failed nation-
state building and this has resulted in Gaelic games, organised on a 32-
county basis, having been played since 1921 in two separate political
jurisdictions. Finally, the Gaelic games movement has been increasingly
affected by socioeconomic trends in Ireland and also in the wider global
economy. The impact on the GAA of material factors is by no means new
given that urbanisation, which accompanied the growth of soccer as a
major sport for both players and spectators, has been consistently gnaw-
ing away at the rural roots of the association virtually since its inception.
However, the pace of change experienced during the past two decades
has been faster than any previous rate and the global and postmodern
impulses which are the result inevitably demand new articulations of

Irishness, which may have little or no time for Gaelic games and the construction of Irishness that is associated with them.

Gaelic Games and the 'New' Ireland

Two frequently cited examples of the Gaelic games' failings in this respect refer to relations with non Gaelic games and the attitude of the GAA to members of the British security forces. However, these two issues, together with the question of commercialism, need to be disaggregated. The debate on the GAA's attitude to 'foreign' games, like that on professionalism, can be legitimately conducted within a discourse on tradition vis à vis modernity. Discussions on Rule 21, however, are best contextualised in terms of different and potentially conflicting visions of modern Ireland. At a conference of the GAA Central Council held on 29 May 1998, a resolution on ending the rule was deferred. Commenting on the failure of the GAA to rescind the ban on security forces' membership forthwith in the wake of the Good Friday Agreement, an *Irish News* editorial commented that 'every aspect of rule 21 is contrary to the spirit of the initiative endorsed by 85 percent of the entire Irish population ten days ago' (Irish News, 1 June 1998).

Cronin, writing long before that decision was made, envisioned that the refusal to delete Rule 21 was evidence that the GAA is locked in a traditional world-view which is at odds with the new Ireland. He argued that 'by refusing to drop rule 21 and clinging onto a self perceived and self important role which the GAA believes it has at the heart of Irish Nationalism, the Association is placing itself at odds with the direction taken by the broad Nationalist community, its political leaders, and the views of many ordinary GAA members' (Cronin 1994: 18f.). Subsequently, however, Cronin (1999: 168) has acknowledged, in connection with the issue of Rule 21, that 'while it may appear that the GAA is existing in an historical backwater and is not prepared to deal with the current realities of the changing situation in Northern Ireland, the broad nature of its appeal to different manifestations of Irish Nationalism has to be appreciated'. Many opinion formers, however, continued to interpret the GAA's obstinacy with regards to Rule 21 solely in terms of outmoded reaction.

Kevin Myers (1998) observed that, whilst the GAA persisted with its ban on the RUC and the Royal Irish Regiment (RIR), 'there is no ban on the authors of the Omagh holocaust, no ban on the "Real IRA", no ban on kneecappers, no ban on those who have buried a widowed mother by moonlight while her orphan children waited vainly and alone for months for her safe return, no ban on those who hold still the secrets of a dozen secret graves or more, no ban on those who have bombed Northern Ireland senseless'. Speaking in advance of the GAA's special congress, the well-known cleric Monsignor Denis Faul also questioned the need for Rule 21 saying that 'the world would view any ban in sport at the present time in a very unfavourable light, and such an important organisation as the GAA must give very good example'. Even the then British Minister of Sport, Tony Banks, contributed to the debate when he commented, 'I don't want to get involved in it but it does seem to me that anything that opens up the game to the widest number of people is a good thing' (Irish News, 1 June 1998).

Most critical commentaries on the recent activities of the association tend to link this issue to that of the GAA's conservative attitudes towards foreign games and professionalism. Whereas the latter are clearly at odds with attempts to create a new, more inclusive construction of Irishness, the refusal to remove Rule 21 until after policing in the north of Ireland had been reorganised was a legitimate though by no means uncontroversial stance for a Nationalist organisation to adopt. It has been argued that amongst the most pressing political problems of the modern era is the question of how to ensure personal and collective security (Berki 1986). This debate has been directly linked to two particularly troublesome aspects of the Irish peace process – decommissioning of paramilitary weapons and reform of policing in the north of Ireland. It is the latter which was clearly most relevant to discussions about Rule 21.

The RUC as well as the RIR (the successor to the Ulster Defence Regiment), mainly locally recruited branches of the British security apparatus in the north of Ireland, were themselves essentially exclusive. Even if one accepts the argument that Republican violence and the threat thereof had been major factors in preventing higher levels of Catholic recruitment, it remained the case that these organisations consisted primarily of Protestants and consistently allied theselves to a pro-British ethos. Furthermore, in terms of the GAA's direct connections with these elements of the security operation in the North, it is important to recognise the extent of harassment suffered by association members. Worse still, under threat from Unionists at the political level and, with more sinister implications, from Loyalists in paramilitary organisations, GAA members consistently felt that they have received little or no protection from the security forces (Bairner and Darby 1999). Symbolically, moreover, the occupation of a section of the Crossmaglen Rangers Gaelic Athletic Club's property by the British army was regarded as further evidence that the Crown forces were hostile towards the Gaelic games movement. In so far as Gaelic grounds are symbolic spaces, their use for British military installations inevitably had an impact on a wide range of Irish Nationalist opinion. In such circumstances, Rule 21 made sense. The fact that the current GAA president and many other officials supported its removal was indicative of a failure to take account of grassroots sentiments in the North as much as a desire to present the association in a better, less overtly sectarian light.

According to Tom Humphries (1998), 'the GAA appears to be at least a step behind the Nationalist constituency in the North'. But this is, at the very least, questionable. The desire for more inclusive ways of maintaining law and order, far from promoting an old-fashioned exclusive conception of Irishness, could be interpreted as being a contribution to the promotion of a more inclusive Ireland than currently existed. Ironically, however, given the fact that most of the pressure to retain Rule 21 came from the six counties, the debate served to illustrate the extent to which partition has added further to the complexities of Irish identities. In the end, support for the Ulster counties came from Cork, Waterford, Kilkenny and even London. It was clear, however, that it was the attitude of those who were most immediately affected by the actions of the crown forces which ensured that the rule would remain for the time being. For example, it was believed that no Belfast club was in favour of abolition. Indeed, responding to the pro-abolition stance of the GAA president, Galway's Joe McDonagh, West Belfast's *Andersonstown News* declared, 'we in Antrim know far more about Rule 21 and its effect than any Galway man' (Andersonstown News, 30 May 1998). Therefore, far from making a sterile contribution to debates about Irishness, the GAA's dealings with Rule 21 told us a lot about the multidimensional character of contemporary Irish Nationalism. If Rule 21 was appropriate when it was first established, then it was difficult to see in 1998 why, given the circumstances which remained in one part of Ireland, it should be removed. Yet, a failure to understand the mind-set of Northern Nationalists led the GAA president and others to assume that what would be a useful public relations exercise in the Irish Republic could be carried. For many Northern Nationalists, on the other hand, so long as it retained Rule 21 the GAA could continue to play a defining role in identity formation similar to that of the Northern Ireland soccer team as regards Unionist and Loyalist identities (Bairner 1997).

It is one thing for politicians and journalists to polemicise on this issue and to create the impression that the GAA's position on Rule 21 was directly linked to its mentality concerning professionalism and the challenge of 'foreign' games. More disturbing, however, is Cronin's attempt to conflate these issues from an academic perspective. According to Cronin (1994: 19), 'for the GAA the time has come to put the past to one side, accept the realities of the current situation and stop posing as the defenders of the nation'. But questions necessarily arose concerning the precise character of these current realities and, indeed, the views of the Northern Nationalist community which both Cronin and Humphries believe to have been misjudged by the GAA.

Calling for a 'no' vote at the GAA's special congress, Eamonn McCann (1998a) noted 'the complexity of Northern Nationalism'. A substantial 'yes' vote in the referendum on the Good Friday Agreement indicated that an overwhelming majority of Nationalists in the North were willing to concede that, for the time being at least, they would continue to live within the United Kingdom. As McCann pointed out, however, 'to the extent that west Belfast, the Glens of Antrim, Dungiven and south Armagh are willing, even pro tem, to accept that they'll remain in the UK, their sensitivity to the political colouration of the Northern State is sharpened, not dulled'. Inevitably, this involved doing whatever was necessary to bring pressure to bear on discussions about the way in which the new Northern Ireland was to be policed. This may not have been an issue of great importance in large parts of the Republic of Ireland, where support for the Agreement amongst Northern Nationalists has simply been interpreted as revealing an acceptance of a modified form of partition. In reality, however, the question of security has to be answered in such a way as to satisfy Northern Nationalists, if the agreed set of arrangements are to have a viable future. By refusing to rescind Rule 21 the GAA accommodated itself to one contemporary Irish reality whilst at the same time turning its back on another.

The GAA's critics claim that there is a new sense of what is involved in being Irish and that the retention of Rule 21 was evidence that the association remained locked in the past, fated to continually reproduce an outmoded vision of Irish identity. This point might be conceded in relation to the debates on professionalism and foreign games (Bairner and Sugden 1998). In the case of Rule 21, however, it is important to recognise that a large number of those who voted in favour of the Agreement did so in the hope that a truly modern Ireland could be constructed, rather than merely to register their support for certain progressive developments which have been taking place within the existing '26-county Republic'.

In 2001, the GAA finally took the momentous decision to rescind Rule 21. It did so in the wake of the formation of a new policing service in Northern Ireland (the Police Service of Northern Ireland – PSNI). The move was supported by all 26 county boards in the Irish Republic and hailed as a major step forward by British and Irish government officials. The association's critics would no doubt argue that it had finally adjusted to reality. The facts are, however, that the establishment of the PSNI itself represented a new reality, that only one of the six counties of Northern Ireland (Down) voted for change and there remain many Northern Nationalists within the GAA and outside it who believe that a final decision should have been further deferred until such time as it became possible to assess the extent to which the PSNI can truly deliver a form of policing acceptable to all shades of opinion in the north. To paraphrase Yeats, things had certainly changed but by no means utterly.

Football and Irish Nationalism in Northern Ireland

The issue of whether or not the Donegal Celtic association football club should play games against the RUC also involves rival readings of modern Ireland. In this instance, however, additional light is shed by way of the application of postcolonial theory to contemporary Irish reality. According to Murray (1997), 'the term "postcolonial" itself seems, at times, to encompass material and methods that are extremely diverse, with a potential to obscure the use of the word in a constructive manner'. It is one thing to assert that the dominant characteristic of the modern world order is its postcoloniality. But, as Moore-Gilbert (1997: 11) comments, 'such has been the elasticity of the concept "postcolonial" that in recent years some commentators have begun to express anxiety that there may be a danger of it imploding as an analytic construct without any real cutting edge'. In certain respects, the concept is only of limited value to the debate on Irish cultural politics. Ireland is not, and has never been, an unequivocally colonial society. Undeniably it has been colonised and subjected to imperial rule at various stages in its historical development, thereby indicating in some ways the application of the term 'postcolonial'. But, as Jeffery (1996) has argued, Ireland has been both 'colonial' and 'imperial'. Thus, Kibberd (1997) makes the legitimate claim that 'only a rudimentary thinker would deny that the Irish experience is at once post-colonial and post-imperial'.

The promotion of Gaelic games is a clear response to the perception of Ireland as a colonised society. The founders of the GAA believed that sport was being used by the British as part of a broader movement to provide cultural support for imperial rule and contingently to undermine native Irish traditions. From this perspective, the GAA is still confronted by a partially colonised Ireland; hence, the belief in some quarters that Rule 21 should have been retained. However, taking the view that Ireland has been both colonial and imperial, whilst games such as cricket, rugby and association football were introduced to Ireland as a product of British influence, this is not fully described by using the concept of colonialism. More than in any other part of the 'English' Empire, with the possible exception of Scotland, as a result of close physical as well as personal ties, the ruling elite in Ireland were perfectly capable of celebrating British traditions and values without any significant degree of British imposition. Indeed, for such people, educated in many instances in England, the distinction between Ireland and Britain was consistently blurred. Thus, it became possible to play British games and yet regard oneself as patriotically Irish, not least since 'foreign' sports offered the opportunity, largely denied by Gaelic games, to represent one's country (or 'nation') as opposed to one's parish, county or province. This linkage of British games to Irish sport-related Nationalism has been made easier, at least in the twenty-six counties of the Republic of Ireland, since partition. In the North, however, the mainly middle-class British games (rugby union, cricket, hockey) have never attracted the attention of Catholics in large numbers. Of the games brought to Ireland by way of the British connection only association football (or soccer) has been fully embraced by Northern Nationalists – at times alongside Gaelic games but in some cases, particularly in urban areas, as an alternative to the latter. It is against this backdrop that the Donegal Celtic issue must be understood.

As Coyle (1999: 13) notes, 'the intensity and passion with which Belfast embraced the coming of association football was little different from that in other cities throughout Britain'. Furthermore, despite the game's British origins, it was taken up with great enthusiasm by Belfast's Nationalist population, not least because the Catholic Church encouraged playing football not only for rational recreation purposes but also as a remedy against the militant Republicanism with which the GAA was increasingly associated (Coyle 1999). In purely logistical terms, too, association football was better suited to an urban environment than either Gaelic football or hurling.

From 1891 until 1949 the main local football interest for Belfast Nationalists was in Belfast Celtic. Meanwhile Glasgow Celtic, the club which inspired the formation of the latter, also received considerable support from Nationalists not only in Belfast but throughout Ireland. Despite this significant Catholic interest, however, Unionists tended to dominate the game in Northern Ireland and sectarian violence was a prominent feature of local matches, particularly those involving Belfast Celtic. These two factors were largely responsible for Celtic's withdrawal from the Irish League in 1949, a few months after a Boxing Day fixture against Linfield (a Belfast club with a mainly Unionist following) had been affected by serious trouble both on and off the pitch. It was not until the late 1970s, when an emergent Nationalist support attached itself to an old, traditionally 'neutral' Belfast team, Cliftonville, that any form of substitute for Belfast Celtic was found. But Cliftonville has suffered in this sense both from a lack of success on the field of play and from the fact that it is not based in West Belfast, which had been home to Belfast Celtic and which possesses the largest Nationalist population in the city. It is the vacuum created by the demise of Belfast Celtic that Donegal Celtic might be expected to fill.

Donegal Celtic have made considerable progress, having come through various junior leagues to the brink of Irish League membership. The club's rise to prominence, however, has not been without controversy. In particular, an Irish Cup game in 1990 against Linfield was marred by crowd trouble together with the intemperate response of the RUC. Given the club's location in Nationalist West Belfast, it almost goes without saying that few of its officials, players and fans respect the RUC as a neutral police force. The fact that the RUC has a football club which competes in the league through which Donegal Celtic would be required to pass if senior status were to be attained is, therefore, problematic. Indeed, the 1998–9 football season provided evidence of the type of difficulty which would emerge if the two teams were to play in the same league.

Donegal Celtic and the RUC were drawn to play against each other on 14 November 1998 in the semi-final of a prominent junior competition, the Steel and Sons Cup. Initially the mood in the local media, including the *Andersonstown News* of West Belfast, was one of eager anticipation. Many local people, however, expressed disquiet that the club would even contemplate having dealings with the RUC. This attitude hardened as pressure was put on the officials of Donegal Celtic, directly by Relatives for Justice, a group representing the families of people who had been killed by members of the RUC, and more covertly by the Republican movement. After a period of deliberation, the club eventually withdrew from the fixture.

Of course, the problem would not have arisen if the entire sporting community of West Belfast restricted its activities to Gaelic games. By way of the mechanism of Rule 21, Gaelic clubs in the area had been able to limit consensual contact with the RUC to almost negligible proportions. Local association footballers, on the other hand, are engaged in the same sporting activity as the police, together with many other members of the Unionist and Loyalist communities. From a purist perspective, this may reveal the dangers of playing with the enemy. Yet the Irish Nationalists who followed Belfast Celtic, who nowadays support Cliftonville and who would like to see Donegal Celtic competing at the game's highest level in the north of Ireland, are no less Irish and, in many instances, no less Republican than those who restrict their sporting activities exclusively to Gaelic games. These rival opinions were reflected in the range of comments which the Donegal Celtic controversy provoked.

Many Nationalists welcomed the eventual outcome. Their analysis was reflected in the words of Fr. Des Wilson (1998) who argued that 'it is for the elected representatives of the people to make clear whether the RUC is acceptable or not to their own people and what should be done about future policing'. However, the *Irish News*, the main Nationalist daily newspaper in the north of Ireland, took a very different line in an editorial arguing that 'Nationalists are wrong to force a vulnerable football club to take up cudgels against the RUC on their behalf' (Irish News, 14 November 1998). Even the Republican and socialist journalist Eamonn McCann (1998b) commented that 'people in west Belfast, and in other areas, not all of them Nationalist, have good grounds for iffyness about the RUC. But a political party which burdens a football club with "responsibility" for carrying this view is simply refusing to shoulder its own responsibilities'. Whatever the merits of these respective positions, one thing is certain: the affair highlighted divisions within the Nationalist sporting community as well as within Northern Nationalism as a whole.

With specific reference to sport, one local journalist, John Haughey (1998), wryly commented, 'I couldn't help but ponder on the irony that the Sinn Féin president was asking a sporting club to cancel a fixture on the same day another sports club from West Belfast were playing a major GAA semi-final.' This raises the possibility that the attitude of some Republicans to the Donegal Celtic–RUC fixture was almost as much an attack on a foreign game as on a sectarian police force. As regards Northern Nationalism more generally, one prominent Republican journalist observed, with a degree of sadness, that 'in the Donegal Celtic debacle, the Nationalist community turned on itself and it wasn't a pretty sight' (O' Muilleoir 1998). Whether nationalist football teams will find it easier to fulfil fixtures against the new PSNI remains to be seen. For the time being, indeed, the name of the RUC has been retained for football purposes.

Conclusion: Sport and Irish National Identity

Taken together, these two episodes drawn from the world of Irish sport tell us a great deal about competing representations of Irish national identity at the start of the new millennium. The debate on Rule 21 provides insights into the very real differences between Nationalist attitudes in the two parts of Ireland, particularly concerning the purpose and meaning of the peace process. The Donegal Celtic affair, on the other hand, indicated divisions within Northern Nationalism not only with regards to sport but also in terms of broader political analysis and strategy. While divisions in the Unionist camp were responsible for many of the difficulties which arose during the summer of 1998 and have reemerged at regular intervals thereafter, this study suggests that there are equally troublesome differences of opinion within the Nationalist and Republican communities which may have serious and damaging implications for peace-building initiatives.

Nevertheless, with specific reference to the two issues that form the heart of this discussion, changes are afoot. The GAA's decision to remove Rule 21 is undoubtedly significant although it is not without its nationalist and republican critics. It clearly reflects changes within the GAA itself although not necessarily a transformation in Northern Nationalist opinion. In the meantime, an advisory panel report to the Minister for Culture, Arts and Leisure on the future of association football in Northern Ireland has recommended that 'in order to introduce a truly open, inclusive and progressive league structure in Northern Ireland, the Irish League should form the top of a "pyramid" system that enables progression from the grassroots through to senior football' (Hamilton et al. 2001). This should in theory benefit a number of clubs based in Nationalist areas. On their own, neither the removal of Rule 21 nor the increased involvement of Nationalists in Irish League soccer can be taken as evidence that the peace process can be saved. They will be useful indicators, however, of the extent to which both Nationalists and Republicans are willing to engage positively with a changing Northern Ireland.

References

Anderson, B. 1983. *Imagined Communities: Reflections on the Origins and Spread of Nationalism*. London.

Bairner, A. 1996. 'Sportive Nationalism and Nationalist Politics. A Comparative Analysis of Scotland, Sweden and the Republic of Ireland', in *Journal of Sport and Social Issues*, vol. 20, no. 3 (1996), pp. 314–35.

———1997. '"Up to their knees"? Football, Sectarianism, Masculinity and Protestant Working–Class Identity', in *Who are 'the People'? Unionism, Protestantism and Loyalism in Northern Ireland*, ed. Peter Shirlow and Mark McGovern. London, pp. 95–113.

———1999a. 'Civic and Ethnic Nationalism in the Celtic Vision of Irish Sport', in *Sport in the Making of Celtic Cultures*, ed. G. Jarvie. Leicester, pp. 12–25.

———1999b. 'Soccer, Masculinity, and Violence in Northern Ireland. Between Hooliganism and Terrorism', in *Men and Masculinities*, vol. 1, no. 3 (1999), pp. 284–301.

Bairner, A. and Shirlow, P. 1998. 'Loyalism, Linfield and the Territorial Politics of Soccer Fandom in Northern Ireland', in *Space and Polity*, vol. 2, no. 2 (1998), pp. 163–177.

Bairner, A. and Sugden, J. 1998. 'Representing the Nation: the Gaelic Athletic Association and Representations of Irishness', (unpublished paper, presented to the Anthropological Association of Ireland).

Bairner, A. and Darby, P. 1999. 'Divided Sport in a Divided Society. Northern Ireland', in *Sport in Divided Societies*, ed. J. Sugden and A. Bairner. Aachen, pp. 51–72.

Berki, R. N. 1986. *Security and Society. Reflections on Law, Order and Politics*, London.

Coyle, P. 1999. *Paradise Lost and Found: The Story of Belfast Celtic*. Edinburgh.

Cronin, M. 1994. 'Sport and a Sense of Irishness', in *Irish Studies Review* 9 (1994), pp. 13–17.

———1996. 'Defenders of the Nation? The Gaelic Athletic Association and Irish National Identity', in *Irish Political Studies* 11 (1996), pp. 1–19.

———1999. *Sport and Nationalism in Ireland. Gaelic Games, Soccer and Irish Identity since 1884*. Dublin.

Cronin, M. and Mayall, D., ed. 1998. *Sporting Nationalisms. Identity, Ethnicity, Immigration and Assimilation*. London.

de Búrca, M. 1980. *The GAA. A History*. Dublin

———1999. 'The Gaelic Athletic Association and Organized Sport in Ireland', in *Sport in the Making of Celtic Cultures*, ed. G. Jarvie. Leicester, pp. 100–111.

Free, M. 1998. '"Angels with Drunken Faces"? Travelling Republic of Ireland Supporters and the Construction of Irish Immigrant Identity in England', in *Fanatics! Power, Identity and Fandom in Football*, ed. A. Brown. London.

Graham, B. 1997. 'Ireland and Irishness. Place, Culture and Identity', In *Search of Ireland. A Cultural Geography*, ed. Brian Graham. London, pp. 1–15.

Hamilton, B. et al. 2001. *Creating a Soccer Strategy for Northern Ireland: Report by the Advisory Panel to the Minister for Culture, Arts and Leisure*. Belfast.

Haughey, J. 1998. 'Brave Celtic Get Right Result', in *Irish News*, 9 November 1998.

Healy, P. 1998. *Gaelic Games and the Gaelic Athletic Association*. Cork.

Holmes, M. 1994. 'Symbols of National Identity. The Case of the Irish Football Team', in *Irish Political Studies* 9 (1994), pp. 91–8.

Horan, L. 1998. *The Irish Sports Almanac*. Inishowen.

Humphries, T. 1996. *Green Fields. Gaelic Sport in Ireland*. London.

——1998. 'A Classic Example of a GAA Own Goal', in *Irish Times*, 8 November 1998.

Jeffery, K. 1996. 'Introduction', in *'An Irish Empire'? Aspects of Ireland and the British Empire*, ed. K. Jeffery. Manchester, pp. 1–24.

Kearney, R. 1997. *Post-Nationalist Ireland*. London.

Kibberd, D. 1997. 'Modern Ireland: Postcolonial or European?', in *Not On Any Map: Essays on Postcoloniality and Cultural Nationalism*, ed. S. Murray. Exeter, pp. 81–100.

MacClancy, J. 1996. 'Sport, Identity and Ethnicity', in *Sport, Identity and Ethnicity*, ed. J. MacClancy. Oxford, pp. 1–20.

Mandle, W. F. 1987. *The Gaelic Athletic Association and Irish Nationalist Politics, 1884–1924*. London.

Mangan, J. A., ed. 1996. *Tribal Identities: Nationalism, Europe, Sport*. London.

McCann, E. 1998a. 'Politics Take Precedence Over Sport', in *Sunday Tribune*, 1 November 1998.

McCann, E. 1998b. 'Vote No to Changes to GAA's Rule 21', *Sunday Tribune*, 24 May 1998.

Messner, M. A. 1992. *Power At Play: Sports and the Problem of Masculinity*. Boston.

MooreGilbert, B. 1997. *Postcolonial Theory: Contexts, Practices, Politics*. London.

Mullan, M. 1995. 'Opposition, Social Closure, and Sport. The Gaelic Athletic Association in the 19th Century', in *Sociology of Sport Journal* 12 (1995), pp. 268–89.

Murray, S. 1997. 'Introduction', in *Not On Any Map: Essays on Postcoloniality and Cultural Nationalism*, ed. S. Murray. Exeter, pp. 1–18.

Myers, K. 1998. 'An Irishman's Diary', *Irish Times*, 19 August 1998.

Ó Muilleoir, Máirtín 1998. Ní Neart Go Cur Le Chéile, in *Andersonstown News*, 21 November 1998.

Smyth, W. J. 1997. 'A Plurality of Irelands', in *In Search of Ireland: A Cultural Geography*, ed. Brian Graham. London, pp. 19–42.

Sugden, J. and Bairner, A. 1986. 'Northern Ireland. Sport in a Divided Society', in *The Politics of Sport*, ed. Lincoln Allison. Manchester, pp. 90–117.

——1993a. Sport, Sectarianism and Society in a Divided Ireland. Leicester.

——1993b. 'National Identity, Community Relations and the Sporting Life in Northern Ireland', in *The Changing Politics of Sport*, ed. by Lincoln Allison. Manchester, pp. 171–206.

Sugden, J. and Harvie, S. 1995. *Sport and Community Relations in Northern Ireland*. Coleraine.

Wilson, D. 1998. 'Time to Play the Right Game', in *Andersonstown News*, 14 November 1998.

Chapter Twelve

Conclusion: The Peace Process since 1998*

Stefan Wolff

In this concluding chapter I will reexamine the Good Friday Agreement in the light of the arguments put forward by the contributors to this volume. In doing so, I will assess the peace process in Northern Ireland since 10 April 1998 and analyse the impact that the Good Friday Agreement had on it.

With the conclusion of the Agreement, the peace process in Northern Ireland moved into a qualitatively new stage, which, in relation to other conflicts, is often described as post-conflict reconstruction. In the case of Northern Ireland, this would be a misleading term, as many contributors to this volume have pointed out: the fundamental conflict between the proponents of two competing visions of national belonging is far from over; (some of) the conflict parties have merely agreed on a new framework in which they want to pursue these distinct visions. From this perspective, it is more appropriate then to speak of post-agreement reconstruction. In order to examine and assess this latest stage in Northern Ireland's current peace process, I will look at three distinct, yet closely related, dimensions of any post-agreement reconstruction process: the building of political institutions, economic development, and social reconstruction. Following a conceptual clarification of 'post-agreement reconstruction', I proceed in three steps. First, I outline the dynamics of post-agreement reconstruction in Northern Ireland. Second, I look at some general developments in each of the three dimensions and examine to what extent they have been influenced by past and present conditions in Northern Ireland and whether, and how much, they have contributed to achieving a degree of sustainability in the peace process. Finally, I draw some conclusions as to whether the current post-agreement reconstruction efforts will be able to succeed in bringing a permanent and stable peace to Northern Ireland.

* The following is partly based on research carried out since summer 2001, which is supported by a grant from the British Academy. It draws on earlier findings published in Wolff (2002). Special thanks are due to Caroline Kennedy-Pipe.

Post-agreement Reconstruction: Conceptual Clarification

Protracted ethnonational conflicts shape the societies in which they take place in many different, yet almost always exclusively negative ways, resulting in a lack of functioning or legitimate political institutions, weak economic performance, nonexisting or polarised structures of civil society, and antagonised elites. Thus, the setting in which post-agreement reconstruction is to begin is often unfavourable in the extreme for the task to be accomplished. However, without a comprehensive programme aimed at rebuilding a conflict-torn society, no settlement would be worth the paper on which it had been written. Post-agreement reconstruction is an extraordinarily complex challenge, and in order to understand its dynamics, a number of distinct dimensions need to be examined, including the various elements it needs to involve, its place in the overall timeline of conflict settlement, the factors that will determine its success, and the indicators by which its success can reliably be measured.

Elements of Post-agreement Reconstruction

The essential aim of post-agreement reconstruction is to create a set of political, economic and social structures in accordance with an agreed conflict settlement that allow the conduct of a nonviolent, just and democratic political process. As such, it is distinct from similar efforts made to facilitate the negotiation processes at the end of which a settlement can be agreed.

It is important to bear in mind the multidimensionality of post-agreement reconstruction and take a holistic and long-term view of transforming conflicts, as 'rushed agreements aimed primarily at stopping conflict may not be the best base on which to try to build a viable democratic state' (Harris and Reilly 1998). The nature of post-agreement reconstruction also means that reconstruction is, in fact, a misleading term, as it really involves 'the creation of new, sustainable, institutions which are more democratic, fair and responsive to the needs, concerns, and aspirations of an entire population' (Bush 1998: 34). That is, the aim is to establish institutions that are superior to those that existed before the violent escalation of the conflict in that they do not contain the same failures that led to the conflict in the first place. In order to achieve this, post-agreement reconstruction needs to address three different areas – building (political) institutions, economic recovery, and establishing conditions conducive for the development of civil society.

At the level of political institutions, one of the foremost tasks is the restoration of law and order and of a judicial system. Equally important is the setting up of a system for democratically accountable government bound by the rule of law. While democratic accountability is important in the long run and from the perspective of consolidating an inclusive and democratic political process after conflict, it is critical to realise that democratic elections alone are insufficient to guarantee this particular outcome. In most cases of agreed settlements, elections figure prominently as part of the rebuilding of political institutions, yet at the wrong time and based on the 'wrong' electoral system they can just as easily destroy a beginning post-agreement reconstruction process by giving opponents of an agreement an opportunity to polarise public opinion, to encourage 'ethnic' voting, and to limit the room for manoeuvre and compromise for moderate political leaders. Thus, institution-building needs to focus on establishing a system of governance that is appropriate for the particular conflict and that is created in a way and by people most suitable for the particular conflict situation. This can mean both immediate elections or elections after a transitory period. The primary task of the institutions set up in accordance with an agreed settlement is to create conditions that are conducive to the success for a comprehensive programme of post-agreement reconstruction. From this perspective, the roots of potential success or failure of post-agreement reconstruction may lie in the agreed settlement itself. At the same time, however, the way in which the implementation of an agreement is carried out, and thus how politicians act during the implementation stage, is another major factor that has bearing on the eventual success or failure of post-agreement reconstruction. This means, with respect to Northern Ireland, that the analysis of post-agreement reconstruction needs to include a thorough examination of the Good Friday Agreement and its suitability, or lack thereof, to serve as a framework for sustainable peace, as well as an assessment of how actions by political and paramilitary leaders have affected its implementation.

At the level of economic reconstruction, the task is normally one of transforming a conflict-driven economy into a robust 'peace economy' with sustainable levels of growth, benefiting all communities. This includes the integration of former combatants into the economic process. In Northern Ireland, there are two additional economic problems that are directly related to the consequences of the particular nature of the conflict over the past thirty-some years. On the one hand, the most obvious effect of the conflict on the economy, apart from overall economic decline and high unemployment rates, has been the disproportionately strongly developed security sector, providing employment almost exclusively to Protestants.[1] Downsizing the security sector will therefore also

---

1 This has been a result of discrimination against Catholics within the police service and the army as well as of peer pressure in the Nationalist/Republican community not to join security forces.

primarily affect Protestants, thus potentially contributing to disaffection and resentment. The other major economic problem in Northern Ireland during the years of conflict (and before) has been the decline in its traditional industries (mainly linen and shipbuilding), also affecting suppliers and service industries, which combined with low levels of inward and Foreign Direct Investment. This resulted in high levels of unemployment throughout the period from the late 1960s onwards. The worst-affected population group has been that of Roman Catholic males, who, at persistently high levels of unemployment, were on average more than twice as likely not to have a job than Protestant males. The challenge for post-agreement reconstruction in the area of the economy, therefore, is not merely one of creating new jobs, but also one of addressing long-standing and potential new inequalities in the labour market.

With regard to civil society, conflict-torn societies are either faced with a complete lack of any civil society, or with a strongly polarised one, that is, the existence of two separate civil societies. To (re)build civil society is crucial for the long-term consolidation of democracy, and thus for the establishment of social and political processes in which conflict issues are addressed by nonviolent means. After often decades of conflict, this is clearly an extremely difficult task. It requires both trust and reconciliation between (formerly) antagonised communities, which may take years to establish. This is very much the case in Northern Ireland where the levels of social and political participation, cooperation and trust within each community is quite high compared to those across the communities. In addition, as Murray and Shirlow have shown for the Nationalist/Republican community and as McAuley has pointed out for the Unionist/Loyalist tradition, dynamics within each community indicate that there are further significant divisions affecting the functioning of civil society in Northern Ireland. The task therefore is one of creating new patterns of, and structures for, interaction that allow new organisations to develop as well as to increase the level of contact and cooperation between already existing organisations. Clearly, for both economic recovery and the (re)building of civil society, political institutions play a key role in providing an appropriate legislative framework as well as necessary funding or co-funding.

Post-agreement Reconstruction as a Component of Conflict Transformation

Taking a holistic and long-term view of transforming conflicts, this process includes three stages: negotiation, implementation and operation of an agreed settlement. Admittedly, this is a rather crude description of a far more complex and multifaceted process, but it allows determining relatively precisely the place of post-agreement reconstruction in the implementation and operation stages. To the extent that post-agreement reconstruction is concerned with the building of (political) institutions, it forms part of the implementation stage. Where it involves programmes aimed at economic recovery and establishing conditions conducive for the development of civil society, post-agreement reconstruction needs to be an element in both the implementation and operation stages of conflict settlement. To be sure, there is certain degree of parallelism and overlap between the dimensions of post-agreement reconstruction. However, as most settlement agreements, including the Good Friday Agreement, are primarily about the building of viable political institutions that enable the former conflict parties to resolve their differences by means other than violence, institution-building is a crucial element of the implementation stage of any agreement and as such a precondition for its operation. It is equally important to realise that institution-building itself is not sufficient for successful post-agreement reconstruction, but without it, it is very unlikely that economic reconstruction or the development of civil society will have any prospects of success. In the case of Northern Ireland, the problem is less one of nonexisting institutions, than one of institutions that are legitimate in the eyes of both communities. Post-agreement reconstruction as an element in the overall settlement of the conflict therefore needs to address the issue of creating and sustaining institutional legitimacy across the range of existing and new institutions.

Factors Determining the Dynamics and Outcome of Post-agreement Reconstruction

Apart from the overall suitability of the agreed settlement for the conflict in question, the factors determining the dynamics and outcome of post-agreement reconstruction can be grouped in a number of relatively broad categories – interethnic and intraethnic relations in the actual conflict zone; in case of a regionally confined conflict within a state, the situation in this state in general needs to be taken into account as well; the same goes for cases in which one of the ethnic groups in the conflict has a kinship relation with a neighbouring state; and, almost as a matter of cause, the broader international context and the actors within it need to be considered. More precisely, the particular nature of the Northern Ireland conflict suggests that the factors displayed in Table 12.1 are those most likely to determine the dynamics and outcome of the post-agreement reconstruction process.

Table 12.1: Factors Determining the Dynamics and Outcome of Post-agreement Reconstruction in Northern Ireland

Northern Ireland	UK/Republic of Ireland	International
General ● Power differential and its interpretation ● Performance and legitimacy of government organs and their institutional set-up *Intraethnic* ● Group identity, awareness and solidarity ● Party-political homogeneity ● Basis for and degree of mobilisation ● Policy agendas and policies of major intragroup actors and their mutual perception *Interethnic* ● Ethnic stratification of society and its perception ● Relationship between ethnic groups, their members and leaders ● Influence of identity-related aspects on intergroup policies ● Policy agendas and policies of the principal conflict parties and their mutual perception	● Policy aims of the two governments and the way in which they are perceived in Northern Ireland ● Means by which aims are sought to realise ● Role and degree of involvement in the post-agreement reconstruction process ● Approach vis-à-vis each other and the two communities in Northern Ireland ● Domestic and international policy constraints	● Motivation of international actors for their involvement ● Availability and commitment of resources ● Skill and determination of intervention

Indicators to Measure the Success of Post-agreement Reconstruction

Bush (1998: 21f.) suggests grouping indicators for the success of post-agreement reconstruction into five categories – security, psychological, social, political and judicial indicators. Apart from the fact that a separate category of economic indicators would need to be added to this classification, in the context of Northern Ireland it seems more sensible to measure success in each of the three main dimensions of post-agreement reconstruction – institution building (political, security and judicial indicators), economic recovery and the rebuilding of civil society (social and psychological indicators). Table 12.2 below specifies the relevant direct and indirect indicators in each of the three dimensions for Northern Ireland.

Table 12.2: Indicators to Measure the Success of Post-agreement Reconstruction in Northern Ireland

Institution-building	Economic recovery	Rebuilding of civil society
Political indicators ● Level and type of political participation (e.g. pro- or anti-Agreement) ● Vote share of political parties (moderates, cross-communal, extremists, parties linked to paramilitary organisations) ● Performance and legitimacy of government institutions ● Significance of 'symbols' (flags, police, etc.) *Security indicators* ● Conflict-related killings and other forms of violence, including intraethnic 'policing' and internal feuds ● Conduct of security forces (arrests, detention, treatment) ● Decommissioning ● Demilitarisation ● Reform of the policing system *Judicial indicators* ● Rule of law ● Even-handed law enforcement ● Prisoner release and prison conditions ● Human rights bill and commission ● Judicial enquiries in past	● Growth rates ● Level of inward investment ● Level of FDI ● Unemployment rates (total and community-specific) ● Community participation in, and support for, regeneration and development	*Social indicators* ● Level of residential segregation ● Level of integrated education ● Level of intermarriage ● Number of intra- and cross-communal organisations ● Number of cross-communal local print and electronic media *Psychological indicators* ● Perception of security situation (individual and collective) ● Perceptions of 'others', including persistence of stereotypes and prejudice ● Level of confidence in future

The Nature and Characteristics of the Northern Ireland Conflict

In order to assess properly the nature and characteristics of the Northern Ireland conflict, and, more importantly, their impact on a society during the process of post-agreement reconstruction, a number of aspects need to be considered. Apart from a purely academic (and no less subjective) assessment of what this conflict really is about, it is vitally important to examine what views about the conflict, and thus about its possible solutions, are held within the society in question and by whom. This I have done at some length in the introductory chapter, when I outlined the nature of the Northern Ireland conflict as an ethnonational one and the different solutions proposed for its settlement by the various conflict parties.

It is equally significant to consider the conduct of the conflict itself: how long and how intense has it been, have there been any previous attempts to settle it, and if so, why they have failed. Again, the introductory chapter provides some analysis of relevant developments up to 1998.

Finally, there is the question of the long-term impact of the conflict on society. While no conflict simply erupts in a peaceful and harmonious society, but is normally preceded by more or less lengthy periods of latent conflict, political radicalisation, and group antagonisation, a prolonged period of violent conflict, as Northern Ireland has seen over thirty years, leaves its mark on society in many different ways that all affect post-agreement reconstruction, such as victimisation of civilians, economic decline and social segregation, to name just a few.

The Intensity of the Northern Ireland Conflict

By global standards of death tolls in violent interethnic conflicts, the one in Northern Ireland has not been very intense. Between 1969 and 1994, when the first IRA and Loyalist cease-fires were announced in the current peace process, about 3,200 people had been killed (Fay et al. 1998). Yet, these statistics only tell half the story. Apart from killings, paramilitaries have committed many more acts of violence, such as beatings, kneecappings, and intimidation, which were directed both at the alleged enemy and members of their own communities. These many forms of violence have had a significant impact on community relations in Northern Ireland, whose examination can provide a good understanding of the degree to which the conflict as a whole has affected society.

Violence, and its increasing acceptance as a means to achieve political objectives among some sections of both communities, has had an impact on community relations and vice versa at three levels – segregation, polarisation and alienation (see Hamilton 1990). Violence may not be the primary cause for, or result of, any of these three dimensions of community relations, yet there is a strong interrelation between them.

Segregation, although it has been a long-term trend, has increased as a result of intercommunal violence. This was the case especially in the late 1960s and early 1970s, but on a lower level it has continued in subsequent decades. While intimidation from the 'other' community and fear of violence have contributed to increasing residential segregation, peer pressure from within one's own community has also played a role in establishing the largely segregated structure of residence in Northern Ireland today. Segregation has important consequences in societies affected by interethnic conflict because it makes it easier to develop and maintain stereotypes about the other community and its intentions towards one's own community. Because of this, there will be even less understanding of the position of the other community, which, in its rejection, increases homogeneity and solidarity within one's own community. On this basis, violence against this other community becomes more easily acceptable and justifications for its use are more readily available. One other feature of segregation that contributes to this phenomenon in Northern Ireland is the maintenance of a confession-based school system, with only few opportunities for integrated schooling.

The degree to which both communities differ in their perceptions of the nature of the Northern Ireland conflict and its potential solutions is influenced by more or less informed judgements about the other community and its political agenda. Violence and the interpretation of violent acts is likely to reinforce the degree of polarisation between the two communities. At the same time, significant differences in views of what could be an acceptable and desirable future for Northern Ireland, and the inability to reach an agreement on this by peaceful means, increased the preparedness of some sections within each community to engage in violence to either achieve their goals or, at least, to prevent the other community from achieving theirs.

The lack of political progress over almost thirty years of violent conflict and the inability of the security forces to provide protection from acts of terrorist violence has also contributed, though unequally, to an increasing alienation of both communities from the British state and its institutions. While this has always been a feature of the relationship between the Nationalist/Republican community and the Stormont and later the British political systems, alienation has also affected the Unionist/Loyalist community, especially after the Anglo-Irish Agreement and after the recent Good Friday Agreement. The sense of being left alone with unresolved problems has triggered processes in both communities in which paramilitary organisations have partly replaced organs of the state. This is more obvious and widespread within sections of the Republican community, where paramilitaries not only 'protect' their community from sectarian attacks, but also police it and provide a number of community 'services'. Unionist and Loyalist alienation from Britain has its origins in the days of partition when national political parties withdrew from campaigning in Northern Ireland, thus encouraging the build-up of an almost exclusively sectarian party system for the decades to come. The creation of a parliament in Northern Ireland was not the preferred option of Unionists, because it marked Northern Ireland as different from the rest of the United Kingdom, yet having a parliament elected by popular vote was at the same time perceived as a safeguard against a British sell-out, and thus still an option with a fairly positive connotation.[2]

2   Personal communication from Antony Alcock.

Community relations that are based on the historic experience of inequality, deprivation and discrimination are more likely to form the background against which intercommunal violence can develop and escalate. Yet the acceptability of violence has not only affected inter- but also intracommunity relations. Feuds between rival paramilitary groups in each community, such as the Loyalist turf wars of summer 2000, and punishment beatings, intimidation and expulsions of individuals and entire families have contributed to a deterioration of social relations, decline in trust in the effectiveness of state institutions to perform essential functions, and widespread disillusionment with the political process in Northern Ireland for several decades.

It has, therefore, been important to reduce the level of violence and 'to take the gun out of politics', but the various policies applied to do so have had different degrees of success, and have had and will have distinct consequences. However, while there is no correlation between the reduction of inequality, deprivation and discrimination and the general downward trend in death tolls recorded in the Northern Ireland conflict over the past two decades (McGarry and O'Leary 1996: 288ff.), positive correlation exists in relation to increasing residential segregation, but it is hard to say whether and where a causal relationship exists.[3] Most likely, the reduction of death tolls since the early 1970s can be attributed to a number of factors – improved capabilities of the security forces, better security cooperation between the British and Irish governments, and changed tactics and political agendas of the paramilitary organisations and the extremist political parties in both communities (McGarry and O'Leary 1996; O'Duffy and O'Leary 1990).

The Long-term Impact of the Conflict on Northern Irish Society

The overall pattern of conflict intensity has also been affected by various (failed) attempts to settle the conflict in Northern Ireland. The most significant and instructive of these were the Sunningdale and Anglo-Irish Agreements of 1973 and 1985 and the Good Friday Agreement of 1998, which I have discussed in some detail in the introductory chapter, concluding that what had primarily changed were contextual circumstances, which increased the acceptability of power-sharing among some sections of the political elites in both communities and their respective constituencies. These positive changes within Northern Ireland have also been pointed out

---

3   Residential segregation, for example, can work both ways. On the one hand, living among one's own community may increase security because of enhanced 'defence capabilities', but on the other, it is the clearest indication of community membership, thus also increasing the risk of either being singled out for an attack or becoming a victim of random violence targeted at the whole community.

by Valerie Morgan in her discussion of the role of women in the peace process, although she also notes that the predominantly patriarchal structure of Northern Irish society has not yet been fundamentally altered as a result of the conclusion of the Good Friday Agreement. Similarly, Farry and Murray have shown that among the cross-community Alliance Party and within the Nationalist SDLP determination and skill combined to grasp the opportunity offered by the peace process in the mid- to later 1990s, partly made possible by the policy shifts in Sinn Féin that Peter Shirlow has analysed in his contribution. While general war weariness on the part of the wider population in Northern Ireland certainly was among the contributing factors that made the agreement possible, Irvin and Byrne have shown that external (economic) factors must not be underestimated in their contribution either. At the same time, however, the analyses provided by Bryan, Bairner and McAuley point to the persistence of patterns of prejudice, unease and fear, and their political manipulation and instrumentalisation, which are among the main reasons for the difficulties that Northern Ireland has experienced in the implementation process of the Good Friday Agreement so far.

Although the Good Friday Agreement provides a comprehensive institutional framework for the settlement of the Northern Ireland conflict, its implementation and operation so far has been hampered by the different expectations and interpretations that exist within each of the two communities in Northern Ireland regarding the final outcome of the implementation process. This, in turn, has led to four key problems that have, over time, become the core stumbling blocks of implementation and thus of success or failure of the current peace process: decommissioning, the reform of the policing system, normalisation of the security situation, and the stability of the institutions set up under the Good Friday Agreement. In addition, there are a number of other issues to which the two communities attach equally high symbolic value, such as parades and flags. While the latter might not have the same political significance, together with the other core problems they reflect quite clearly the persisting divisions in Northern Ireland; and it is the apparent inability to overcome these divisions, not even at the elite level, that has important consequences for the process of post-agreement reconstruction.

The situation in Northern Ireland today is characterised both by the legacy of thirty years of failed conflict resolution and by the hopes and aspirations connected with the Good Friday Agreement. The former solidified the distrust between significant sections of both communities, manifesting itself in attitudes such as 'Unionists will never fairly share power' and 'Republicans will never give up violence'. Yet, intercommunal distrust is only part of the story. Relationships between the two communities and British and Irish authorities were equally strained. While Nationalists/Republicans primarily distrusted the British government's proclaimed neutrality in the conflict and saw the RUC as an 'Orange' police force, Unionists/Loyalists were not only fearful of a British sell-out, but also regarded the Irish government as patron-state of Nationalists and in pursuit of a reunification agenda.

Given these past and present dynamics of the intercommunal conflict in Northern Ireland, there are, in each of the three dimensions of post-agreement reconstruction, aspects that are of particular significance as indicators of success and failure. Among the political indicators for institution-building, these are the vote share obtained by different political parties, the performance and legitimacy of government institutions, and the significance of community-specific symbols. In relation to security indicators, the level of violence, decommissioning and demilitarisation, and police reform are important as they allow an assessment of the progress of post-agreement reconstruction. Aspects of the judicial process to which both communities attach particular importance are the way in which the law is enforced, the speed of prisoner release, and the conduct of judicial enquiries in the past. Economically, community-specific unemployment rates, that is, the employment differential between the two communities, can be deemed significant, as can the degree to which members of both communities partake in regeneration projects and the level to which they benefit from them. As far as the rebuilding of (civil) society is concerned, the provision of integrated education and the number of intercommunal organisations and local media are important among social indicators, while the perception of the security situation and of the agenda and policies of the respectively other community, are among psychological indicators.

This is not to deny the significance of all other indicators listed in Table 12.2 above. Rather, the purpose of this singling-out exercise is to provide the basis for context-related analysis of post-agreement reconstruction in Northern Ireland and to allow for an adequate assessment of its current status.

The Process of Post-agreement Reconstruction in Northern Ireland so far

Institution Building

Not surprisingly, the two communities and the political parties representing them have interpreted the Good Friday Agreement in very different fashions. As McAuley has shown, these interpretations reached from 'destruction of the union with Britain' (DUP, UKUP) to 'strengthening the union' (UUP, PUP) in the Unionist/Loyalist community, and, as Murray and Shirlow have pointed out, from 'basis for a (permanent) settlement' (SDLP) to 'transitional arrangement on the road to a united Ireland' (Sinn Féin) in the Nationalist/Republican community. In addition, Morgan and Farry in their studies of what constitutes the small, but nevertheless important, cross-communal political space, have demonstrated that these political forces, too, can recognise themselves and their agendas in the Good Friday Agreement. This, of course, reflects the different political traditions from which the parties come and what they perceive to be the core interests of their electorate. The Good Friday Agreement itself has not been able to fundamentally change these different aspirations (nor was it reasonable to expect this). Northern Irish society continues to be divided along traditional lines of community-based politics. The stability of the political process will therefore essentially depend upon the skill and determination of all the leading politicians to work within the established set of arrangements and to manage and accommodate the diverse expectations about what the long-term political and constitutional perspectives for Northern Ireland are under the Good Friday Agreement. This is particularly significant in relation to how the performance and thus legitimacy of the new institutions in Northern Ireland will be assessed across the two communities. At the same time, this process is also fraught with extreme difficulty in the face of two long-term problems – policing and decommissioning – and the highly emotional nature of symbolic and ritualistic politics in Northern Ireland in relation to, among other things, flags and parades.

Against the background of very different community experiences and levels of identification with the police forces in Northern Ireland, the issue of policing has remained one of the most contentious areas of disagreement, even after the two major parties in the assembly, the UUP and the SDLP, have agreed to nominate representatives to the Policing Board and thus ended the impasse in the implementation of the government's plans for police reform. The fundamental conflict here has not been, and is not now, so much over whether there should be a reform of the policing system, but over the degree to which such a reform should be carried out. While Nationalist/Republican opinion tended towards radical reform, up to the disbanding of the RUC, Unionist attitudes, although recognising the need for a more representative police force, favoured less decisive measures. This difference in approach had not least to do with the widespread feeling among Unionists/Loyalists that the RUC was 'our' police force, as compared to the Nationalist/Republican perception of the RUC being 'their' police force. Clearly, from this point of view, both communities had very different expectations about the degree of reform necessary. The Good Friday Agreement did not make any specific provisions in relation to a reform of the police service, but left details to further negotiations and the recommendations of an independent commission. The terms of reference for the work of this independent commission were quite tight.[4] The recommendations of the Patten

4   Annex A of the provisions on 'Policing and Justice' stipulates in relation to the independent commission that 'its proposals on policing should be designed to ensure that policing arrangements, including composition, recruitment, training, culture, ethos and symbols, are

Report (Independent Commission on Policing for Northern Ireland 1999) sought to find an acceptable middle ground, but were not received very well in either community – Unionists and Loyalists felt they were going too far, particularly with respect to the proposed name change, while especially Republicans had hoped for even farther-reaching reforms. Under the Police (Northern Ireland) Act 2000, which became law on 23 November 2000, and the Implementation Plan, the British government committed itself to a number of deliverables suggested by the Patten Report. These include the new Policing Board representing both communities, new arrangements for accountability, a new code of ethics, a new name, a new badge and flag, a human rights-orientated training and development programme and balanced recruitment to the police force in order to achieve greater representativeness. The implementation of these commitments was initially at best sporadic, which further contributed to a climate of uncertainty in which the issue could be used for polarising Northern Irish society, which essentially played into the hands of hardliners on both sides.

As early as June 1998, the British and Irish governments had put in place the legal and regulatory framework for the proposed Independent International Commission on Decommissioning (IICD) in a bilateral Agreement (1998) that followed earlier steps taken on decommissioning since 1995.[5] However, apart from a symbolic act of decommissioning in December 1998 by the Loyalist Volunteer Force, nothing happened on the decommissioning front until 2 December 1999, when the IRA announced the appointment of a representative to liaise with the IICD, followed by similar moves on the part of the Ulster Volunteer Force (UVF) and the Ulster Freedom Fighters (UFF). After some ups and downs in the engagement with the IICD, in a statement of 6 May 2000 the IRA (2000) committed itself to put IRA weapons 'completely and verifiably ... beyond use' and announced as a confidence building measure that 'contents of a number of ... arms dumps will be inspected by agreed third parties who will report that they have done so to the IICD. The dumps will be reinspected regularly to ensure that the weapons have remained silent.' Following the appointment of Cyril Ramaphosa and Marti Ahtisaari, several inspections took place, confirming that the weapons seen were secure and had not been used. However, even inten-

---

such that in a new approach Northern Ireland has a police service that can enjoy widespread support from, and is seen as an integral part of, the community as a whole.' It goes on to outline in relative detail how the proposals of the independent commission are to contribute to enabling the RUC to police in a peaceful society.

5 These included the two governments' decision on 28 November 1995 to establish an International Body to provide an independent assessment of the decommissioning issue, the 1997 Decommissioning Act in the Republic of Ireland and the Northern Ireland Arms Decommissioning Act of the same year in the United Kingdom, and the Joint Communiqué issued on 29 July 1997 by the Irish Minister for Foreign Affairs and the British Secretary of State for Northern Ireland on completing preparations for the establishment of an Independent Commission on decommissioning.

sive discussions between the IICD and representatives from the IRA, UVF and UFF had not managed to move the decommissioning issue any further after May 2000, when a deadline had been set by the British and Irish governments on the full implementation of the Good Friday Agreement by June 2001. The subsequent stand-off on decommissioning was characterised by mutual recriminations. The IRA claimed in a statement on 8 March 2001 that the British government had failed to 'deliver on the agreement made with us on May 5th, 2000' (IRA 2001a). According to an IICD report of June 2001, 'the UVF will not consider decommissioning before they know the IRA's intentions and hear their declaration that the war is over', while the UFF found it 'difficult to discuss decommissioning further with us while members of the UFF were continuing to be interned' (IICD 2001). Among political parties, the picture is similar – Unionists refuse to sit in government with Sinn Féin as long as there is no move on decommissioning, Sinn Féin insists that they are in no position to dictate to the IRA and that there should be no link between individual aspects of implementation.

To make matters even worse, on 14 August 2001, the process moved back to square one. Following UUP leader David Trimble's resignation as First Minister as of 1 July, there was (according to the provisions in the Agreement) a six-week period in which a new First Minister had to be found. Trimble's resignation, intended to to put pressure on the IRA, seemed to pay off when a surprise announcement by the IRA (2001b) on 9 August confirmed 'that the IRA leadership has agreed a scheme with the IICD, which will put IRA arms completely and verifiably beyond use'. However, this was deemed insufficient by the UUP to agree to put forward a candidate for the election of First Minister. Given a choice between suspension and new elections, the British government opted for a 24-hour suspension of the institutions, hoping that another six weeks of 'breathing space' would provide sufficient time to facilitate an agreement between the parties that would bring the UUP back into government. The prospects for that, however, quickly faded away after the IRA (2001c) announced on 14 August that, because of the renewed suspension, 'the conditions therefore do not exist for progressing' on the basis of their earlier proposal for decommissioning and that they were therefore withdrawing their proposal.

Faced with the imminent collapse of the political institutions created by the Good Friday Agreement, and under considerable national and international pressure following the terrorist attacks on the USA and the arrest of three alleged IRA members in Colombia, Sinn Féin publicly called on the IRA in October 2001 to begin decommissioning their weapons, which was followed by a subsequent announcement of the IICD that a first set of arms and other equipment had been put beyond use. While this prevented the feared collapse of the institutions in October 2001, it remains to be seen how far decommissioning can in fact 'save' a peace process that is confronted with numerous other difficulties as well. Notwithstanding those, it is also significant, and indicative of further progress on the decommissioning front in the near future, that the British government proposed an amendment to the current decommissioning legislation, extending the amnesty period from the end of February 2002 initially until 2003, with possible further extensions until 2007. Despite Unionist and Conservative concerns that this would take the pressure off the paramilitary groups, the Northern Ireland Decommissioning (Amendment) Bill was passed in the House of Commons on 9 January 2002 and sent to the House of Lords.

Having lived through thirty years of 'the Troubles', both the constitutional and paramilitary camps have had rather similar experiences, yet their interpretations and conclusions were fundamentally different. What complicates the issue further is the fact that it seems difficult for the hardcore in each community to understand that the security of one's own group, based on the continued ability to defend oneself with arms, is very often perceived as a threat by the respective other group. Mistrust and the experience of suffering over decades are unlikely to be transformed into trust and mutual understanding in the short term. On the other hand, even if decommissioning takes place, it might give a false sense of security as it does not involve a disruption of the existing paramilitary structures nor a destruction of the paramilitaries' capability to rearm themselves at any time.

As a further element of the security sector reform, the British government has undertaken a number of steps towards a normalisation of the security situation in Northern Ireland, including a reduction in the numbers and role of armed forces,[6] the removal of security installations,[7] the replacement of the Emergency Provisions Act by a new UK-wide Terrorism Act, and the closure of the so-called holding centres in Castlereagh and Strand Road. In this context of security sector reform, it must also not be forgotten that since 1998, 444 prisoners who qualified for early release were set free in Northern Ireland and fifty-seven in the Republic.

Similarly to security sector reform, the parades issue is highly contentious between the two communities, which, as Bryan has shown in his contribution to this volume, is again related to the rather different experiences historically and the notions connected with it. Clearly, parades form an important aspect of Unionist identity. The commitment to recognition of equal chances for both traditions in Northern Ireland to be

---

6 By July 2001, the number of troops in Northern Ireland had been reduced by 3,500, military patrolling had decreased by 50% since 1995, the number of Army helicopter flying hours had gone down by 21%, and one of the six Royal Irish Regiments had been disbanded. Following the first substantive act of decommissioning by the IRA, the Army presence in Northern Ireland was further reduced and has dropped to less than 13,500 troops on 59 bases by January 2002.

7 By July 2001, forty-two military installations had been closed, demolished or vacated, and 102 cross-border roads had been re-opened between the Northern Ireland and the Republic.

expressed and developed requires respect for the right to hold parades. Equally, however, it requires the respect for the feelings of the National-ist community, many of whom feel offended by what they perceive as triumphalist and sectarian manifestation of Unionist supremacy. Yet again, the division between the communities is not as clear-cut. The Nationalist community does not in general dispute the right of Unionists to march and perform their rituals, but rather demands equal respect for the feelings of its members, that is, to abstain from marching through mainly Catholic estates. The Unionist community, on the other hand, is prepared to make certain concessions, such as not having their bands play while marching through Nationalist residential areas, but they insist on their right to march on the 'Queen's/King's highway' and see any lim-itation of this right as violation of their basic civil liberties and as a threat to their traditional way of life. This highly symbolic nature of parades becomes particularly apparent if one considers the following figures: in 1999/2000 there were of 3,403 parades. Of these, fewer than ten percent (297) were contentious and referred to the Parades Commission, which imposed route restrictions on 152 parades (Parades Commission 2000). Yet, this relatively small number of contentious parades, and in particu-lar the Orange Order parades in Portadown/Drumcree, still have the ability to reinforce existing communal divides and increase the alien-ation of both communities from each other and (depending on the decision reached by the Commission and its enforcement by the police) of at least one of them from the political institutions in Northern Ireland. This has meant that the Parades Commission has so far not been very successful in brokering any long-term deal between the opposing sides in any of the main areas of contention, all of which are predominantly Catholic housing estates. The Commission's aim to establish 'important principles that are essential to a successful pluralist society' (Parades Commission 1999) has so far not effected a change in attitudes or even of circumstances in which this would be possible.[8] However, it also needs to be stated that the 2001 parades passed without the levels of violence that had characterised the marching season in previous years.

The debate over flags, that is, on what days and buildings the Union Jack (and Irish tricolours) should be flown, also points to the persistence of deep intercommunal divisions. In the words of the former Secretary of State for Northern Ireland, Peter Mandelson (2000), 'in Northern Ireland symbols matter a lot ... Symbols represent the different identities and different tra-ditions of those who live in this part of the United Kingdom and, like other

8 The 2000 report of the Commission indirectly admits this failure, of which the public in Northern Ireland is very much aware. In a special survey, only 15 percent of respondents con-sidered the work of the Commission successful. However, the Commission was also able to point out a number of advances: parades in 1999 were conducted largely peacefully, and over 80 percent of respondents in the same survey stated that there was a need for dialogue and engagement with the commission in order to resolve contentious parades issues (Parades Commission 2000).

symbols, flags have historically been a source of conflict that has driven people apart'. That this is not only a matter of the past became obvious in the deliberations of an Ad Hoc Committee set up by the Northern Ireland Assembly on 11 September 2000 to consider the draft Regulations by the Secretary of State under the Flags (Northern Ireland) Order 2000.[9]

The verdict on other indicators in this area is equally mixed. Even though the recent elections indicated a continued interest in political issues among the majority of the population, the results also confirm a tendency (although not as strong as in 1974) of a weakening of the moderate middle ground and a strengthening of more extremist parties in either of the two communities. As Murray and McAuley have shown, the SDLP and UUP lost votes and seats to Sinn Féin and the DUP, respectively, in the parliamentary and local council elections in June 2001, and this is likely to have long-term implications for the peace process.

The overall trend of decreasing violence has been reversed since 2001 with acts of spontaneous and organised mob and paramilitary violence once again becoming a feature of Northern Irish politics. The months-long stand-off and clashes between Catholics and Protestants around the Holy Cross Girls' Primary School in the Ardoyne area North Belfast, the murder of a Catholic postal worker and the, subsequently withdrawn, UDA threat against Catholic school teachers and postal workers, as well as the threat by the Republican paramilitary group INLA against the Protestant staff at a Marks & Spencer distribution centre testify to the persistence of sectarian divisions and mindsets in Northern Ireland. However, what is equally, if not more significant, is that the murder of the Catholic postal worker was not only widely condemned by representatives from all major political parties in Northern Ireland, but also led to thousands of people from both communities participating in rallies against hatred and sectarianism. By the same token, it is interesting to observe that the clashes around the Holy Cross Girls' Primary School did not spread across Northern Ireland or even led to wider rioting in Belfast itself, as similar events did over the past years. What this indicates is a decreasing acceptance of violence as a useful means to achieve political aims, and as such points to a change in the overall political climate in Northern Ireland over the past several years that must not be underestimated in its significance for post-agreement reconstruction.

The appointment of a Human Rights Commissioner, the release of paramilitary prisoners, and the initiation of public inquiries into unresolved issues, such as Bloody Sunday and allegations of security forces collusion in high-profile killings over the past thirty years,[10] have individually addressed specific needs of both communities.

---

9   See Ad Hoc Committee (2000).

10 As part of the political package agreed between the UK and Irish governments in summer 2001, it was agreed to appoint an international and independent judge to investigate the following cases: Pat Finucane, Rosemary Nelson, Robert Hamill, Harry Breen and Bob Buchanan, Lord Justice and Lady Gibson, and Billy Wright.

The Economic Dimension of Post-agreement Reconstruction

Developments in relation to the economic recovery of Northern Ireland allow the painting of a more optimistic picture in terms of growth rates, investment, unemployment, and community involvement in specific reconstruction projects.

Sustained economic growth in Northern Ireland since the early 1990s has not only been reflected in actual GDP growth figures, but has also had a positive impact on unemployment, pay increases and economic confidence among businesses in the region. In the first half of the 1990s, unemployment had been around or above 100,000 people until 1994, but then declined sharply to 40,000 by March 2001, equalling 5.1 percent of the total workforce. Both communities have almost equally benefited from economic recovery in the 1990s: between 1990 and 1999 Catholic unemployment has fallen by 45 percent, Protestant unemployment has fallen by almost 42 percent (NISRA 2001). However, it is still almost twice as likely for Catholics to be unemployed than it is for Protestants, which means that the unemployment differential between the two communities has not yet sufficiently been addressed. What is more, the latest available comprehensive labour market survey of autumn 2001 indicates that, rather than narrowing, the gap between Protestant and Catholic unemployment rates is in fact increasing. Compared to the previous quarter (covering the period June-August 2001), Protestant unemployment dropped from 4.4% to 4.0%, while that among Catholics increased from 8.5% to 9.0%. Especially for the significant category of males, it is now more than 2.5 times as likely for a Catholic to be unemployed than it is for a Protestant (10.9% compared to 4.2%). This has been despite the fact that the Labour government recognised the need to effect change in this area and committed itself to reducing such inequality as one of the key targets of its 'New Targeting Social Need' (New TSN) initiative in November 1999 (New TSN 1999). New TSN had been mentioned as a key instrument in the creation of a fairer and more prosperous society in Northern Ireland in the Good Friday Agreement, yet its objectives are in many ways broader than one would expect in the context of post-agreement reconstruction, and there are very few references to the particularity of the situation in Northern Ireland as being one of transition after three decades of conflict.[11]

As Irvin and Byrne have shown, more explicit references to the conflict and to building the conditions of sustainable peace in Northern Ireland were made in the 'European Union Special Support Programme for Peace and Reconciliation in Northern Ireland and the Border Counties of Ire-

---

11 In an almost typical case of British understatement, the introductory paragraph to the first New TSN Annual Report reads: 'New TSN is about the way the Government, its Departments and public bodies approach some of the most important problems in society, *including some which are special to Northern Ireland* ' (New TSN 1999, my emphasis).

land', which was initiated in 1995, taking advantage of the opportunities offered by the first round of cease-fires announced in 1994.[12] The strategic aim of the programme was set as reinforcing 'progress towards a peaceful and stable society and to promote reconciliation by increasing economic development and employment, promoting urban and rural regeneration, developing cross-border cooperation and extending social inclusion'. The first phase of the EU programme, Peace I, ran from 1995 to 1999, allocating a total of €503m,[13] 80 percent of which was spent on projects in Northern Ireland, and the remainder was allocated to projects in the Republic of Ireland. A total of around 15 percent of all funds were invested in cross-border initiatives. There are eight sub-programmes: employment, urban and rural regeneration, cross-border, social inclusion, productive investment, partnerships, technical assistance, and flagships. Probably the most interesting one from the perspective of post-agreement reconstruction is the one on district partnerships, which is administered by a company specifically established for that purpose in 1996, the Northern Ireland Partnership Board Limited (NIPB). The EU-defined rationale behind the partnership sub-programme was to 'harness the energies and talents of local groups in pursuit of common goals' so as to 'benefit all communities ... while concentrating on those areas and people who have suffered most from the conflict' (my emphasis). A KPMG evaluation report (NIPB 2000) of the partnership programme and the work of NIPB found that 70 percent of partnership funds were allocated to social inclusion projects, that 65 percent of projects operated in an area identified by TSN, that 68 percent of all initiatives under the programme were cross-community in nature and that 25 percent had a cross-border element. A survey carried out for this report among project participants revealed that the coming together of community leaders was the key impact of the partnership sub-programme. This is also reflected in the following figures: of 601 participants polled,

- 60 percent stated that as a result of the sub-programme, cooperation between the communities increased
- 58 percent agreed that relations between the two communities had improved over the first three years of the sub-programme

12 Additionally, Northern Ireland has also benefited from other EU programmes: Belfast and Londonderry received funding from the URBAN Initiative for inner-city regeneration, and from the INTERREG Programme, which promotes the creation and development of cross-border networks in order to address negative effects of peripherality in Northern Ireland and the border counties of the Republic of Ireland.

13 On 25 March 1999, the European Union Council agreed a new Peace Programme for Northern Ireland and the border counties, committing €500 million over a five-year period beginning in 2000.

- 63 percent said that their participation had enabled them to understand better the views of the respectively other community
- 90 percent were convinced that the partnerships sub-programme had a positive impact on peace and reconciliation in their specific community.

Clearly, these figures are impressive, but they may not be totally representative of the views of society in Northern Ireland as a whole. As the report itself indicates, there is an inherent danger of such initiatives reaching only those people who already share a commitment to peace and reconciliation and are prepared to compromise and engage with the other community, while those who are hardline opponents of any compromise do not participate at all. As a consequence, they do not share in the benefits, and often interpret this as confirming their opposition to the peace process in general. This implies that if the outreach of these and similar programmes cannot be increased, significant intercommunal divides will remain, as will intracommunal ones, with both having the potential to endanger the long-term stability of the Good Friday Agreement.

New Structures for Northern Ireland's Civil Society?

There can be little doubt that a functioning civil society is a key ingredient for any viable democratic political process, as it provides the structures and opportunities for citizen participation and engagement, including access to the public discourse for otherwise underrepresented or marginalised interests. A particular consequence of the conflict in Northern Ireland on society there has been that there are, in fact, two civil societies with relatively little overlap. This is mostly a result of the deep divisions in Northern Ireland, including the fact that significant levels of residential segregation persist. While indicators of social capital, such as trust and membership in civic organisations, are rather high in Northern Ireland, these figures can not be taken as an indication for a well-integrated civil society that goes beyond communal boundaries. Therefore, the success or failure so far of post-agreement reconstruction in the area of civil society is best measured in terms of the establishment of new structures within which the two existing civil societies can be integrated and within which existing organisations, which have grown historically and reflect the character of one particular community, such as the Orange Order or the Gaelic Athletics Association, can be complemented by new organisations that are not primarily based within a single community. Such a 'new' civil society could become a major political factor in Northern Ireland, to contribute to a sustained and stable peace process, and in their distinct analyses Morgan, Bairner, Byrne and O'Reilly have examined different trends in this area and demonstrated the need for more progress in building new structures for a Northern Irish civil society.

A significant step in this direction was taken through the establishment, on 16 February 1999, of sixty-person-strong Civic Forum under the aegis of the Office of the First Minister and the Deputy First Minister. According to the Good Friday Agreement, the Forum is to act as a consultative mechanism on social, economic and cultural issues, as well as on any independent consultative forum established in relation to North-South cooperation.[14] The members of the Civic Forum are representatives from the business community (7), from agriculture and fisheries (3), from the trade unions (7), from the voluntary sector (18), from the churches (5), from culture (4), from arts and sports (4), victims (2), from community relations (2), from education (2) and from the office of the First Minister and his Deputy (6). Even though the Forum is not a body exclusively made up of members of civil society, the attempt to bring together representatives from the private sector, the political institutions, the voluntary sector, and other parts of Northern Irish society is important in so far as it raises the profile of civil society organisations, increases their public presence, and offers opportunities for them to cooperate beyond communal boundaries. The period since its inauguration, however, has been characterised by a remarkable degree of inactivity and it remains to be seen whether the Civic Forum can accomplish these tasks.

A somewhat older body with relevance for the development of civil society is the Central Community Relations Unit, which was set up in 1987 and whose central task is to increase the degree of mutual understanding between the two communities in Northern Ireland. This is fairly well incorporated with initiatives on education (integrated education and the programme on Education for Mutual Understanding and Cultural Heritage) and a variety of initiatives directly sponsored by the government that fund the development of specific local responses to community relations problems. However, the results of all these programmes are not far-reaching enough yet to make it possible to speak of a functioning and integrated civil society in Northern Ireland. Apart from some occasional local projects and a number of high-profile initiatives, the situation in Northern Ireland to date is one that reflects deep communal divisions in all sectors of public life, including civil society. While some progress has been made, in particular in relation to victims groups, there is still a general lack of cross-communal civil society organisations. In particular in relation to parades, language and sports, as Byrne, O'Reilly and Bairner have

---

14 See Paragraph 24, Strand One, and Paragraph 19, Strand Two, of the Good Friday Agreement.

shown, the problem is not only the lack of cross-communal organisations but deliberate attempts by some to actively exclude members of the other community and to prevent meaningful contacts between existing organisations with roots in different communities.

This underlines the importance of fostering contact and cooperation between the two communities in other sectors. Successful and mutually beneficial cooperation in the economy and politics have the potential to work as precedents for closer interaction in civil society, too. However, there is no automatism in this. An integrated civil society cannot be imposed on the two communities, but has to grow organically. As the Good Friday Agreement, together with earlier government initiatives, provides some of the structures for such a new civil society, it is not unlikely that, over time, new cross-communal organisations will emerge to complement existing ones and help to fuse them into one overarching civil society in which both communities can find spaces to express, preserve and develop their distinct identities as well as to work together on issues of mutual concern.

Conclusions

Almost four years after the conclusion of the Good Friday Agreement, Northern Ireland remains a deeply divided society, shaped by over thirty years of violent interethnic conflict. The general elections on 7 June 2001, which saw the moderate Unionists and Nationalists weakened at the expense of Sinn Féin and the DUP, have confirmed a trend of increasing divisions and a declining willingness to compromise and cooperate. On the other hand, recent positive developments in relation to policing and decommissioning might allow a more optimistic assessment of the future of the peace process.

However, the persistence of divisions and mutual suspicion in itself is not surprising – the time it takes to move a conflict-torn society away from long-established patterns of prejudice and distrust is measured in generations, not years. The point of this concluding analysis is therefore not to decry the failure of the Good Friday Agreement to achieve a miracle, but to lay the foundations for a critical examination of the post-agreement reconstruction process so far and to assess its future prospects and requirements.

Table 12.3 provides a general assessment of the situation in Northern Ireland as of November 2001, in relation to individual indicators of post-agreement reconstruction.

Table 12.3: The Status of Post-agreement Reconstruction in Northern Ireland

INDICATOR	STATUS
Institution-building	
Political Indicators	
Participation	Remains high, but contributes to polarisation
Vote share	Increased for extremists at the expense of moderates
Performance of government institutions	Good
Legitimacy of government institutions	Remains low among significant sections in both communities, leading to institutional instability
Significance of community-specific symbols	Remains high
Security Indicators	
Violence	Has increased since 2000
Conduct of security forces	Fair
Decommissioning	Significant progress with the beginning of actual IRA decommissioning in October 2001
Demilitarisation	Initial progress continues after the beginning of IRA decommissioning
Police reform	Progresses according to the British government's implementation plan
Judicial Indicators	
Rule of Law	Exists
Law enforcement	Even-handed
Prisoner release	All eligible prisoners released
Human Rights Commission	Set up, but largely inactive
Judicial enquiries into past	Set up, but contribute to polarisation, rather than reconciliation
Economic Recovery	
Growth rates	Remain above 3% since 1998
Investment	High in 1997/98, but remains at high levels since
Unemployment (total)	Significantly down for both communities since 1998
Unemployment (community-specific)	Employment differential remains almost unchanged
Community participation in regeneration	Apparent, but insufficient improvement for most deprived areas
Rebuilding of (civil) society	
Social indicators	
Residential segregation	Remains at high levels
Integrated education	Remains at low levels
Intermarriage	Remains at low levels
Intracommunal organisations	Many and slightly increasing
Intercommunal organisations	Remain few
Intercommunal local media	Remain few
Psychological indicators	
Perception of security situation	Gradual sense of improvement
Perception of others	Significant lack of trust remains
Level of confidence in future of	
Good Friday Agreement	Decreases, particularly among Unionists

Note: ▨ indicates important issue.   Note: ▨ indicates negative impact.

A simple computation exercise alone reveals that with regard to fourteen out of twenty-nine indicators the current status of post-agreement reconstruction has had a negative impact, that is, has failed to provide conditions for sustainable peace. Even more significantly, out of the eighteen indicators deemed important because of the specificities of the conflict in Northern Ireland, the current status of eleven reveals a negative impact. With the exception of judicial and security indicators in the area of institution-building, the failure of post-agreement reconstruction to contribute to sustainable peace is resounding. The question that therefore arises is whether this failure is due to bad implementation of the Good Friday Agreement as the 'founding document' of the post-agreement reconstruction process, or whether the roots for failure lie much deeper, namely in the Agreement itself and its unsuitability as a framework for sustainable peace in Northern Ireland.

At a very general level, there has always been a degree of uncertainty about whether the Good Friday Agreement could really deliver on its promise: a rigid framework for consociationalism, it required the two communities to accept a political process which essentially tried to square the circle of Nationalist and Unionist aspirations, that is, a united Ireland and continued strong links with Great Britain. For this to be possible, it would have been necessary for both communities to drop their maximum demands, that is, in particular to accept the proposed North-South institutions as a compromise structure within which both groups' aspirations and concepts of national belonging could be accommodated. The change in attitude necessary for this acceptance to happen, however, has not been forthcoming, and it is questionable whether it really could be expected to appear on the horizon within only a few years after entire group identities have been constructed around this Irish dimension for decades if not centuries. Therefore, it could be argued that the Agreement was fundamentally flawed from the beginning, and nothing that politicians in Belfast, Dublin and London were doing would have prevented the inevitable failure of the implementation process. Yet, this is too easy an answer and too easy a way out, especially for politicians in Northern Ireland, who bear a fair share of the responsibility for the difficulties that the implementation of the Good Friday Agreement has experienced so far – but they also deserve credit for the progress that has been made.

Within Northern Ireland, the emotionalisation in particular of decommissioning and police reform by politicians of both communities, combined with largely simulative politics on both issues and a crucial lack of leadership, has created a situation characterised by mutually reinforcing conceptions of resentment and entitlement among large sections in both communities. Political leaders, by playing to, and thereby often actually encouraging and strengthening, alleged fears and myths among their electorates, have managed to boost self-perceptions of victimhood and perceptions of victimisation at the hands of the other community. Clearly, divisions, prejudice and stereotype have long been features of intercommunal relations in Northern Ireland, but since 1998 politicians in both communities have done little to overcome these. Neither has it helped that Unionists and Loyalists have tried to prevent any substantial reform of the police forces in Northern Ireland, nor has the initial rejection by Nationalists and Republicans of the proposals on the table contributed in any way to creating a situation of normality in which a Northern Irish police force could have been created that would have been acceptable to both communities. By the same token, the damaging linkage between decommissioning and Unionist participation in the power-sharing government has left it for paramilitaries to decide the progress, if any, of the implementation process. The initially merely verbal gestures from the IRA were obviously unacceptable to Unionist leaders, who had created a 'sideshow' over the decommissioning issue although it was fairly obvious that any actual decommissioning of whatever quantity of arms and explosives would be merely symbolic – exploitable as defeat of the IRA while completely unverifiable as to the extent of paramilitary equipment actually surrendered, let alone sufficient to prevent rearmament. Strong leadership could have been expressed on both sides: Sinn Féin could have publicly declared its strong support for decommissioning much earlier, while the UUP should not have allowed itself to make power-sharing dependent on decommissioning. This would have made it possible for a political process in Northern Ireland to develop in which the work of the institutions created under the Good Friday Agreement would have dominated the public and political discourses, and not decommissioning. Thus, legitimate political leaders could have retained control instead of surrendering it to paramilitaries. While this has changed as of October 2001 with the beginning of IRA decommissioning, the damage done to the peace process over the first three-and-a-half years of one impasse chasing another will be more difficult to undo and has been a major contributor to Unionist support for the Good Friday Agreement falling from about 55 percent in May 1998 to just over 42 percent in September 2001 (Hearts and Minds Survey 2001).

The government in London, too, is not free of blame. In contrast to the situation in 1973/74 when there was a lack of involvement and support for the then pro-Agreement parties, the period since 1998 is characterised by some kind of overinvolvement. On the one hand, London deserves to be commended for its determination to bring a lasting peace to Northern Ireland. On the other hand, however, the strong role that the British government has retained in Northern Irish politics and its dues ex machina-like rescue attempts of the agreement have taken away control, and thus responsibility, from politicians in Northern Ireland, making it possible for them to have a convenient scapegoat to blame other than themselves for any failure. While the first suspension of the institutions in February 2000 may have been justifiable, the situation in August 2001 was different. Calling elections to the Assembly would have given the people in Northern Ireland a chance to deliver their verdict on the post-agreement reconstruction process so far, and would also have corresponded to the wishes of a relative majority of people in Northern Ireland who preferred this option to either another one-day or an indefinite suspension of the Assembly (Hearts and Minds Survey 2001). The outcome of these elections would, in all likelihood, have altered the balance of power between the political parties, but it would not have meant the automatic end of the peace process. Instead of the current climate of political engineering, it might have served as a reminder for the people and politicians in Northern Ireland that it is their future that is at stake. In retrospect, however, the government's decision not to call elections has paid off in so far as IRA decommissioning has begun and an Assembly is still in place that includes a majority, and more favourable distribution, of members in favour of the agreement.

Thus, in conclusion, the prospects of the Good Friday Agreement having a long-term positive impact on the peace process, and thus on politics and society in Northern Ireland, are not bad. However, the Agreement is only one step in a much longer process of transforming the ethnonational conflict at the heart Northern Ireland's problems. To maintain the current positive momentum in this process will require skill and determination of all those involved in the Northern Irish peace process in London and Dublin, Brussels and Washington, and foremost in Belfast itself.

References

Ad Hoc Committee. 2000. *Report on Draft Regulations proposed under Article 3 of The Flags (Northern Ireland) Order 2000.*
http://www.ni-assembly.gov.uk/Flags/adhoc1-00r.htm

Agreement between the Government of the United Kingdom of Great Britain and Northern Ireland and the Government of the Republic of Ireland Establishing the Independent International Commission on Decommissioning. 1998.
http://www2.nio.gov.uk/press/970826c.htm

Bush, Kenneth, 1998. *A Measure of Peace: Peace and Conflict Impact Assessment of Development Projects in Conflict Zones.* Ottawa.

Fay, M. T., Morrissey, M. and Smyth, M. 1998. The Cost of the Troubles Study: Mapping Troubles-Related Deaths in Northern Ireland, 1969–1994. Derry/Londonderry.

Hamilton, Andrew. 1990. *Violence and Communities.* Coleraine.

Harris, Peter and Reilly, Ben. 1998. *Democracy and Deep-Rooted Conflict: Options for Negotiators.* Stockholm.

Hearts and Minds Survey. 2001. Conducted by PricewaterhouseCoopers on 10 and 11 September 2001.

http://news.bbc.co.uk/hi/english/uk/northern_ireland/newsid_1552000/1552632.stm

Independent Commission on Policing for Northern Ireland. 1999. A New Beginning: Policing in Northern Ireland. Belfast: HMSO, 1999

Independent International Commission on Decommissioning. 2001. Report of the Independent International Commission on Decommissioning, 30 June 2001. http://cain.ulst.ac.uk/events/peace/docs/iicd300601.htm

IRA. 2000. 'Statement by the Irish Republican Army (IRA), issued (at midday) Saturday 6 May 2000'. http://cain.ulst.ac.uk/events/peace/docs/ira060500.htm

———2001a. 'Statement by the Irish Republican Army (IRA), issued 8 March 2001'. http://cain.ulst.ac.uk/events/peace/docs/ira080301.htm

———2001b. 'Statement by the Irish Republican Army (IRA), issued 9 August 2001'. http://news.bbc.co.uk/hi/english/uk/northern_ireland/newsid_1481000/1481529.stm

———2001c. 'Statement by the Irish Republican Army (IRA), issued 14 August 2001'. http://news.bbc.co.uk/hi/english/uk/northern_ireland/newsid_1490000/1490164.stm

Mandelson, Peter. 2000. Commons Hansard Debates Text for Tuesday 16 May 2000: Column 263, http://www.parliament.the-stationery-office.co.uk/pa/cm199900/cmhansrd/vo000516/debtext/00516-37.htm#column_263

McGarry, John. and O'Leary, Brendan. 1996. Explaining Northern Ireland: Broken Images. Oxford.

New TSN Targeting Social Need. 1999. An agenda for targeting social need and promoting social inclusion in Northern Ireland. http://www.dfpni.gov.uk/ccru/contents.htm

NIPB Northern Ireland Partnership Board. 2000. Evaluation Report. http:www/nipb.org/KPMGReport.htm

NISRA (Northern Ireland Statistics & Research Agency). 2001. A Profile of Protestants and Roman Catholics in the Northern Ireland Labour Force. Belfast.

O'Duffy, Brendan and O'Leary, Brendan. 1990. 'Violence in Northern Ireland, 1969-June 1989', in The Future of Northern Ireland, ed. John McGarry and Brendan O'Leary. Oxford.

O'Leary, Brendan and McGarry, John. 1993. The Politics of Antagonism: Understanding Northern Ireland. London.

Parades Commission. 1999. Annual Report. http://www.paradescommission.org/annual1/annual.htm

———2000. Annual Report. http://www.paradescommission.org/annual2/annual.htm

Wolff, S. 2002. 'The Peace Process in Northern Ireland since 1998: Success or Failure of Post-agreement Reconstruction', in Civil Wars, vol. 5, no. 1 (2002).

INDEX

By the Same Author

DISPUTED TERRITORIES
The Transnational Dynamics of Ethnic Conflict Settlement

Stefan Wolff

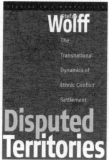

Ethnic conflicts have shaped the twentieth century in significant ways. While the legacy of the last century is primarily one of many unresolved conflicts, the author contends that Western Europe has a track record in containing and settling ethnic conflicts which provides valuable lessons for conflict management elsewhere. The author identifies the factors at work in disputes over borders from Northern Ireland to Alsace, South Tyrol and elsewhere, demonstrating that they can also provide the seeds for their resolution.

Stefan Wolff was educated at the University of Leipzig, Germany. He received an MPhil from the University of Cambridge and a PhD from the London School of Economics. He is currently Lecturer in the Department of European Studies at the University of Bath.

Hardback ISBN 1-57181-516-3 £47.00 / $75.00 / €82.00
Studies in Ethnopolitics

By the Same Author

COMING HOME TO GERMANY?
The Integration of Ethnic Germans from Central and Eastern Europe in the Federal Republic since 1945

Edited by **David Rock** and **Stefan Wolff**

The end of World War II led to one of the most significant forced population transfers in history: the expulsion of over 12 million ethnic Germans from Central and Eastern Europe between 1945 and 1950 and the subsequent emigration of another four million in the second half of the twentieth century. Although unprecedented in its magnitude, conventional wisdom has it that the integration of refugees, expellees, and Aussiedler was a largely successful process in postwar Germany. While the achievements of the integration process are acknowledged, the volume also examines the difficulties encountered by ethnic Germans in the Federal Republic and analyses the shortcomings of dealing with this particular phenomenon of mass migration and its consequences.

David Rock teaches in the Department of Modern Languages at the University of Keele. **Stefan Wolff** is lecturer in the Department of European Studies at the University of Bath.

Hardback ISBN 1-57181-718-2 **£47.00 / $69.95 / €77.25**
Paperback ISBN 1-57181-729-8 **£17.00 / $25.00 / €28.00**
256 pages, bibliog., index
Volume 4 of *Culture and Society in Germany*

www.berghahnbooks.com

CHALLENGING ETHNIC CITIZENSHIP
German and Israeli Perspectives on Immigration

Edited by **Danny Levy** and **Yfaat Weiss**

In contrast to most other countries, both Germany and Israel have descent-based concepts of nationhood and have granted members of their nation (ethnic Germans and Jews) who wish to immigrate automatic access to their respective citizenship privileges. Therefore these two countries lend themselves well to comparative analysis of the integration processes of immigrant groups, who were formally part of the collective "self" but have become increasingly transformed into "others."

This volume brings together a group of leading scholars specializing in German and Israeli immigration from the perspectives of their various disciplines. This is reflected in the richness of the empirical and theoretical material offered, involving historical developments, demographic changes, sociological problems, anthropological insights, and political implications.

Daniel Levy is Assistant Professor in the Sociology Department at the State University of New York, Stony Brook. His publications reflect his research interests in the comparative sociology of immigration in Europe and collective memory studies. **Yfaat Weiss** studied at the universities of Tel-Aviv and Hamburg and is presently a senior lecturer in the Department for Jewish History at Haifa University. She has written on Eastern European Jewry in Germany and on Zionism and the State of Israel.

Hardback ISBN 1-57181-291-1 £47.00 / $75.00 / €82.00
Paperback ISBN 1-57181-292-X £17.00 / $25.00 / €28.00
288 pages, bibliog., index

EUROPE'S NEW RACISM
Causes, Manifestations and Solutions
Edited by **The Evens Foundation**

Europe has seen a tremendous rise in popularity of new rightist political parties in the last two decades or so, claiming the cultural supremacy of the so-called native Europeans over foreign immigrants. In this volume, European scholars from Russia to Britain have come together in an effort to determine the causes of this resurgence of rightist and anti-democratic ideologies. They furthermore suggest actions that might help combat racism more effectively.

Nora Räthzel, 'Developments in Theories of Racism' – Marc Verlot, 'Understanding Institutional Racism' – John Solomos & Liza Schuster, 'Hate Speech, Violence and Contemporary Racisms' – Natan Lerner, 'The Role of International Law' – Bas de Gaay Fortman, 'Racism and Poverty in a Human Rights Perspective' – Robert Maier, 'Does a Supranational Europe Stimulate and/or Combat Racism?' – Gudrun Hentges, 'Refugee and Asylum Policy Influenced by Europeanisation' – Maykel Verkuyten, 'Ethnic Relations in Local Contexts: Beyond a Dualist Approach to Identities and Racism' – Béla Greskovits, 'Economic Globalisation and Racism in Eastern and Western Europe' – Giovanna Campani, 'The Role and Forms of Education' – Jagdish S. Gundara, 'Racism, Devolution and Education in the European Union' – Rik Pinxten and Marijke Cornelis, 'What Interculturalism Could Bring a Solution to Racism?'

The Evens Foundation is a public, non-profit organization, founded in the late 1990s, whose aims are to promote peaceful co-existence through intercultural and artistic education contributing to the further integration of Europe.

Hardback ISBN 1-57181-332-2 £47.00 / $75.00 / €77.25
Paperback ISBN 1-57181-333-0 £17.60 / $25.00 / €28.00
Available, 256 pages, bibliog., index